FOR REFERENCE
Do Not Take From This Room

The Big Book of Children's Reading Lists

SEP 2007

The Big Book of Children's Reading Lists

100 Great, Ready-to-Use Book Lists for Educators, Librarians, Parents, and Children

Nancy J. Keane

LIBRARIES UNLIMITED
A Member of the Greenwood Publishing Group
Westport, Connecticut • London

Library of Congress Cataloging-in-Publication Data

Keane, Nancy J.
The big book of children's reading lists : 100 great, ready-to-use book lists for educators, librarians, parents, and children / by Nancy J. Keane.
p. cm.
Includes index.
ISBN 1-59158-334-9 (pbk : alk. paper)
1. Children—Books and reading. 2. Children's literature—Bibliography. 3. Children's libraries—Book lists. 4. School libraries—Book lists. I. Title.
Z1037.K29 2006
028.5'5—dc22 2006007470

British Library Cataloguing in Publication Data is available.

Copyright © 2006 by Libraries Unlimited

All rights reserved. No portion of this book may be reproduced, by any process or technique, without the express written consent of the publisher. An exception is made for reproducibles, which may be copied for library educational and classroom use only.

Library of Congress Catalog Card Number: 2006007470
ISBN: 1-59158-334-9

First published in 2006

Libraries Unlimited, 88 Post Road West, Westport, CT 06881
A Member of the Greenwood Publishing Group, Inc.
www.lu.com

Printed in the United States of America

The paper used in this book complies with the Permanent Paper Standard issued by the National Information Standards Organization (Z39.48–1984).

10 9 8 7 6 5 4 3 2

Dedicated to my children, Aureta and Alex,
and my grandchildren, Aiden and Jordan

EAST NORTHPORT PUBLIC LIBRARY
EAST NORTHPORT, NEW YORK

Contents

Acknowledgments

I would like to thank the people who have helped with this book, either directly or indirectly. There is no way I could have done this by myself.

First, I would like to thank my children and grandchildren for forgiving me during those times when I couldn't be with them because I was writing. Yes, Aiden, Mimi does have more time to play now. I promise.

I have been fortunate to have colleagues contribute lists to this book. First is Pooja Makhijani, an essayist, journalist, and writer of children's literature. She is the editor of *Under Her Skin: How Girls Experience Race in America* and the author of *Mama's Saris,* a picture book. I would also like to thank Charity Huechteman, Children's Associate Librarian at Brentwood Library in Springfield, Missouri. The professionals on the e-lists LM_NET, yalsa-bk, and childlit also helped by suggesting titles for the lists.

I would like to thank my colleagues in New Hampshire, who always have titles to share and stories to tell. I am fortunate to be acquainted with such talented people.

And I have to give a big thank you to my editor, Barbara Ittner. This is the second time I have had the opportunity to work with her, and I have learned a great deal. When I had trouble picturing parts of the book, Barb was always able to refocus me and lead me in the direction I needed to go. I am looking forward to working with her again soon.

Introduction

One good read leads to another, and a good book often leaves young readers hungry for more. Whether you and your school use basal readers, leveled reading, or a literature-based program, you are probably often called upon to extend the reading beyond the current materials. But how do you find those supplemental materials easily? How do you lead children to the next book? This guide provides reading lists that support extended reading demands.

Every day librarians plan activities for children that involve using literature. They may have some books in mind, or maybe not. It is time consuming to search for books that support the specific themes of a lesson. This book provides valuable reading lists to support public and school librarians in their work with children.

An unlimited number of reading lists could be created to assist professionals in their work. The 100 lists in this book have been chosen in consultation with working elementary teachers and public librarians and through discussions on professional e-mail lists. They are based on some of the most common needs of educators and librarians who work with young readers. The book is divided into three parts: "School Subjects," "Character and Values," and "Genres and Themes." Additional contributions were made by Pooja Makhijani and Charity Huechteman.

You'll find fiction and nonfiction books in these lists. All were in print as of August 2005. Although the emphasis is on books published within the last ten years, older titles are included if they are still in print and offer valuable additions to the lists. Information for each title includes the author, title, publisher, date of publication, and number of pages. Nonfiction books are designated by (NF) following the number of pages. A brief annotation describes the plot or premise of the book. Books are grouped by age level, with picture books under the heading "Books for Children of All Ages". Most of these books can be used with children of all ages and are not necessarily restricted to use with younger children. Books that have appeal for upper elementary students are listed under the heading "Books for Children Ages 8–12". Again, these books are not restricted to these age levels but are suggested for upper elementary students. These lists include primarily chapter books. Since the age range 8 to 12 is a large span, you are strongly advised to review the materials before using them with younger children. It is important to look beyond recommended interest level when suggesting books to students.

These lists can be used in a variety of ways. They can be photocopied and handed out to teachers as suggested reading. They can be enlarged and posted in the library, put on the library Web site or into the library's newsletter; or can be used to create book displays. There is room at the top of each to allow for personalization—add your school or library logo, or even some copyright-free clip art. Have fun. Be creative. Be resourceful.

However you use the lists, it is hoped that you will find them to be valuable resources and aids for suggesting reading materials.

Part 1

School Subjects

Adjectives

Books for Children of All Ages

Beaton, Clare. ***How Loud Is a Lion?*** Barefoot Books, 2002. 24pp.
Various animals of the jungle are presented through descriptive adjectives and repeating text.

Berenstain, Stan. ***The Berenstain Bears Ready, Get Set, Go!*** Random House, c1988. 32pp.
The Bear family engage in competitive sports events while demonstrating to the reader the comparison of adjectives.

Brett, Jan. ***The Mitten: A Ukrainian Folktale.*** Putnam, c1989. 32pp.
Several animals sleep snugly in Nicki's lost mitten, until the bear sneezes.

Carle, Eric. ***"Slowly, Slowly, Slowly," Said the Sloth.*** Philomel Books, c2002. 27pp.
Challenged by the other jungle animals for his seemingly lazy ways, a sloth living in a tree explains the many advantages of his slow and peaceful existence.

Fox, Mem. ***Where Is the Green Sheep?*** Harcourt, c2004. 32pp.
A story about many different sheep, and one that seems to be missing.

Provensen, Alice. ***A Day in the Life of Murphy.*** Simon & Schuster Books for Young Readers, c2003. 32pp.
Murphy, a farm terrier, describes a day in his life: he gets fed in the kitchen, hunts mice, goes to the vet, returns to the house for dinner, investigates a noise outside, and retires to the barn for sleep.

Books for Children Ages 8–12

Cleary, Brian P. ***Hairy, Scary, Ordinary: What Is an Adjective?*** Carolrhoda Books, c2000. 32pp. (NF)
Rhyming text and illustrations of comical cats present numerous examples of adjectives, from "hairy, scary, cool, and ordinary" to "tan and tall," "funny, frisky, smooth, and small."

Frasier, Debra. ***Miss Alaineus: A Vocabulary Disaster.*** Harcourt, . c2000. 34pp.
When Sage's spelling and definition of a word reveal her misunderstanding of it to her classmates, she is at first embarrassed but then uses her mistake as inspiration for the vocabulary parade.

Heller, Ruth. ***Many Luscious Lollipops: A Book About Adjectives.*** Grosset & Dunlap, c1989. 44pp. (NF)
Brief text in rhyme and pictures introduces adjectives and their uses.

From Nancy J. Keane, *The Big Book of Children's Reading Lists: 100 Great, Ready-to-Use Book Lists for Educators, Librarians, Parents, and Children.* Westport, CT: Libraries Unlimited, 2006. Copyright © 2006 by Libraries Unlimited.

Idioms

Books for Children of All Ages

Allard, Harry. *The Stupids Step Out.* Houghton Mifflin, 1974. 30pp.
The Stupid family and their dog Kitty have a fun-filled day doing ridiculous things.

Arnold, Tedd. *Even More Parts: Idioms from Head to Toe.* Dial Books for Young Readers, c2004. 30pp.
A young boy is worried about what will happen to his body when he hears such expressions as "I'm tongue tied," "don't give me any of your lip," and "I put my foot in my mouth."

Arnold, Tedd. *More Parts.* Dial Books for Young Readers, c2001. 32pp.
A young boy is worried about what will happen to his body when he hears such expressions as "give him a hand," "laugh your head off," and "hold your tongue."

Denim, Sue. *The Dumb Bunnies.* Scholastic, c1994. 32pp.
Follows the adventures of the Dumb Bunnies, a family of rabbits who do everything without any rhyme or reason.

Gwynne, Fred. *A Chocolate Moose for Dinner.* Aladdin Paperbacks, c1976. 47pp. (NF)
A little girl pictures the things her parents talk about, such as a chocolate moose, a gorilla war, and shoe trees.

Gwynne, Fred. *The King Who Rained.* Aladdin Paperbacks, 1980. c1970. 40pp. (NF)
Confused by the different meanings of words that sound alike, a little girl imagines such unusual sights as "a king who rained" and "the foot prince in the snow."

Gwynne, Fred. *A Little Pigeon Toad.* Aladdin Paperbacks, c1988. 47pp. (NF)
Humorous text and illustrations introduce a variety of homonyms and figures of speech.

Parish, Peggy. *Amelia Bedelia.* HarperCollins, 1992. 63pp.
A literal-minded housekeeper causes a ruckus in the household when she attempts to make sense of some instructions.

Stanley, Diane. *Raising Sweetness.* Putnam, c1999. 32pp.
Sweetness, one of eight orphans living with a man who is an unconventional housekeeper, learns to read and writes an important letter to improve their situation.

Stanley, Diane. *Saving Sweetness.* Putnam, c1996. 32pp.
The sheriff of a dusty Western town rescues Sweetness, an unusually resourceful orphan, from nasty old Mrs. Sump and her terrible orphanage.

From Nancy J. Keane, *The Big Book of Children's Reading Lists: 100 Great, Ready-to-Use Book Lists for Educators, Librarians, Parents, and Children.* Westport, CT: Libraries Unlimited, 2006. Copyright © 2006 by Libraries Unlimited.

Idioms

Books for Children Ages 8–12

Edwards, Wallace. ***Monkey Business.*** Kids Can Press, 2004. 26pp. (NF)
Contains an introduction to idioms through a collection of animal portraits and illustrations.

Leedy, Loreen. ***There's a Frog in My Throat!: 440 Animal Sayings a Little Bird Told Me.*** Holiday House, c2003. 48pp. (NF)
Presents the meanings of over 400 common phrases that make references to animals, along with vivid illustrations.

Terban, Marvin. ***In a Pickle and Other Funny Idioms.*** Clarion Books, c1983. 64pp. (NF)
Thirty common English phrases, such as "a chip off the old block" and "cry over spilled milk" are illustrated and explained.

Terban, Marvin. ***Mad as a Wet Hen!: And Other Funny Idioms.*** Clarion Books, c1987. 64pp. (NF)
Illustrates and explains over 100 common English idioms, in categories including animals, body parts, and colors.

Terban, Marvin. ***Punching the Clock: Funny Action Idioms.*** Clarion Books, c1990. 63pp. (NF)
Introduces and explains more than 100 expressions that mean something different than the separate words within them, such as "raise the roof," "hold your horses," and "carry a tune."

From Nancy J. Keane, *The Big Book of Children's Reading Lists: 100 Great, Ready-to-Use Book Lists for Educators, Librarians, Parents, and Children.* Westport, CT: Libraries Unlimited, 2006. Copyright © 2006 by Libraries Unlimited.

Long and Short "A"

Long "A"

Books for Children of All Ages

Aardema, Verna. ***Bringing the Rain to Kapiti Plain: A Nandi Tale.*** Dial Books for Young Readers, c1981. 32pp.
A cumulative rhyme relating how Ki-pat brought rain to the drought-stricken Kapiti Plain.

Bang, Molly. ***The Paper Crane.*** Greenwillow Books, c1985. 32pp.
A mysterious man enters a restaurant and pays for his dinner with a paper crane that magically comes alive and dances.

Moncure, Jane Belk. ***My "A" Sound Box.*** Child's World, c2001. 30pp.
A little boy fills his sound box with words beginning with the letter "a."

Salzmann, Mary Elizabeth. ***Aa.*** Abdo. c2000. 24pp.
A picture book presenting lots of word examples that use the long vowel sound of "a." (NF)

Short "A"

Books for Children of All Ages

Chapman, Joan. ***An Ant: Learning the Short A Sound.*** PowerKids Press, 2002. 23pp. (NF)
Introduces young learners to the short "a" sound through a story about an ant.

Cox, Phil Roxbee. ***Fat Cat on a Mat.*** Usborne, EDC, 1999. 16pp.
After accidentally knocking a bird's nest out of a tree, Fat Cat decides to help the eggs hatch, in this book made up of simple phonic words.

Doudna, Kelly. ***Aa.*** Abdo. c2000. 24pp.
Presents pictures of objects spelled with the short vowel "a."

Flack, Marjorie. ***Angus and the Cat.*** Farrar, Straus & Giroux, 1997, c1932. 32pp.
Angus the Scottie dog spends three days chasing the new cat that has come to live at his house, but when the cat disappears, Angus misses his new friend.

From Nancy J. Keane, *The Big Book of Children's Reading Lists: 100 Great, Ready-to-Use Book Lists for Educators, Librarians, Parents, and Children.* Westport, CT: Libraries Unlimited, 2006. Copyright © 2006 by Libraries Unlimited.

Long and Short "A"

Flack, Marjorie. ***Ask Mr. Bear.*** Simon & Schuster Books for Young Readers, 1960. 34pp.
Danny does not know what to give his mother for her birthday, so he asks many animals for their help.

Flanagan, Alice K. ***Cats: The Sound of Short "A."*** Child's World, c2000. 23pp.
Simple text and repetition of the letter "a" help readers learn how to use this sound.

Gag, Wanda. ***Millions of Cats.*** Putnam, c1956. 32pp.
An old man sets out in search of a pet for his lonely wife and returns with millions of cats, all claiming to be the most beautiful of the bunch.

Gibbons, Gail. ***The Seasons of Arnold's Apple Tree.*** Harcourt Brace, c1984. 32pp.
As the seasons pass, Arnold enjoys a variety of activities as a result of his apple tree. Includes a recipe for apple pie and a description of how an apple cider press works.

Karlin, Nurit. ***The Fat Cat Sat on the Mat.*** HarperTrophy, 1998. c1996. 32pp.
Rat tries to get the fat cat off the mat and back to his usual resting place in the vat.

Minden, Cecilia. ***Akiko, Miss Alice, and the Dance Class: The Sound of Short A.*** Child's World, c2005.
Introduces the short "a" sound through the story of Akiko's tap dance class with Miss Alice.

Moncure, Jane Belk. ***Short "A" and Long "A" Play a Game.*** Child's World, c2002. 32pp.
Introduces the long and short "a" sounds through color illustrations of objects such as a flag, a cake, and acorns.

Moncure, Jane Belk. ***Word Bird Makes Words with Cat.*** Child's World, c2002. 32pp.
When his father brings home new word puzzles, Word Bird makes up words with his friend Cat, and each new word leads them into a new activity.

Most, Bernard. ***There's an Ant in Anthony.*** Mulberry, 1992. c1980. 32pp.
After discovering an "ant" in his own name, Anthony searches for the word "ant" in other words.

Seuss, Dr. ***The Cat in the Hat.*** Random House, c1985. 61pp.
A fantastic cat entertains two children in a most unusual way.

From Nancy J. Keane, *The Big Book of Children's Reading Lists: 100 Great, Ready-to-Use Book Lists for Educators, Librarians, Parents, and Children.* Westport, CT: Libraries Unlimited, 2006. Copyright © 2006 by Libraries Unlimited.

Long and Short "E"

Long "E"

Books for Children of All Ages

Braidich, Shelby. ***Meet Me on the Farm: Learning the Long E Sound.*** PowerKids Press, 2002. 23pp. (NF)
Pairs words and pictures to teach young readers the basic phonetic applications of the long "e" sound.

Klingel, Cynthia Fitterer. ***What a Week: The Sound of Long E.*** Child's World, c2000. 23pp.
Simple text and repetition of the letter "e" help readers learn how to use the "long e" sound.

Minden, Cecilia. ***Eve's Green Garden—The Sound of Long E.*** Child's World, c2004. 24pp.
Simple text featuring the long "e" sound describes how Eve plants and cares for a vegetable garden.

Moncure, Jane Belk. ***My "E" Sound Box.*** Child's World, c2001. 30pp.
A little boy fills his sound box with many words beginning with the letter "e."

Moncure, Jane Belk. ***Short "E" and Long "E" Play a Game.*** Child's World, c2002. 32pp.
A brief story in which characters representing the short "e" sound and the long "e" sound look for these vowels in different words.

Salzmann, Mary Elizabeth. ***Ee.*** Abdo, c2001. 24pp. (NF)
A picture book presenting lots of word examples that use the long vowel sound of "e."

Shapiro, Arnold L. ***Mice Squeak, We Speak: A Poem.*** Puffin, 2000, c1997. 32pp.
Illustrations and simple text describe the ways various animals communicate, such as "owls hoot," "pigs squeal," and "bees buzz."

Shaw, Nancy. ***Sheep in a Jeep*****.** Houghton Mifflin, c1986. 32pp.
Records the misadventures of a group of sheep that go riding in a jeep.

Shaw, Nancy. ***Sheep on a Ship.*** Houghton Mifflin, 1989. 32pp.
Sheep on a deep-sea voyage run into trouble when it storms, and they are glad to come paddling into port.

From Nancy J. Keane, *The Big Book of Children's Reading Lists: 100 Great, Ready-to-Use Book Lists for Educators, Librarians, Parents, and Children.* Westport, CT: Libraries Unlimited, 2006. Copyright © 2006 by Libraries Unlimited.

Long and Short "E"

Short "E"

Books for Children of All Ages

Doudna, Kelly. ***Ee.*** Abdo. c2000. 24pp. (NF)
Presents pictures of objects spelled with the short vowel "e."

Flanagan, Alice K. ***Ben's Pens: The Sound of Short "E."*** Child's World, c2000. 23pp.
Simple text and repetition of the letter "e" help readers learn how to use this sound.

Krauss, Ruth. ***The Happy Egg.*** HarperCollins, c2005.
After an egg hatches, it can do many of the same things birds can do.

Metz, Lynn. ***Every Egg: Learning the Short E Sound.*** PowerKids Press, 2002. 23pp. (NF)
Introduces young learners to the short "e" sound through a story about eggs.

Moncure, Jane Belk. ***Short "E" and Long "E" Play a Game.*** Child's World, c2002. 32pp.
A brief story in which characters representing the short "e" sound and the long "e" sound look for these vowels in different words.

Moncure, Jane Belk. ***Word Bird Makes Words with Hen.*** Child's World, c2002. 32pp.
When his father brings him some new word puzzles, Word Bird makes up more words with his friend Hen, and each word that they make up leads them into a new activity.

From Nancy J. Keane, *The Big Book of Children's Reading Lists: 100 Great, Ready-to-Use Book Lists for Educators, Librarians, Parents, and Children.* Westport, CT: Libraries Unlimited, 2006. Copyright © 2006 by Libraries Unlimited.

Long and Short "I"

Long "I"

Books for Children of All Ages

Battistoni, Ilse. ***I Fight Fires: Learning the Long I Sound.*** PowerKids Press, 2002. 23pp. (NF)
Presents the long "i" sound in simple sentences that describe what a firefighter does, and includes an activity list for teachers.

Berenstain, Stan. ***The Bike Lesson.*** Beginner Books/Random House, c1992. 61pp.
Papa Bear keeps getting into trouble when he tries to show Junior how to ride a bike.

Carlson, Nancy L. ***I Like Me!*** Puffin Books, 1990. c1988. 32pp.
By admiring her finer points and showing that she can take care of herself and have fun even when there's no one else around, a charming pig proves the best friend you can have is yourself.

Hazen, Barbara Shook. ***Tight Times.*** Puffin Books, 1983. c1979. 32pp.
A small boy, not allowed to have a dog because times are tight, finds a starving kitten in a trash can on the same day his father loses his job.

Kirk, David. ***Little Miss Spider.*** Scholastic Press/Callaway, 1999. 31pp.
On her very first day of life, Little Miss Spider searches for her mother and finds love in an unexpected place.

Minden, Cecilia. ***Isaac on the Farm: The Sound of Long I.*** Child's World, c2005. 24pp.
Introduces the long "i" sound through the story of Isaac's visit to his grandparents' farm.

Moncure, Jane Belk. ***Short "I" and Long "I" Play a Game.*** Child's World, c2002. 32pp.
A brief story in which characters representing the short "i" sound and the long "i" sound look for these vowels in different words.

Noyed, Robert B. ***Smiles: The Sound of Long I.*** Child's World, c2000. 23pp.
Simple text and repetition of the letter "i" help readers learn how to use this sound.

Steig, William. ***Brave Irene.*** Farrar, Straus & Giroux, 1986. 32pp.
Plucky Irene, a dressmaker's daughter, braves a fierce snowstorm to deliver a new gown to the duchess in time for the ball.

Waber, Bernard. ***Ira Sleeps Over.*** Houghton Mifflin, c1972. 48pp.
A little boy is excited at the prospect of spending the night at his friend's house but worries how he'll get along without his teddy bear.

Short "I"

Books for Children of All Ages

Ballard, Peg. ***Little Bit: The Sound of Short "I."*** Child's World, c2000. 23pp.
Simple text and repetition of the letter "i" help readers learn how to use this sound.

From Nancy J. Keane, *The Big Book of Children's Reading Lists: 100 Great, Ready-to-Use Book Lists for Educators, Librarians, Parents, and Children.* Westport, CT: Libraries Unlimited, 2006. Copyright © 2006 by Libraries Unlimited.

Long and Short "I"

Braidich, Shelby. ***Little Pigs, Big Pigs: Learning the Short I Sound.*** PowerKids Press, 2002. 23pp. (NF)
Simple sentences introduce readers to the short "i" sound, describing pigs, where they live, and what they do.

Doudna, Kelly. ***India and Iggy***. Abdo, c2005. 23pp. (NF)
Presents a series of words, sentences, and rebus riddles that introduce early readers to the short "i" sound.

Hoban, Tana. ***Is It Red? Is It Yellow? Is It Blue?: An Adventure in Color.*** Greenwillow Books, c1978. 32pp. (NF)
Illustrations and brief text introduce colors and the concepts of shape and size.

Hoban, Tana. ***Is It Rough? Is It Smooth? Is It Shiny?*** Greenwillow Books, c1984. 32pp. (NF)
Color photographs without text introduce objects of many different textures, such as pretzels, foil, hay, mud, a kitten, and bubbles.

Hutchins, Pat. ***Titch.*** Aladdin Paperbacks, 1993, c1971. 30pp.
Titch feels left out because he is so much smaller than his brother and sister, until he gets a little seed that grows bigger than anything they have.

Keats, Ezra Jack. ***Whistle for Willie.*** Viking Press, c1964. 33pp.
A young boy tries to learn how to whistle so that he can call his dog, like all the bigger boys do.

Lionni, Leo. ***Inch by Inch.*** HarperCollins, 1994. c1960. 31pp.
To keep from being eaten, an inchworm measures a robin's tail, a flamingo's neck, a toucan's beak, a heron's legs, and a nightingale's song.

Lionni, Leo. ***It's Mine!*** Knopf (distributed by Random House), 1996. c1985. 32pp.
Three selfish frogs quarrel over who owns their pond and island, until a storm makes them value the benefits of sharing.

Lionni, Leo. ***Swimmy.*** Pantheon, c1968. 32pp.
Swimmy, a small black fish, finds a way to protect a school of small red fish from their natural enemies.

Lobel, Arnold. ***Small Pig.*** HarperCollins, c1969. 63pp.
Because the farmer's wife insists on cleaning his mud puddle, a little pig runs away to the city, where he becomes permanently stuck in what he thought was another mud puddle.

Maccarone, Grace. ***Itchy, Itchy Chicken Pox.*** Scholastic. c1992. 30pp.
Peppy rhymes present the humorous side of a common ailment.

McPhail, David M. ***Fix-it.*** Puffin Books, 1987, c1984. 24pp.
When the fix-it man is trying to repair the television and her parents are trying to entertain her, Emma becomes so interested in reading that she no longer cares about TV.

Meier, Joanne D. ***Isabel's Favorite Things—The Sound of Short I.*** Child's World, c2004. 24pp.
In simple text featuring the short "i" sound, Isabel and her mother discuss an upcoming family trip on a ship.

Moncure, Jane Belk. ***Short "I" and Long "I" Play a Game.*** Child's World, c2002. 32pp.
A brief story in which characters representing the short "i" sound and the long "i" sound look for these vowels in different words.

From Nancy J. Keane, *The Big Book of Children's Reading Lists: 100 Great, Ready-to-Use Book Lists for Educators, Librarians, Parents, and Children.* Westport, CT: Libraries Unlimited, 2006. Copyright © 2006 by Libraries Unlimited.

Long and Short "O"

Long "O"

Books for Children of All Ages

Greene, Carol. ***Snow Joe.*** Childrens Press, c1982. 31pp.
Throw. Blow. Whoa! Joe does many things with snow.

Hanson, Anders. ***Olga and Olaf.*** Abdo, c2005. 23pp. (NF)
Presents a series of words, sentences, and rebus riddles that introduce early readers to the long "o" sound.

Minden, Cecilia. ***Olivia by the Ocean: The Sound of Long O.*** Child's World, c2005. 24pp.
Introduces the long "o" sound through the story of Olivia's walk by the ocean.

Moncure, Jane Belk. ***Short "O" and Long "O" Play a Game.*** Child's World, c2002. 32pp.
Introduces the long and short "o" sounds through color illustrations of objects such as a mop, an oboe, and oatmeal.

Noyed, Robert B. ***On My Boat: The Sound of Long O.*** Child's World, c2000. 23pp.
Simple text about a boat and repetition of the letter "o" help readers learn how to use the "long o" sound.

Richter, Abigail. ***By the Ocean: Learning the Long O Sound.*** PowerKids Press, 2002. 23pp. (NF)
Pairs words and pictures to teach young readers the basic phonetic applications of the long "o" sound.

Salzmann, Mary Elizabeth. ***Oo.*** Abdo Publishing, c2000. 24pp. (NF)
A picture book presenting lots of word examples that use the long vowel sound of "o."

Tresselt, Alvin R. ***White Snow, Bright Snow.*** Lothrop, Lee & Shepard, c1988. 32pp.
When it begins to look, feel, and smell like snow, everyone prepares for a winter blizzard.

Wadsworth, Olive A. ***Over in the Meadow: A Counting Rhyme.*** North-South Books, c2002. 24pp.
A variety of meadow animals pursuing their daily activities introduce the numbers one through ten.

Short "O"

Books for Children of All Ages

Benchley, Nathaniel. ***Oscar Otter***. HarperTrophy, c1994. 64pp.
The adventures of a young otter as he discovers he has much to learn from his father.

From Nancy J. Keane, *The Big Book of Children's Reading Lists: 100 Great, Ready-to-Use Book Lists for Educators, Librarians, Parents, and Children.* Westport, CT: Libraries Unlimited, 2006. Copyright © 2006 by Libraries Unlimited.

Long and Short "O"

Crews, Donald. ***Ten Black Dots.*** Greenwillow Books, c1986. 29pp.
A counting book which shows what can be done with ten black dots—one can make a sun, two a fox's eyes, or eight the wheels of a train.

DeRubertis, Barbara. ***Foxy Fox.*** Kane Press, 1997. 32pp.
Introduces the short "o" sound through a story about Foxy Fox, whose work-shy ways may cost him his job at the store.

Emberley, Barbara. ***Drummer Hoff.*** Simon and Schuster Books for Young Readers, 1987. c1967. 32pp.
A cumulative folk song in which seven soldiers build a magnificent cannon, but Drummer Hoff fires it off.

Flanagan, Alice K. ***Hot Pot: The Sound of Short "O."*** Child's World, c2000. 23pp.
Simple text and repetition of the letter "o" help readers learn how to use this sound.

Hanson, Anders. ***Olive and Oscar.*** Abdo, c2005. 23pp. (NF)
Presents an introduction to the letter "o", in simple text with photographs, and contains words and short sentences of people, places, and things that begin with the letter "o."

McKissack, Pat. ***Flossie & the Fox.*** Dial Books for Young Readers, c1986. 32pp.
A wily fox, notorious for stealing eggs, meets his match when he encounters a bold little girl in the woods who insists upon proof that he is a fox before she will be frightened.

Meier, Joanne D. ***Oliver's Box—The Sound of Short O*** Child's World, c2004.
Simple text featuring the sound of the short "o" describes a game Oliver loves to play.

Metz, Lynn. ***On the Job: Learning the Short O Sound.*** PowerKids Press, 2002. 23pp. (NF)
Pairs pictures and words to help young readers learn the basic phonetic applications of the short "o" sound.

Moncure, Jane Belk. ***Short "O" and Long "O" Play a Game.*** Child's World, c2002. 32pp.
Introduces the long and short "o" sounds through color illustrations of objects such as a mop, an oboe, and oatmeal.

Seuss, Dr. ***Fox in Socks.*** Beginner Books, c1993. 61pp.
A collection of easy-to-read tongue twisters.

Seuss, Dr. ***Hop on Pop.*** Beginner Books, c1963. 64pp.
Pairs of rhyming words are introduced and used in simple sentences, such as "Day. Play. We play all day. Night. Fight. We fight all night."

Wilson, Karma. ***A Frog in the Bog.*** M.K. McElderry Books, c2003. 32pp.
A frog in the bog grows larger and larger as he eats more and more bugs, until he attracts the attention of an alligator who puts an end to his eating.

From Nancy J. Keane, *The Big Book of Children's Reading Lists: 100 Great, Ready-to-Use Book Lists for Educators, Librarians, Parents, and Children.* Westport, CT: Libraries Unlimited, 2006. Copyright © 2006 by Libraries Unlimited.

Long and Short "U"

Long "U"

Books for Children of All Ages

Minden, Cecilia. ***Umeko and the Music Show—The Sound of Long U.*** Child's World, c2004.
Umeko appears in a music show and sings with her friends, in simple text featuring the long "u" sound.

Moncure, Jane Belk. ***Short "U" and Long "U" Play a Game.*** Child's World, c2002. 32pp.
Short "u" and Long "u" introduce the long and short "u" sounds.

Noyed, Robert B. ***Cute!: The Sound of Long U.*** Child's World, c2000. 23pp.
Simple text about babies and repetition of the letter "u" help readers learn how to use the "long u" sound.

Pinkney, Andrea Davis. ***Sleeping Cutie.*** Harcourt Brace, c2004. 32pp.
Cutie LaRue is perfect in nearly every way, but her sleeplessness causes problems for her parents until they send for a new toy that introduces Cutie to the Dreamland Nightclub.

Salzmann, Mary Elizabeth. ***Uu.*** Abdo Publishing, c2000. 24pp. (NF)
A picture book presenting lots of word examples that use the long vowel sound of "u."

Vastola, Pam. ***Huge Animals: Learning the Long U Sound.*** PowerKids Press, 2002. 23pp. (NF)
Introduces young learners to the long "u" sound through a story about huge animals.

Short "U"

Books for Children of All Ages

Bailey, Jacqui. ***Sun Up, Sun Down: The Story of Day and Night.*** Picture Window Books, 2004. c2003. 31pp.
Follows the sun from dawn to dusk to explain how light rays travel, how shadows are formed, how the moon lights up the night sky, and more.

Ballard, Peg. ***Fun!: The Sound of Short U.*** Child's World, c2000. 23pp.
Simple text about playing and repetition of the letter "u" help readers learn how to use the "short u" sound.

Gibbons, Gail. ***Sun Up, Sun Down.*** Harcourt Brace, c1983. 32pp. (NF)
Describes the characteristics of the sun and the ways in which it regulates life on earth.

From Nancy J. Keane, *The Big Book of Children's Reading Lists: 100 Great, Ready-to-Use Book Lists for Educators, Librarians, Parents, and Children.* Westport, CT: Libraries Unlimited, 2006. Copyright © 2006 by Libraries Unlimited.

Long and Short "U"

Jones, Jeff. ***Just Bugs: Learning the Short U Sound.*** PowerKids Press, 2002. 23pp. (NF)
Introduces young learners to the short "u" sound through a story about bugs.

Lewis, Kevin. ***My Truck Is Stuck!*** Hyperion Books for Children, c2002. 32pp.
A dump truck causes quite a traffic jam when it gets stuck in a hole.

Minden, Cecilia. ***Umberto's Summer Day—The Sound of Short U.*** Child's World, c2004.
Simple text featuring the sound of the short "u" describes some of the ways a boy enjoys a summer day.

Moncure, Jane Belk. ***Short "U" and Long "U" Play a Game.*** Child's World, c2002. 32pp.
Short "u" and Long "u" introduce the long and short "u" sounds.

Monsell, Mary Elise. ***Underwear!*** Whitman, c1988. 24pp.
Bismark the Buffalo is grumpy and unlovable until his friends teach him how to laugh and show him that wearing colorful underwear can be great fun.

Prelutsky, Jack. ***The Baby Uggs Are Hatching.*** Mulberry, 1989. c1982. 32pp.
A collection of twelve humorous poems about such strange creatures as the sneepy and the quossible.

Scheunemann, Pam. ***Ulma and Upton.*** Abdo, c2005. 23pp. (NF)
Presents a series of words, sentences, and rebus riddles that introduce early readers to the short "u" sound.

Scheunemann, Pam. ***Unity and Uri.*** Abdo, c2005. 23pp. (NF)
Presents an introduction to the letter "u", in simple text with photographs, and contains words and short sentences of people, places, and things that begin with the letter "u."

Udry, Janice May. ***Thump and Plunk.*** HarperTrophy, c2000. 23pp.
When Thump thumps Plunk's doll Plunkit, an argument starts which their mother resolves.

Whitney, Louise Doak. ***B Is for Buckaroo: A Cowboy Alphabet.*** Sleeping Bear Press, c2003. 40pp. (NF)
The letters of the alphabet are represented by words, set in short rhymes with additional information, relating to cowboys and ranch life.

Yolen, Jane. ***Sleeping Ugly.*** Putnam & Grosset Group, 1997. c1991. 64pp.
Princess Miserella, a beautiful but mean-spirited girl, Plain Jane, and a fairy all fall victim to a sleeping spell, and when Prince Jojo comes along, a youngest son with no money or property, he makes a surprising but wise choice of who to kiss first.

From Nancy J. Keane, *The Big Book of Children's Reading Lists: 100 Great, Ready-to-Use Book Lists for Educators, Librarians, Parents, and Children.* Westport, CT: Libraries Unlimited, 2006. Copyright © 2006 by Libraries Unlimited.

Native American

Books for Children of All Ages

Bruchac, Joseph. ***Between Earth & Sky: Legends of Native American Sacred Places.*** Harcourt Brace & Co. c1996. 32pp.

Through the guidance of his uncle and the retelling of various Native American legends, a young boy learns that everything living and inanimate has its place, should be considered sacred, and given respect.

Bruchac, Joseph. ***The First Strawberries: A Cherokee Story.*** Dial Books for Young Readers, c1993. 32pp.

A quarrel between the first man and the first woman is reconciled when the Sun causes strawberries to grow out of the earth.

Bruchac, Joseph. ***The Great Ball Game: A Muskogee Story.*** Dial Books for Young Readers, c1994. 32pp.

Bat, who has both wings and teeth, plays an important part in a game between the birds and the animals to decide which group is better.

Bruchac, Joseph. ***How Chipmunk Got His Stripes: A Tale of Bragging And Teasing.*** Dial Books for Young Readers, c2001. 32pp.

When Bear and Brown Squirrel have a disagreement about whether Bear can stop the sun from rising, Brown Squirrel ends up with claw marks on his back and becomes Chipmunk, the striped one.

Bruchac, Joseph. ***Raccoon's Last Race: A Traditional Abenaki Story.*** Dial Books for Young Readers, c2004. 32pp.

Tells the story of how Raccoon, the fastest animal on earth, loses his speed because he is boastful and breaks his promises.

Ehlert, Lois. ***Mole's Hill: A Woodland Tale.*** Harcourt Brace, c1994. 34pp.

When Fox tells Mole she must move out of her tunnel to make way for a new path, Mole finds an ingenious way to save her home.

Goble, Paul. ***The Legend of the White Buffalo Woman.*** National Geographic Society, c1998. 32pp.

A Lakota Indian legend in which the White Buffalo Woman presents her people with the Sacred Calf Pipe which gives them the means to pray to the Great Spirit.

Goble, Paul. ***Remaking the Earth: A Creation Story from the Great Plains of North America.*** Orchard Books, c1996. 32pp.

In this Algonquin "Earth Diver" creation myth, woven from the ideas of several traditional tales, the water birds and animals left behind when the old world was flooded dive for mud so that the Creator can make dry land again.

From Nancy J. Keane, *The Big Book of Children's Reading Lists: 100 Great, Ready-to-Use Book Lists for Educators, Librarians, Parents, and Children.* Westport, CT: Libraries Unlimited, 2006. Copyright © 2006 by Libraries Unlimited.

Native American

Martin, Rafe. ***The Rough-Face Girl.*** G.P. Putnam's Sons, c1992. 32pp.
In this Algonquin Indian version of the Cinderella story, the Rough-Face Girl and her two beautiful but heartless sisters compete for the affections of the Invisible Being.

McDermott, Gerald. ***Coyote: A Trickster Tale from the American Southwest.*** Harcourt Brace, c1994. 32pp.
Coyote, who has a nose for trouble, insists that the blackbirds teach him how to fly, but the experience ends in disaster for him.

McDermott, Gerald. ***Raven: A Trickster Tale from the Pacific Northwest.*** Harcourt Brace, c1993. 32pp.
Raven, a Pacific Coast Indian trickster, sets out to find the sun.

Medicine Crow, Joseph. ***Brave Wolf and the Thunderbird: Tales of the People.*** National Museum of the American Indian, Abbeville Press, c1998. 31pp.
While hunting, Brave Wolf is snatched by a huge Thunderbird and taken to her nest on a high cliff so he can protect her chicks from a monster.

Pollock, Penny. ***The Turkey Girl: A Zuni Cinderella Story.*** Little, Brown, c1996. 32pp.
In this Native American variant of a familiar story, some turkeys make a gown of feathers for the poor girl who tends them so that she can participate in a sacred dance, but they desert her when she fails to return as promised.

San Souci, Robert D. ***Sootface: an Ojibwa Cinderella Story.*** Dragonfly, 1997. c1994. 32pp.
In this Ojibwa retelling of the Cinderella story, a Native American maiden called Sootface, who is mocked and mistreated by her two older sisters, wins a mighty invisible warrior for her husband with her kind and honest heart.

Steptoe, John. ***The Story of Jumping Mouse: A Native American Legend.*** Lothrop, Lee & Shepard, c1984. 40pp.
The gifts of Magic Frog and his own hopeful and unselfish spirit bring Jumping Mouse finally to the Far-Off Land where no mouse goes hungry.

Stevens, Janet. ***Coyote Steals the Blanket: A Ute Tale.*** Holiday House, c1993. 32pp.
Coyote receives his comeuppance when he tries to take something that does not belong to him.

Van Laan, Nancy. ***Rainbow Crow: A Lenape Tale.*** Knopf, c1989. 36pp.
When the weather changes and the ever-falling snow threatens to engulf all the animals, it is Crow who flies up to receive the gift of fire from the Great Sky Spirit.

Zeman, Ludmila. ***The First Red Maple Leaf.*** Tundra Books, c1997. 24pp.
A young boy saves his people and brings summer back to his frozen land when he performs a good deed and saves a goose that was caught in the onslaught of Iceheart and his frigid storms.

From Nancy J. Keane, *The Big Book of Children's Reading Lists: 100 Great, Ready-to-Use Book Lists for Educators, Librarians, Parents, and Children.* Westport, CT: Libraries Unlimited, 2006. Copyright © 2006 by Libraries Unlimited.

Native American

Books for Children Ages 8–12

Bruchac, Joseph. ***The Boy Who Lived with the Bears: And Other Iroquois Stories.*** Parabola Books, 2003. 63pp.

Presents a collection of traditional Iroquois tales in which animals learn about the importance of caring and responsibility and the dangers of selfishness and pride.

Bruchac, Joseph. ***The Earth Under Sky Bear's Feet: Native American Poems of the Land.*** Putnam & Grosset, 1998. c1995. 32pp.

A collection of tales about the Big Dipper from various North American Indian cultures.

Bruchac, Joseph. ***Thirteen Moons on Turtle's Back: A Native American Year of Moons.*** Philomel Books, c1992.

Celebrates the seasons of the year through poems from the legends of such Native American tribes as the Cherokee, Cree, and Sioux.

Curry, Jane Louise. ***Hold Up the Sky: And Other Native American Tales from Texas and the Southern Plains.*** M.K. McElderry Books, c2003. 159pp.

Retells twenty-six tales from Native Americans whose traditional lands were in Texas and the Southern Plains, and provides a brief introduction to the history of each tribe.

Dalal, Anita. ***Myths of the Native Americans.*** Raintree Steck-Vaughn, c2002. c2001. 48pp.

Presents ten Native American myths accompanied by color illustrations, and includes a general introduction, a glossary, and a list of related resources. Covers such figures as Old Man Coyote, Wisagatcak, Sedna, and Raven.

De Paola, Tomie. ***The Legend of the Bluebonnet: an Old Tale of Texas.*** Putnam, 1993. c1983. 30pp.

A retelling of the Comanche Indian legend of how a little girl's sacrifice brought the flower called bluebonnet to Texas.

Goble, Paul. ***The Return of the Buffaloes: A Plains Indian Story About Famine and Renewal of the Earth.*** National Geographic Society, 2002. c1996. 32pp.

Based on a Lakota legend in which a mysterious woman returns the buffalo and the other animals to the Indian people.

Hausman, Gerald. ***The Story of Blue Elk.*** Clarion Books, c1998. 32pp.

In this traditional tale, a great magic elk helps a mute Native American boy find his voice.

Oughton, Jerrie. ***How the Stars Fell into the Sky: A Navajo Legend.*** Houghton Mifflin, 1992. 28pp.

A retelling of the Navajo legend that explains the patterns of the stars in the sky.

From Nancy J. Keane, *The Big Book of Children's Reading Lists: 100 Great, Ready-to-Use Book Lists for Educators, Librarians, Parents, and Children.* Westport, CT: Libraries Unlimited, 2006. Copyright © 2006 by Libraries Unlimited.

Native American

Ross, Gayle. ***How Rabbit Tricked Otter and Other Cherokee Trickster Stories.*** Parabola Books, 2003. 79pp.
Fifteen traditional tales follow the adventures of Rabbit, the Cherokee trickster.

Spider Spins a Story: Fourteen Legends from Native America. Rising Moon, c1997. 63pp.
Presents tales from various native peoples, including the Kiowa, Zuni, Cherokee, Hopi, Lakota, and Muskogee, all featuring a spider character.

Taylor, C. J. ***How Two-Feather Was Saved from Loneliness: an Abenaki Legend.*** Tundra Books, c1990. 22pp.
Retells the Abenaki Indian legend of how both fire and corn came into the world.

Taylor, C. J. ***How We Saw the World: Nine Native Stories of the Way Things Began.*** Tundra Books, c1993. 32pp.
Presents nine Native American legends that provide insight into how North America was seen by its first inhabitants.

Taylor, C. J. ***The Messenger of Spring.*** Tundra Books, Tundra Books of Northern New York, c1997. 24pp.
New Dawn comes to bring Iceman a message, and as he delivers that message, he melts the winter ice and snow Iceman has left, bringing to life the joy of spring.

Taylor, C. J. ***The Monster from the Swamp: Native Legends of Monsters, Demons and Other Creatures.*** Tundra Books, Tundra Books of Northern New York, c1995. 32pp.
Legends of the Mohawk, Tlingit, Malecite, Micmac, Cheyenne, Comanche, Gwich'in, and Seneca tribes, including two that have never appeared in written form before.

Taylor, C. J. ***Peace Walker: The Legend of Hiawatha and Tekanawita.*** Tundra Books, c2004. 45pp.
The author draws upon her Mohawk heritage and the stories she heard from the elders to tell the story of the formation of the Iroquois Confederacy and the peace walker, Hiawatha, who strove to bring the warring nations together.

Van Laan, Nancy. ***Shingebiss: An Ojibwe Legend.*** Houghton Mifflin, c1997. 32pp.
Shingebiss the duck bravely challenges the Winter Maker and manages to find enough food to survive a long, harsh winter.

Wargi, Kathy-jo. ***The Legend of Sleeping Bear.*** Sleeping Bear Press, c1998. 48pp.
In this retelling of an Ojibwe Indian tale, a mother bear loses sight of her two cubs as they all attempt to escape a forest fire by swimming across Lake Michigan.

The Wonderful Sky Boat: And Other Native American Tales of the Southeast. Margaret K. McElderry Books, c2001. 142pp.
A collection of twenty-seven Native American tales of the Southeast, including trickster tales, "how and why" stories, and stories of the supernatural.

From Nancy J. Keane, *The Big Book of Children's Reading Lists: 100 Great, Ready-to-Use Book Lists for Educators, Librarians, Parents, and Children.* Westport, CT: Libraries Unlimited, 2006. Copyright © 2006 by Libraries Unlimited.

Central and South American

Books for Children of All Ages

Ada, Alma Flor. ***Dreaming Fish.*** Alfaguara/Santillana, c2000. 32pp.
Contains a collection of poetry by noted Spanish poets from Puerto Rico, Mexico, and Argentina, and includes Hispanic folklore by Alma Flor Ada and F. Isabel Campoy.

DeSpain, Pleasant. ***The Dancing Turtle: A Folktale from Brazil.*** August House LittleFolk, c1998. 32pp.
After being caught by a hunter, a clever turtle uses her wits and her talent playing the flute to trick the hunter's children into helping her escape.

Gonzalez, Lucia M. ***Señor Cat's Romance and Other Favorite Stories from Latin America.*** Scholastic, 2001. c1997. 46pp.
A collection of popular tales told to young children in places such as Argentina, Cuba, Colombia, Nicaragua, and Mexico.

Gugler, Laurel Dee. ***Monkey Tales.*** Annick Press (distributed in the United States by Firefly Books), c1998. 38pp.
Contains illustrated retellings of three monkey tales from different cultures around the world.

Keens-Douglas, Richardo. ***The Trial of the Stone: A Folktale Retold.*** Annick Press (distributed in the United States by Firefly Books), c2000. 32pp.
An illustrated telling of the Asian and South American folktale in which a boy loses his breakfast money after hiding it under a stone, and the stone is put on trial for stealing it.

Knutson, Barbara. ***Love and Roast Chicken: A Trickster Tale from the Andes Mountains.*** Carolrhoda Books, c2004. 40pp.
In this folktale from the Andes, a clever guinea pig repeatedly outsmarts the fox that wants to eat him for dinner.

Lilly, Melinda. ***Mira and the Stone Tortoise.*** Rourke Press, c1999. 30pp.
After befriending a clever tortoise while lost in the Brazilian rain forest, a young Kulina girl helps it avoid becoming her father's dinner.

Little Book of Latin American Folktales. Douglas & McIntyre (distributed in the United States by Publishers Group West), c2003. 132pp.
A collection of ten short Latin American folktales.

MacDonald, Margaret Read. ***A Hen, a Chick, and a String Guitar: Inspired by a Chilean Folk Tale.*** Barefoot Books, c2005. 28pp.
A cumulative tale from Chile that begins with a hen and ends with sixteen different animals and a guitar. Includes an audio CD.

From Nancy J. Keane, *The Big Book of Children's Reading Lists: 100 Great, Ready-to-Use Book Lists for Educators, Librarians, Parents, and Children.* Westport, CT: Libraries Unlimited, 2006. Copyright © 2006 by Libraries Unlimited.

Central and South American

Maggi, Maria Elena. ***The Great Canoe: A Karina Legend.*** Douglas & McIntyre (distributed in the United States by Publishers Group West), c2001. 37pp.

The Carib Indians are warned by their sky god to build canoes to escape a worldwide flood, but few believe them.

McDermott, Gerald. ***Jabuti, the Tortoise: A Trickster Tale from the Amazon.*** Harcourt, c2001. 32pp.

All the birds enjoy the songlike flute music of Jabuti, the tortoise, except Vulture, who, jealous because he cannot sing, tricks Jabuti into riding his back toward a festival planned by the King of Heaven.

Mora, Pat. ***The Race of Toad and Deer.*** Douglas & McIntyre (distributed in the United States by Publishers Group West), c2001. 32pp.

With the help of his friends, Tio Sapo, the toad, defeats the overconfident Tio Venado, the deer, in a race.

Pitcher, Caroline. ***Mariana and the Merchild: A Folk Tale from Chile.*** Eerdmans Books for Young Readers, c2000. 26pp.

A childless old woman is given a merbaby to raise until the child can safely return to the sea.

Van Laan, Nancy. ***The Magic Bean Tree: A Legend from Argentina.*** Houghton Mifflin, 1998. 32pp.

A young Quechuan boy sets out on his own to bring the rains back to his parched homeland and is rewarded by a gift of carob beans that come to be prized across Argentina.

Books for Children Ages 8–12

Dalal, Anita. ***Myths of Pre-Columbian America.*** Raintree Steck-Vaughn, c2002. 48pp.

Recounts the myths of pre-Columbian America and explains how they reflect the environment, way of life, and religion of the people who created them.

Delacre, Lulu. ***Golden Tales: Myths, Legends, and Folktales from Latin America.*** Scholastic, 2001. c1996. 73pp.

Collection of twelve myths, legends, and folktales reflecting the history of Latin America before and after the arrival of the Spaniards in 1492. drawing from the traditions of thirteen countries and four native cultures.

Lilly, Melinda. ***Huatya Curi and the Five Condors: A Huarochiri Myth.*** Rourke Press, c1999. 31pp.

Huatya Curi, also known as Potato Eater, son of the mountain spirit Paria Caca, challenges a greedy king and wins a worthy bride, releasing his father from his icy mountain prison.

Metaxas, Eric. ***The Monkey People.*** Abdo, 2005. c1995. 38pp.

The people in a village in the Amazon rain forest grow so lazy that they eagerly allow a strange man to create monkeys from leaves to do everything for them.

Pirotta, Saviour. ***Stories from the Amazon***. Raintree Steck-Vaughn, c2000. 48pp.

Retellings of traditional stories from the people of the Amazon rain forests, including "The Legend of the Sun God," "The Tree of Life," and "The Sad Song of the Moon."

From Nancy J. Keane, *The Big Book of Children's Reading Lists: 100 Great, Ready-to-Use Book Lists for Educators, Librarians, Parents, and Children.* Westport, CT: Libraries Unlimited, 2006. Copyright © 2006 by Libraries Unlimited.

African

Books for Children of All Ages

Aardema, Verna. ***Anansi Does the Impossible!: An Ashanti Tale.*** Aladdin Paperbacks, 2000. c1997. 32pp.
Anansi and his wife outsmart the Sky God and win back the beloved folktales of their people.

Aardema, Verna. ***Rabbit Makes a Monkey of Lion: A Swahili Tale.*** Puffin Books, 1993. c1989. 30pp.
With the help of his friends Bush-rat and Turtle, smart and nimble Rabbit makes a fool of the mighty but slowwitted king of the forest.

Aardema, Verna. ***Why Mosquitoes Buzz in People's Ears: A West African Tale.*** Dial Books for Young Readers, c1975. 32pp.
Reveals the meaning of the mosquito's buzz.

Claire, Elizabeth. ***The Sun, the Wind, and Tashira: A Hottentot Tale from Africa.*** Mondo, 1994. 22pp.
The sun and the wind try to please a young girl by bringing colors into her life in the dry and dusty place where she lives in southern Africa.

Gregorowski, Christopher. ***Fly, Eagle, Fly!: An African Tale.*** Margaret K. McElderry Books, c2000. 32pp.
A farmer finds an eagle and raises it to behave like a chicken, until a friend helps the eagle learn to find its rightful place in the sky.

Haley, Gail E. ***A Story, a Story: An African Tale.*** Aladdin Paperbacks, c1970. 36pp.
Recounts how most African folktales came to be called "Spider Stories."

Kimmel, Eric A. ***Anansi and the Magic Stick.*** Holiday House, c2001. 32pp.
Anansi the Spider steals Hyena's magic stick so he won't have to do the chores, but when the stick's magic won't stop, he gets more than he bargained for.

Kimmel, Eric A. ***Anansi and the Talking Melon.*** Holiday House, c1994. 32pp.
Anansi, a clever spider, tricks Elephant and some other animals into thinking the melon in which he is hiding can talk.

Kimmel, Eric A. ***Anansi Goes Fishing.*** Holiday House, c1992. 32pp.
Anansi the Spider plans to trick Turtle into catching a fish for his dinner, but Turtle proves to be smarter and ends up with a free meal. Explains the origin of spider webs.

Kimmel, Eric A. ***Rimonah of the Flashing Sword: A North African Tale.*** Holiday House, c1995. 32pp.
A traditional Egyptian version of "Snow White."

Martin, Francesca. ***Clever Tortoise: A Traditional African Tale.*** Candlewick Press, 2000. 35pp.
Clever Tortoise leads the other jungle animals in teaching bullying Elephant and Hippopotamus a lesson by tricking them into engaging in a tug of war with each other.

From Nancy J. Keane, *The Big Book of Children's Reading Lists: 100 Great, Ready-to-Use Book Lists for Educators, Librarians, Parents, and Children.* Westport, CT: Libraries Unlimited, 2006. Copyright © 2006 by Libraries Unlimited.

African

McDermott, Gerald. ***Anansi the Spider: A Tale from the Ashanti.*** H. Holt, 1972. 41pp.
In trying to determine which of his six sons to reward for saving his life, Anansi the Spider is responsible for placing the moon in the sky.

McDermott, Gerald. ***Zomo the Rabbit: A Trickster Tale from West Africa***. Harcourt Brace, c1992. 32pp.
Zomo the Rabbit, an African trickster, sets out to gain wisdom.

Steptoe, John. ***Mufaro's Beautiful Daughters: An African Tale.*** Lothrop, Lee & Shepard, c1987. 32pp.
Mufaro's two beautiful daughters, one bad-tempered, one kind and sweet, go before the king, who is choosing a wife.

Books for Children Ages 8–12

Badoe, Adwoa. ***The Pot of Wisdom: Ananse Stories.*** Douglas & McIntyre (distributed in the United States by Publishers Group West), c2001. 63pp.
A collection of ten stories about Ananse, the African spider trickster.

Barbosa, Rogerio Andrade. ***African Animal Tales.*** Volcano Press, 1993. 62pp.
A collection of ten African animal tales.

Bryan, Ashley. ***Ashley Bryan's African Tales, Uh-Huh.*** Atheneum Books for Young Readers, c1998. 198pp.
An illustrated collection of traditional African myths, legends, and folktales.

Courlander, Harold. ***The Cow-Tail Switch and Other West African Stories.*** H. Holt, 1986. 143pp.
Contains seventeen stories gathered from the Ashantis of West Africa.

McIntosh, Gavin. ***Hausaland Tales from the Nigerian Marketplace.*** Linnet Books, c2002. 98pp.
A collection of twelve traditional tales from the Hausa people of Nigeria.

Mollel, Tololwa M. ***The Orphan Boy: A Maasai Story***. Clarion Books, c1990. 32pp.
Though delighted that an orphan boy has come into his life, an old man becomes insatiably curious about the boy's mysterious powers.

Nelson Mandela's Favorite African Folktales. W.W. Norton, c2002. 143pp.
A collection of traditional stories from different parts of Africa, featuring varied characters and themes, some familiar, some newer.

Paye, Won-Ldy. ***Why Leopard Has Spots: Dan Stories from Liberia.*** Fulcrum Kids, 1999, c1998. 50pp.
A collection of stories from the Dan ethnic group of Liberia.

Washington, Donna L. ***A Pride of African Tales.*** HarperCollins/Amistad, c2004. 70pp.
Presents vividly illustrated versions of six folktales from Congo, Ghana, and other regions of Africa, and lists further resources for each story.

From Nancy J. Keane, *The Big Book of Children's Reading Lists: 100 Great, Ready-to-Use Book Lists for Educators, Librarians, Parents, and Children.* Westport, CT: Libraries Unlimited, 2006. Copyright © 2006 by Libraries Unlimited.

Asian

Chinese folklore has a separate list.

Books for Children of All Ages

Backstein, Karen. ***The Blind Men and the Elephant.*** Scholastic, c1992. 48pp.
A retelling of the fable from India about six blind men who each get a limited understanding of what an elephant is by feeling only one part of it. (India)

Barkow, Henriette. ***Buri and the Marrow: An Indian Folk Tale.*** Mantra, 2000. 24pp.
An old woman traveling to her daughter's home convinces a fox, a tiger, and a lion not to eat her until her return trip, and then she must plot with her daughter to come up with a plan to fool them. Presented in English and Urdu. (India)

Berger, Barbara. ***All the Way to Lhasa: A Tale from Tibet.*** Philomel Books, c2002. 32pp.
A boy and his yak persevere along the difficult way to the holy city of Lhasa and succeed where others fail. (Tibet)

Blia Xiong. ***Nine-in-One, Grr! Grr!: A Folktale from the Hmong People of Laos.*** Children's Book Press, c1989. 30pp.
When the great god Shao promises Tiger nine cubs each year, Bird comes up with a clever trick to prevent the land from being overrun by tigers. (Laos)

Bowler, Ann Martin. ***Gecko's Complaint: A Balinese Folktale.*** Periplus (distributed by Tuttle Publishing), c2003. 32pp.
A Balinese folktale in which a gecko's griping about enthusiastic fireflies sets off a chain of complaints that is finally resolved by the jungle's lion chief. (Indonesia)

Brown, Marcia. ***Once a Mouse—: A Fable Cut in Wood.*** Atheneum Books for Young Readers, c1961. 32pp.
As it changes from mouse, to cat, to dog, to tiger, a hermit's pet also becomes increasingly vain. (India)

Brucker, Meredith Babeaux. ***Anklet for a Princess: A Cinderella Story from India.*** Shen's Books, 2002. 32pp.
Cinduri, hungry and ragged, is befriended by Godfather Snake, who feeds her delicacies and dresses her in gold cloth and anklets with bells and diamonds, to meet the prince. (India)

Charles, Veronika Martenova. ***The Crane Girl.*** Stoddart, c1992. 32pp.
Feeling that the arrival of a new baby has stopped her parents from loving her, Yoshiko goes to live among the cranes, whose magic transforms her into one of their young for a while. (Japan)

Claire, Elizabeth. ***The Little Brown Jay: A Tale from India.*** Mondo Publishing, 1994. 22pp.
A retelling of a traditional Indian tale in which a little bird helps the beautiful Princess Maya through a selfless act of love. (India)

Climo, Shirley. ***The Korean Cinderella.*** HarperCollins, c1993. 46pp.
In this version of "Cinderella" set in ancient Korea, Pear Blossom, a stepchild, eventually comes to be chosen by the magistrate to be his wife. (Korea)

From Nancy J. Keane, *The Big Book of Children's Reading Lists: 100 Great, Ready-to-Use Book Lists for Educators, Librarians, Parents, and Children.* Westport, CT: Libraries Unlimited, 2006. Copyright © 2006 by Libraries Unlimited.

Asian

Coburn, Jewell Reinhart. ***Angkat: The Cambodian Cinderella.*** Shen's Books, c1998. 32pp.
A Cambodian version of "Cinderella" in which a poor girl marries a prince, is killed by her jealous stepfamily, and then, through her virtue, returns to become queen. (Cambodia)

Coburn, Jewell Reinhart. ***Jouanah: A Hmong Cinderella.*** Shen's Books, c1996. 32pp.
Despite a cruel stepmother's schemes, Jouanah, a young Hmong girl, finds true love and happiness with the aid of her dead mother's spirit and a pair of special sandals. (Hmong)

Farley, Carol J. ***Mr. Pak Buys a Story.*** Whitman, c1997. 32pp.
The unusual story that a wealthy couple's servant buys from a thief proves to be well worth the price. (Korea)

French, Fiona. ***Little Inchkin: A Tale of Old Japan.*** Frances Lincoln Children's Books (distributed in the United States by Publishers Group West), 2004, c1994. 28pp.
In feudal Japan, little Inchkin, though only a few inches tall, becomes an honored Samurai swordsman. (Japan)

Ginsburg, Mirra. ***The Chinese Mirror.*** Harcourt Brace, c1988. 32pp.
A retelling of a traditional Korean tale in which a mirror brought from China causes confusion within a family as each member looks in it and sees a different stranger. (Korea)

Heine, Theresa. ***Elephant Dance.*** Barefoot Books, 2004. 44pp.
Grandfather tells many stories about his native India in answer to Ravi and Anjali's questions, such as the tale of a procession of elephants on the feast of Divaali when he was a boy. Includes facts about life in India, a list of cooking spices, and descriptions of Indian animals. (India)

Heo, Yumi. ***The Green Frogs: A Korean Folktale.*** Houghton Mifflin, c1996. 32pp.
A folktale about two green frogs who always disobey their mother, explaining why green frogs cry out whenever it rains. (Korea)

Hodges, Margaret. ***The Boy Who Drew Cats.*** Holiday House, c2002. 30pp.
A young boy's obsession with drawing cats changes his life. (Japan)

Kako, Satoshi. ***Little Daruma and Little Daikoku: A Japanese Children's Tale.*** Tuttle Publishing, 2003. 30pp.
Little Daruma is jealous of Little Daikoku's magic mallet, which brings all kinds of wonderful things when shaken, but Daruma's mallet doesn't bring the same results as his friend's does. (Japan)

Lee, Jeanne M. ***Toad Is the Uncle of Heaven: A Vietnamese Folk Tale.*** Holt, Rinehart & Winston, 1989. c1985. 30pp.
Toad leads a group of animals to ask the King of Heaven to send rain to the parched earth. (Vietnam)

Leo, Veronica. ***The Three Silver Coins: A Folk Story from Tibet.*** Snow Lion Publications, c1995. 32pp.
Jinpa is a poor but kindly boy who spends all his money to save the lives of a fish, a cat, and a dog and is later rewarded many times over. (Tibet)

McDermott, Gerald. ***The Stonecutter: A Japanese Folk Tale.*** Puffin Books, 1978. c1975. 32pp.
Relates the consequences of a stonecutter's foolish longing for power. (Japan)

From Nancy J. Keane, *The Big Book of Children's Reading Lists: 100 Great, Ready-to-Use Book Lists for Educators, Librarians, Parents, and Children.* Westport, CT: Libraries Unlimited, 2006. Copyright © 2006 by Libraries Unlimited.

Asian

Mosel, Arlene. ***The Funny Little Woman.*** Puffin Books, 1986. c1972. 40pp.
While chasing a dumpling, a little lady is captured by wicked creatures, from whom she escapes. Then she becomes the richest woman in Japan. (Japan)

Myers, Tim. ***Tanuki's Gift: A Japanese Tale.*** M. Cavendish, c2003. 32pp.
One winter, a priest takes in a furry tanuki and the two become friends, but when the tanuki tries to repay the priest, they both learn a lesson. (Japan)

Park, Janie Jaehyun. ***The Tiger and the Dried Persimmon: A Korean Folk Tale.*** Douglas & McIntyre (distributed by Publishers Group West), c2002. 32pp.
A retelling of a classic Korean folk tale in which a tiger is brought down by his own vanity and foolishness. (Korea)

Rowe, William Woodin. ***A Dog's Tooth.*** Snow Lion Publications, c1998. 31pp.
A retelling of the Tibetan tale of deception and faith, in which a young man who fails to obtain a sacred relic for his dying mother gives her a dog's tooth instead. (Tibet)

San Souci, Daniel. ***In the Moonlight Mist: A Korean Tale.*** Caroline House/Boyds Mills Press, 1999. 32pp.
A good-hearted woodcutter finds a heavenly wife in this retelling of a Korean folk tale. (Korea)

San Souci, Daniel. ***The Rabbit and the Dragon King: Based on a Korean Tale.*** Boyds Mills Press, 2002. 32pp.
Thanks to a quick-witted rabbit and a seaworthy turtle, a dragon king who is ill regains his desire to live. (Korea)

Say, Allen. ***Under the Cherry Blossom Tree: An Old Japanese Tale.*** Houghton Mifflin. 1997. c1974. 31pp.
A cherry tree growing from the top of the wicked landlord's head is the beginning of his misfortunes and a better life for the poor villagers. (Japan)

Sierra, Judy. ***The Gift of the Crocodile: A Cinderella Story.*** Simon & Schuster Books for Young Readers, c2000. 40pp.
In this Indonesian version of "Cinderella," a girl named Damura escapes her cruel stepmother and stepsister and marries a handsome prince, with the help of Grandmother Crocodile. (Indonesia)

Sierra, Judy. ***Tasty Baby Belly Buttons.*** Knopf (distributed by Random House), c1999. 38pp.
Urikohime, a girl born from a melon, battles the monstrous onis, who steal babies to eat their tasty belly buttons. (Japan)

Snyder, Dianne. ***The Boy of the Three-Year Nap.*** Houghton Mifflin, c1988. 32pp.
A poor Japanese woman maneuvers events to change the lazy habits of her son. (Japan)

So, Meilo. ***Gobble, Gobble, Slip, Slop: A Tale of a Very Greedy Cat.*** Knopf (distributed by Random House), c2004. 30pp.
In this story based on a folktale from India, a very greedy cat eats five hundred cakes, his friend the parrot, the nosy old woman, and much more. (India)

From Nancy J. Keane, *The Big Book of Children's Reading Lists: 100 Great, Ready-to-Use Book Lists for Educators, Librarians, Parents, and Children.* Westport, CT: Libraries Unlimited, 2006. Copyright © 2006 by Libraries Unlimited.

Asian

So-un, Kim. ***The Deer and the Woodcutter: A Korean Folktale.*** Tuttle Publishing, c2005. 32pp.
Presents an illustrated Korean folktale about why the rooster crows at dawn. (Korea)

Thornhill, Jan. ***The Rumor: A Jataka Tale from India.*** Maple Tree Press (distributed by Firefly Books), c2002. 32pp.
A retelling of a traditional story from India about a constantly worried hare who starts a stampede after a noise in the grove convinces her the world is breaking apart. (India)

Verma, Jatinder Nath. ***The Story of Divaali***. Barefoot Books, 2002. 40pp.
Retells the Hindu tale of a heroic prince and his bride who are separated by the demon prince Ravana, until the Monkey Army of Hanuman, god of the wind, helps them. Includes facts about Divaali, the festival celebrating Rama and Sita's return to their kingdom. (India)

Weitzman, David. ***Rama and Sita: A Tale from Ancient Java.*** D. R. Godine, 2002. 32pp.
Banished by his father to a dark forest, Prince Rama loses his wife Sita to the demon prince Ravana, but the Monkey King offers to help rescue her. (Indonesia)

Williams, Laura E. ***The Long Silk Strand.*** Bell Books/Boyds Mills Press, 2000. c1995. 32pp.
In this newly created tale set in ancient Japan, a young girl climbs a long silk strand hanging from heaven and discovers her grandmother waiting for her. (Japan)

Wisniewski, David. ***The Warrior and the Wise Man.*** Mulberry Paperback Book, 1998. c1989. 32pp.
An emperor gives his twin sons, one a warrior and one a wise man, a quest to see which will rule his kingdom. (Japan)

Books for Children Ages 8–12

Bodkin, Odds. ***The Crane Wife.*** Harcourt Brace, c1998. 32pp.
A retelling of the traditional Japanese tale about a poor sail maker who gains a beautiful but mysterious wife skilled at weaving magical sails. (Japan)

Clayton, Sally Pomme. ***Tales Told in Tents: Stories from Central Asia.*** Frances Lincoln Children's Books (distributed in the United States by Publishers Group West), c2004. 60pp.
Presents twelve folklore stories and proverbs along with full-color illustrations depicting the culture of Central Asia. (Central Asia)

Garland, Sherry. ***Children of the Dragon: Selected Tales from Vietnam.*** Harcourt, c2001. 58pp.
An illustrated collection of Vietnamese folktales, with explanatory notes following each story. (Vietnam)

Korean Children's Favorite Stories. Tuttle Publishing, 2004. c1955. 95pp.
Presents illustrated retellings of thirteen traditional Korean stories for children. (Korea)

Naidu, Vayu. ***Stories from India*** Raintree Steck-Vaughn, c2000. 48pp.
A collection of traditional stories retold from the folktales and epics of India, including "Dead Man Walking," "Valmiki—the Highway Poet," and "The Goddess with her Hands Full." (India)

Paterson, Katherine. ***The Tale of the Mandarin Ducks.*** Penguin Books, 1995, c1990. 40pp.
A pair of mandarin ducks, separated by a cruel lord who wishes to possess the drake for his colorful beauty, reward a compassionate couple who risk their lives to reunite the ducks. (Japan)

From Nancy J. Keane, *The Big Book of Children's Reading Lists: 100 Great, Ready-to-Use Book Lists for Educators, Librarians, Parents, and Children.* Westport, CT: Libraries Unlimited, 2006. Copyright © 2006 by Libraries Unlimited.

Balkan

Books for Children of All Ages

Demi. ***The Hungry Coat: A Tale from Turkey.*** Margaret K. McElderry Books, c2004. 34pp.
After being forced to change into a fancy new coat to attend a party, Nasrettin Hoca tries to feed his dinner to the coat, reasoning that it was the coat that was the invited guest. (Turkey)

Gantschev, Ivan. ***The Three Little Rabbits: A Balkan Folktale.*** North-South Books, 2002. 26pp.
A Balkan variation on "The Three Little Pigs." Three young rabbits set out on their own, but only one of them follows her father's advice on how to be safe from a hungry fox. (Balkan Peninsula)

Manna, Anthony L. ***Mr. Semolina-Semolinus: A Greek Folktale.*** Aladdin Paperbacks, 2004. c1997. 32pp.
Areti, a Greek princess, makes a man fit for her to love from almonds, sugar, and semolina, but he is stolen away by a jealous queen. Areti searches the world for him. (Greece)

Philip, Neil. ***Noah and the Devil: A Legend of Noah's Ark from Romania.*** Clarion Books, 2001. 26pp.
A retelling of the story of Noah's ark, embellished with elements from Romanian folklore, including how the devil sneaked aboard, the reason Noah threw a cat overboard, and the role of a snake in saving the ark. (Romania)

Rascol, Sabina. ***The Impudent Rooster.*** Dutton Children's Books, c2004. 32pp.
Using his amazing swallowing ability, a rooster foils the evil plans of a greedy nobleman and brings back riches to his poor master. (Romania)

Books for Children Ages 8–12

Barber, Antonia. ***Hidden Tales from Eastern Europe.*** Frances Lincoln Children's Books, 2003, c2002. 45pp.
Presents a collection of seven Eastern European folktales from Russia, Slovenia, Poland, Slovakia, Croatia, Serbia, and Romania about the people and culture of the region.

From Nancy J. Keane, *The Big Book of Children's Reading Lists: 100 Great, Ready-to-Use Book Lists for Educators, Librarians, Parents, and Children.* Westport, CT: Libraries Unlimited, 2006. Copyright © 2006 by Libraries Unlimited.

Caribbean

Books for Children of All Ages

Alvarez, Julia. ***The Secret Footprints.*** Dell Dragonfly Books, 2002. c2000. 37pp.
A story based on Dominican folklore, about the ciguapas, a tribe of beautiful underwater people whose feet are attached backwards, with their toes pointing in the direction from which they have come.

Buffett, Jimmy. ***The Jolly Mon***. Harcourt Brace, c1988. 32pp.
Relates the adventures of a fisherman who finds a magic guitar floating in the Caribbean Sea. Includes the music for the song "Jolly Mon Sing."

Comissiong, Lynette. ***Zebo Nooloo Chinoo***. Macmillan Caribbean, c2002. 31pp.
Young Isha has to find out an old woman's name, but no matter how hard she tries, she cannot guess, so she seeks out the help of a remarkable crab named Sollstine.

Gershator, Phillis. ***Tukuma Tootles the Flute: A Tale from St. Thomas.*** Orchard Books, c1994. 32pp.
When Tukama is captured by a two headed giant and held prisoner by the giant's wife, he uses his flute to escape.

Hallworth, Grace. ***Sing Me a Story: Song-and-Dance Tales from the Caribbean.*** August House LittleFolk, c2002. 45pp.
A collection of five traditional tales from the Caribbean region, each accompanied by a song and instructions for dance steps.

Jaffe, Nina. ***The Golden Flower: A Taino Myth from Puerto Rico.*** Pinata Books, c2005. 32pp.
Contains a Taino origin myth, in simple text with illustrations, and a story from folklore that explains the existence of the forest, sea, and island called Puerto Rico.

Jaffe, Nina. ***Sing, Little Sack!: Canta, Saquito!: A Folktale from Puerto Rico.*** Gareth Stevens. 1999. c1993
Captured and kept inside a sack by a strange little man, a young girl is forced to sing, until her mother hears her song and realizes that it is not the sack that is singing.

Keens-Douglas, Richardo. ***La Diablesse and the Baby: A Caribbean Folktale.*** Annick Press (distributed in the United States by Firefly Books), c1994. 24pp.
Granny will not let the baby be stolen by La Diablesse, a beautiful and mysterious woman with one human foot and one cow foot.

From Nancy J. Keane, *The Big Book of Children's Reading Lists: 100 Great, Ready-to-Use Book Lists for Educators, Librarians, Parents, and Children.* Westport, CT: Libraries Unlimited, 2006. Copyright © 2006 by Libraries Unlimited.

Caribbean

Keens-Douglas, Richardo. ***Mama God, Papa God: A Caribbean Tale.*** Crocodile Books, c1999. 30pp.
Papa God creates light so that he can see Mama God, and then he makes the world because he wants to give her something beautiful.

MacDonald, Amy. ***Please, Malese!: A Trickster Tale from Haiti.*** Farrar, Straus & Giroux, c2002. 32pp.
Using his tricky ways, Malese takes advantage of his neighbors, until they catch on, after which he manages to pull an even bigger trick on them.

Montes, Marisa. ***Juan Bobo Goes to Work: A Puerto Rican Folktale.*** HarperCollins, c2000. 32pp.
A retelling of the Puerto Rican folktale in which a boy named Juan Bobo tries to do exactly as his mother tells him, but keeps getting things all wrong.

San Souci, Robert D. ***Cendrillon: A Caribbean Cinderella.*** Simon & Schuster Books for Young Readers, c1998. 40pp.
A Creole variant of the familiar Cinderella tale set in the Caribbean and narrated by the godmother who helps Cendrillon find true love.

San Souci, Robert D. ***The Twins and the Bird of Darkness: A Hero Tale from the Caribbean.*** Simon & Schuster Books for Young Readers, c2002. 40pp.
When the Bird of Darkness takes Princess Marie, twin brothers Soliday, who is brave and kind, and Salacota, who is cowardly, set off to fight the beast and rescue the princess.

Books for Children Ages 8–12

Breinburg, Petronella. ***Stories from the Caribbean.*** Raintree Steck-Vaughn, c2000. 48pp.
A collection of folktales from the Caribbean, including “Bre-nancy and the 13 Plantains,” “Anana, the Maker,” and “The Flying Slaves.”

Moreton, Daniel. ***La Cucaracha Martina: A Caribbean Folktale***. Turtle Books, c1997. 33pp.
While searching for the source of one beautiful sound, a ravishing cockroach rejects marriage proposals from a menagerie of city animals, woo her with their noises.

San Souci, Robert D. ***The Faithful Friend.*** Simon & Schuster Books for Young Readers, c1995. 40pp.
A retelling of the traditional tale from the French West Indies in which two friends, Clement and Hippolyte, encounter love, zombies, and danger on the island of Martinique.

From Nancy J. Keane, *The Big Book of Children's Reading Lists: 100 Great, Ready-to-Use Book Lists for Educators, Librarians, Parents, and Children.* Westport, CT: Libraries Unlimited, 2006. Copyright © 2006 by Libraries Unlimited.

Chinese

Books for Children of All Ages

Casanova, Mary. ***The Hunter: A Chinese Folktale.*** Atheneum Books for Young Readers, c2000. 32pp.
After learning to understand the language of animals, Hai Li Bu the hunter sacrifices himself to save his village.

Chen, Kerstin. ***Lord of the Cranes: A Chinese Tale.*** North-South Books, 2002, c2000. 33pp.
To test the compassion of the people in the city, the lord of the cranes leaves his home high in the mountains and travels there disguised as a beggar, but only one man, the innkeeper, passes the test.

Demi. ***Kites: Magic Wishes That Fly Up to the Sky.*** Crown, 2000, c1999. 34pp.
Retells the Chinese legend of how kites became so popular, eventually evolving into a celebration called the Double Ninth Festival; includes illustrated instructions on how to make a kite.

Mosel, Arlene. ***Tikki Tikki Tembo.*** H. Holt, c1968. 45pp.
When an eldest son fell in the well, and most of the time getting help was spent pronouncing the name of the one in trouble, the Chinese, according to legend, decided to give all their children short names.

Wang, Rosalind C. ***The Magical Starfruit Tree: A Chinese Folktale.*** Beyond Words Publishing (distributed by Publishers Group West), c1993. 32pp.
A stingy peddler is chastised for his miserly ways by an old beggar with magical powers.

Wang, Rosalind C. ***The Treasure Chest: A Chinese Tale.*** Holiday House, c1995. 32pp.
A rainbow-colored, magic fish helps Laifu protect his bride-to-be from the evil ruler Funtong.

Yep, Laurence. ***The Dragon Prince: A Chinese Beauty & the Beast Tale.*** HarperCollins, c1997. 32pp.
A poor farmer's youngest daughter agrees to marry a fierce dragon in order to save her father's life.

Yolen, Jane. ***The Emperor and the Kite.*** Philomel Books, 1988, c1967. 31pp.
When the emperor is imprisoned in a high tower, his smallest daughter, whom he has always ignored, uses her kite to save him.

Young, Ed. ***Lon Po Po: A Red-Riding Hood Story from China.*** Philomel Books, c1989. 32pp.
Three sisters staying home alone are endangered by a hungry wolf who is disguised as their grandmother.

From Nancy J. Keane, *The Big Book of Children's Reading Lists: 100 Great, Ready-to-Use Book Lists for Educators, Librarians, Parents, and Children.* Westport, CT: Libraries Unlimited, 2006. Copyright © 2006 by Libraries Unlimited.

Chinese

Young, Ed. ***The Lost Horse: A Chinese Folktale.*** Harcourt, 2004. c1998. 32pp.
A retelling of the tale about a Chinese man who owned a marvelous horse and who believed that things were not always as bad, or as good, as they might seem.

Books for Children Ages 8–12

Fang, Linda. ***The Ch'i Lin Purse: A Collection of Ancient Chinese Stories.*** Farrar, Straus & Giroux, 1997, c1995. 127pp.
The author presents nine stories based on some of her favorite ancient Chinese novels and operas.

Heyer, Marilee. ***The Weaving of a Dream: A Chinese Folktale.*** Puffin Books, 1989, c1986. 31pp.
When the beautiful tapestry woven by a poor woman is stolen by fairies, her three sons set out on a magical journey to retrieve it. A retelling of a traditional Chinese tale.

Krasno, Rena. ***Cloud Weavers: Ancient Chinese Legends.*** Pacific View Press, c2003. 96pp.
Presents legends and tales from China, including ancient folktales, that reflect Chinese traditions and virtues; historical tales; and selections from literature.

Louie, Ai Ling. ***Yeh Shen: A Cinderella Story from China.*** Philomel Books, c1982. 31pp.
A young Chinese girl overcomes the wickedness of her stepsister and stepmother to become the bride of a prince.

Pirotta, Saviour. ***Stories from China.*** Raintree Steck-Vaughn, c2000. 48pp.
Presents six stories from China, each with an introductory essay that discusses the myth, legend, or tradition that inspired the story.

Yip, Mingmei. ***Chinese Children's Favorite Stories.*** Tuttle Publishing, c2004. 96pp.
An illustrated collection of thirteen Chinese folktales.

From Nancy J. Keane, *The Big Book of Children's Reading Lists: 100 Great, Ready-to-Use Book Lists for Educators, Librarians, Parents, and Children.* Westport, CT: Libraries Unlimited, 2006. Copyright © 2006 by Libraries Unlimited.

European

German folklore has its own listing.

Books for Children of All Ages

Ada, Alma Flor. ***The Three Golden Oranges.*** Atheneum Books for Young Readers, c1999. 28pp.
Acting on the advice of the old woman on the cliff by the sea, three brothers who wish to find brides go in search of three golden oranges. (Spain)

Ballesteros Rey, Xose. ***The Little White Rabbit: A Popular Portuguese Fairy Tale.*** Kalandraka Ediciones, c2002. 26pp.
A little white rabbit returns to her home to find it invaded by a mean old goat, so she sets out to see if someone will help her reclaim her house. (Portugal)

Bateman, Teresa. ***The Ring of Truth: An Original Irish Tale.*** Holiday House, c1997. 32pp.
After the king of the leprechauns bestows on him the Ring of Truth, Patrick O'Kelley no longer expects to win a blarney contest. (Ireland)

Blair, Eric. ***Tom Thumb.*** Picture Window Books, c2005. 31pp.
A boy the size of his father's thumb has a series of adventures, including stopping a pair of thieves, being swallowed by a cow, and tricking a wolf into bringing him back home. (England)

Brown, Marcia. ***Dick Whittington and His Cat.*** Atheneum Books for Young Readers, c1950. 32pp.
A retelling of the legend about a boy who became mayor of London, who heard his future in the Bells of Bow and made his fortune through his cat. (England)

Carroll, Yvonne. ***Leprechaun Tales.*** Gill & Macmillan, c1999. 64pp.
Presents six illustrated retellings of traditional Irish stories about leprechauns and other "little people." (Ireland)

Climo, Shirley. ***The Irish Cinderlad.*** HarperCollins, c1996. 32pp.
Becan, a poor boy belittled by his stepmother and stepsisters, rescues a princess in distress after meeting a magical bull. (Ireland)

De Paola, Tomie. ***The Clown of God: An Old Story.*** Harcourt Brace, c1978. 46pp.
A once-famous Italian juggler, now old and a beggar, gives one final performance before a statue of Our Lady and the Holy Child. (Italy)

De Paola, Tomie. ***Jamie O'Rourke and the Big Potato: An Irish Folktale.*** Putnam, c1992. 32pp.
The laziest man in all of Ireland catches a leprechaun, who offers a potato seed instead of a pot of gold for his freedom. (Ireland)

De Paola, Tomie. ***The Legend of Old Befana: An Italian Christmas Story.*** Harcourt Brace, c1980. 32pp.
Because Befana's household chores kept her from finding the Baby King, she searches to this day, leaving gifts for children on the Feast of the Three Kings. (Italy)

De Paola, Tomie. ***Strega Nona: An Original Tale.*** Simon & Schuster, c1975. 32pp.
When Strega Nona leaves him alone with her magic pasta pot, Big Anthony is determined to show the townspeople how it works. (Italy)

From Nancy J. Keane, *The Big Book of Children's Reading Lists: 100 Great, Ready-to-Use Book Lists for Educators, Librarians, Parents, and Children.* Westport, CT: Libraries Unlimited, 2006. Copyright © 2006 by Libraries Unlimited.

European

De Paola, Tomie. ***Tony's Bread: An Italian Folktale.*** Putnam & Grosset, c1996. 32pp.
In the grand city of Milano, after meeting a determined nobleman and baking a unique loaf of bread, a baker loses his daughter but gains a bakery. (Italy)

Doyle, Malachy. ***Una and the Sea-cloak.*** Frances Lincoln Children's Books, 2004. 24pp.
A young man travels far and wide to help a sea maiden repair her cloak after she turns up on his shore. (Ireland)

Forest, Heather. ***The Woman Who Flummoxed the Fairies: An Old Tale from Scotland.*** Harcourt Brace, 1996, c1990. 32pp.
Asked to make a cake for the fairies, a clever baker woman must figure out a way to prevent the fairies from wanting to keep her with them always to bake her delicious cakes. (Scotland)

Gal, Laszlo. ***The Parrot: An Italian Folktale.*** Douglas & McIntyre (distributed in the United States by Publishers Group West), c1997. 32pp.
A retelling of an Italian folktale about a prince who becomes a parrot to keep his beloved safe until her father returns. (Italy)

Hogrogian, Nonny. ***The Contest.*** Greenwillow Books, c1976. 32pp.
An Armenian folktale about two robbers courting the same woman. (Armenia)

Huck, Charlotte S. ***Princess Furball.*** Greenwillow Books, c1989. 42pp.
A princess in a coat of a thousand furs hides her identity from a king who falls in love with her. (England)

Kellogg, Steven. ***Jack and the Beanstalk***. Morrow Junior Books, c1991. 46pp.
An illustrated retelling of the classic tale about a boy named Jack who uses his quick wits to outsmart a giant and make a fortune for himself and his widowed mother. (England)

Kellogg, Steven. ***The Three Sillies.*** Candlewick Press, 2004. c1999. 40pp.
A young man believes his sweetheart and her family are the three silliest people in the world, until he meets three others who are even sillier. (England)

Kimmel, Eric A. ***Count Silvernose: A Story from Italy.*** Holiday House, c1996. 32pp.
A washerwoman's clever oldest daughter finds a way to rescue her two foolish sisters from the cruel Count Silvernose. (Italy)

Kimmel, Eric A. ***The Old Woman and Her Pig.*** Holiday House, c1992. 32pp.
When her newly bought pig won't go over the stile, an old woman tries to enlist the aid of some reluctant helpers so that she can get home that night. (England)

Kimmel, Eric A. ***Squash It!: A True and Ridiculous Tale.*** Holiday House, c1997. 26pp.
The King of Spain's fondness for a louse that bit him leads to good fortune for a clever peasant. (Spain)

Kimmel, Eric A. ***Three Sacks of Truth: A Story from France.*** Holiday House, c1993. 32pp.
With the aid of a perfect peach, a silver fife, and his own resources, Petit Jean outwits a dishonest king and wins the hand of a princess. (France)

Lottridge, Celia Barker. ***The Little Rooster and the Diamond Button: A Hungarian Folktale.*** Douglas & McIntyre (distributed in the United States by Publishers Group West), c2001. 32pp.
Little Rooster finds a diamond button, which a sultan takes from him, but he is determined to get it back. (Hungary)

From Nancy J. Keane, *The Big Book of Children's Reading Lists: 100 Great, Ready-to-Use Book Lists for Educators, Librarians, Parents, and Children.* Westport, CT: Libraries Unlimited, 2006. Copyright © 2006 by Libraries Unlimited.

European

Lupton, Hugh. ***Pirican Pic and Pirican Mor*****.** Barefoot Books, 2003. 42pp.
The story of two friends who go off to pick walnuts. The adventure begins after one friend has been picking the walnuts, while the other has eaten every one. Based on a Scottish folktale. (Scotland)

MacDonald, Margaret Read. ***The Old Woman Who Lived in a Vinegar Bottle: A British Fairy Tale.*** August House LittleFolk, 1995. 32pp.
In this British variant of a traditional tale, an ungrateful woman who complains constantly about her house is granted increasingly grandiose wishes by a fairy. (England)

MacDonald, Margaret Read. ***Slop!: A Welsh Folktale.*** Fulcrum Kids, c1997. 24pp.
An old man and old woman unknowingly throw their dinner leftovers onto the tiny house of a little man and his wife. (Wales)

Maddern, Eric. ***Death in A Nut.*** Frances Lincoln Children's Books (distributed in the United States by Publishers Group West), c2005. 28pp.
Jack learns a valuable lesson about life when he tries to keep Old Man Death from taking his mother. (Scotland)

McDermott, Gerald. ***Tim O'Toole and the Wee Folk: An Irish Tale.*** Viking Press, 1990. 31pp.
A very poor Irishman is provided with magical things by the "wee folk," but he must then keep his good fortune out of the hands of the greedy McGoons. (Ireland)

Milligan, Bryce. ***Brigid's Cloak: An Ancient Irish Story.*** Eerdmans Books for Young Readers, 2002. 32pp.
Relates a legend about the Irish slave girl who became Saint Brigid, beginning with a celestial song, a mysterious gift, and a prophecy on the night of her birth. (Ireland)

Nuñez, Marisa. ***The Featherless Chicken: A Popular Portuguese Fairy Tale.*** Kalandraka Ediciones, c2003. 36pp.
A featherless chicken learns that it is okay to be different from others. (Portugal)

O'Connor, Jane. ***The Teeny Tiny Woman.*** Random House, c1986. 32pp.
A teeny tiny woman, who puts a teeny tiny bone she finds in a churchyard away in a cupboard before she goes to sleep, is awakened by a voice demanding the return of the bone. (England)

Orgel, Doris. ***Button Soup.*** Gareth Stevens. c1998. 32pp.
In this modern version of the French folktale "Stone Soup," Rag-Tag Meg shows the neighborhood how to make a delicious pot of soup starting with only water and an old wooden button. (France)

Radunsky, Vladimir. ***Manneken Pis: A Simple Story of a Boy Who Peed on a War.*** Atheneum Books for Young Readers, c2002. 30pp.
A little Belgian boy shows the world just how silly it is to fight, after he pees on a war. (Belgium)

Robertson, M. P. ***The Moon in the Swampland.*** Frances Lincoln Children's Books (distributed by Publishers Group West), 2004. 32pp.
Thomas, a boy who is saved by the Moon from the bogles that inhabit Swampland, leads a rescue team into the swamp when the Moon's failure to appear leads them to believe she has been captured. (England)

From Nancy J. Keane, *The Big Book of Children's Reading Lists: 100 Great, Ready-to-Use Book Lists for Educators, Librarians, Parents, and Children.* Westport, CT: Libraries Unlimited, 2006. Copyright © 2006 by Libraries Unlimited.

European

San Souci, Robert D. ***Brave Margaret: An Irish Adventure.*** Simon & Schuster Books for Young Readers, c1999. 40pp.

In this retelling of an Irish folktale, a brave young woman battles a sea serpent and rescues her true love from a giant. (Ireland)

Schecter, Ellen. ***Diamonds and Toads: A Classic Fairy Tale.*** Gareth Stevens, c1999. 47pp.

After showing kindness to a fairy in disguise, Claire receives the gift of flowers and jewels that fall from her mouth when she speaks, but her bitter sister suffers a less pleasant fate. (France)

Shepard, Aaron. ***King O' the Cats.*** Atheneum Books for Young Readers, c2004. 28pp.

A church sexton, known for his wild tales, has three weird encounters with magical cats and can't convince Father Allen that they really happened, until the priest's cat shows an intense interest in his story. (England)

Shulevitz, Uri. ***The Treasure.*** Farrar, Straus & Giroux, 1986, c1978. 32pp.

A retelling of the traditional English tale in which a poor man follows the advice of his dream and is eventually led to a treasure. (England)

Sierra, Judy. ***The Beautiful Butterfly: A Folktale from Spain.*** Clarion Books, c2000. 32pp.

After choosing a husband for his sweet singing voice, a beautiful butterfly mourns the fact that he is swallowed by a fish, until a king in his underwear reunites the two. (Spain)

Stewig, John W. ***Whuppity Stoorie.*** Holiday House, c2004. 32pp.

In order to cure her ailing pig, an Irish widow agrees to give a strange woman whatever she wants; then the widow must guess the woman's name or give up her baby. (Ireland)

Wahl, Jan. ***Little Johnny Buttermilk: After an Old English Folktale.*** August House LittleFolk, c1999. 36pp.

Little Johnny Buttermilk must escape from the witch who keeps trying to steal his pails of milk, until finally he outwits her once and for all. (England)

Wiesner, David. ***The Loathsome Dragon.*** Clarion Books, c2005. 32pp.

A wicked queen casts a spell over her beautiful stepdaughter, turning her into a loathsome dragon until such time as her wandering brother shall return and kiss her three times. (England)

Zemach, Harve. ***Duffy and the Devil: A Cornish Tale***. Farrar, Straus & Giroux, c1973. 40pp.

The spinning and knitting the devil agrees to do for her win Duffy the Squire's name and a carefree life, until it comes time for her to guess the devil's name. (England)

Zemach, Margot. ***The Three Wishes: An Old Story.*** Farrar, Straus & Giroux, 1993. 32pp.

While working in the forest, a poor woodcutter and his wife free an imp whose tail is caught under a fallen tree. As a reward he gives them three wishes. (France)

From Nancy J. Keane, *The Big Book of Children's Reading Lists: 100 Great, Ready-to-Use Book Lists for Educators, Librarians, Parents, and Children.* Westport, CT: Libraries Unlimited, 2006. Copyright © 2006 by Libraries Unlimited.

European

Books for Children Ages 8–12

Bedard, Michael. ***The Wolf of Gubbio.*** Stoddart Kids (distributed in the United States by General Distribution Services), 2001, c2000. 24pp.

Retells the legend of how St. Francis of Assisi made peace between the people of Gubbio and a ferocious wolf that had been terrorizing the town. (Italy)

Climo, Shirley. ***Magic & Mischief: Tales from Cornwall.*** Clarion Books, c1999. 127pp.

A collection of stories detailing charms, powers, and adventures, each about "some kind of magical being, good or bad" from the small corner of England known as Cornwall. (England)

Cooper, Susan. ***The Silver Cow: A Welsh Tale.*** Aladdin Paperbacks, c1991. 32pp.

The father of a young Welsh boy gifted with a magic cow manages to destroy all the good things the cow has brought to their lives. (Wales)

Doyle, Malachy. ***Tales from Old Ireland.*** Barefoot Books, c2000. 95pp.

Enchanting stories include "The Children of Lir," "Fair, Brown, and Trembling," "The Twelve Wild Geese," "Lusmore and the Fairies," "Son of an Otter," "Son of a Wolf," "The Soul Cages," and "Oisin in Tir na nOg." (Ireland)

Gross, Gwen. ***Knights of the Round Table.*** Random House, c1985. 109pp.

Retells the exploits of King Arthur and his knights of the Round Table. (England)

Heaney, Marie. ***The Names upon the Harp: Irish Myth and Legend.*** Arthur A. Levine Books, 2000. 95pp.

Nine Irish myths and legends are retold in this richly illustrated collection, in which the Mythological, Ulster, and Fenian cycles of early Irish literature are all represented. (Ireland)

Hodges, Margaret. ***Merlin and the Making of the King.*** Holiday House, c2004. 39pp.

A retelling of four Arthurian legends—"The Sword in the Stone," "Excalibur," "The Lady of the Lake," and "The Last Great Battle"—which feature Merlin, King Arthur, and other familiar figures. (England)

Hodges, Margaret. ***Saint George and the Dragon: A Golden Legend.*** Little Brown, c1984. 32pp.

Retells the segment from Spenser's "The Faerie Queene" in which George, the Red Cross Knight, slays the dreadful dragon that has been terrorizing the countryside for years, bringing peace and joy to the land. (England)

Kerven, Rosalind. ***King Arthur.*** DK Publishing, c1998. 64pp.

A retelling of the story of the boy fated to be the "Once and Future King," covering his glorious reign and his tragic, yet triumphant, passing. Illustrated notes throughout the text explain the historical background of the story. (England)

From Nancy J. Keane, *The Big Book of Children's Reading Lists: 100 Great, Ready-to-Use Book Lists for Educators, Librarians, Parents, and Children.* Westport, CT: Libraries Unlimited, 2006. Copyright © 2006 by Libraries Unlimited.

European

Krull, Kathleen. ***A Pot O' Gold: A Treasury of Irish Stories, Poetry, Folklore, and (Of Course) Blarney.*** Hyperion Books for Children, c2004. 181pp.
A collection of stories, folklore, poetry, and songs from Ireland. (Ireland)

Milligan, Bryce. ***The Prince of Ireland and the Three Magic Stallions.*** Holiday House, c2003. 32pp.
In this retelling of an Irish folktale, the prince of Ireland's stepmother curses him to stay no longer than two nights anywhere until he brings her a giant's horses from the western edge of the world. (Ireland)

Morpurgo, Michael. ***Sir Gawain and the Green Knight.*** Candlewick Press, c2004. 114pp.
The quest of Sir Gawain for the Green Knight teaches him a lesson in pride, humility, and honor. (England)

Perrault, Charles. ***The Complete Fairy Tales of Charles Perrault.*** Clarion Books, c1993. 156pp.
Contains the works of Charles Perrault, including Cindrella and others (France).

Philip, Neil. ***Robin Hood.*** DK Publishing, c1997. 64pp.
Recounts the life and adventures of Robin Hood, the legendary outlaw of Sherwood Forest who dedicated himself to fighting tyranny. Illustrated notes throughout the text explain the historical background of the story. (England)

Schmidt, Gary D. ***Saint Ciaran: The Tale of a Saint of Ireland.*** Eerdmans Books for Young Readers, c2000. 40pp.
A story in picture book format of Ireland's first saint, Ciaran of Saighir. (Ireland)

Vittorini, Domenico. ***The Thread of Life: Twelve Old Italian Tales.*** Running Press Kids, 2003, c1995. 80pp.
A collection of folktales from Italy that celebrate fairness, goodness, wisdom, and resourcefulness, as well as explaining why snakes are found under rocks and March has thirty-one days. (Italy)

Young, Richard. ***Stories from the Days of Christopher Columbus: A Multicultural Collection for Young Readers.*** August House, c1992. 160pp.
A collection of traditional tales, fables, and legends from the cultures brought together or affected by the voyages of Columbus, including those of Spain, Portugal, Italy, and the mainland, and island Indian tribes he encountered.

From Nancy J. Keane, *The Big Book of Children's Reading Lists: 100 Great, Ready-to-Use Book Lists for Educators, Librarians, Parents, and Children.* Westport, CT: Libraries Unlimited, 2006. Copyright © 2006 by Libraries Unlimited.

German

Books for Children of All Ages

Blair, Eric. *The Brave Little Tailor: A Retelling of the Grimms' Fairy Tale.* Picture Window Books, c2004. 32pp.
A retelling of the fairy tale in which a tailor kills seven flies with one blow.

Blair, Eric. *The Pied Piper.* Picture Window Books, c2005. 32pp.
Presents an illustrated retelling of the story in which the Pied Piper is hired to free a village rats, but when the villagers refuse to pay him for the service, he lures away their children as well.

Craft, Mahlon F. *Sleeping Beauty*. SeaStar Books, c2002. 32pp.
A beautiful and beloved princess, cursed by the one fairy who was not invited to her christening, pricks her finger on her sixteenth birthday and falls asleep for a hundred years.

Ernst, Lisa Campbell. *The Three Spinning Fairies: A Tale from the Brothers Grimm.* Dutton Children's Books, c2002. 34pp.
Three unusual fairies help a lazy girl try to attain a life of luxury and ease as the prince's wife.

Grimm, Jacob. *Snow White.* Little, Brown, c1974. 48pp.
Retells the tale of the beautiful princess whose lips were red as blood, skin was white as snow, and hair was black as ebony.

Grimm, Wilhelm. *Dear Mili: An Old Tale.* Michael di Capua Books, 1995. c1988. 40pp.
A new Grimm tale, part of a letter written by Wilhelm to a little girl in 1816, came to light in 1983. A mother sends her daughter into the forest to save her from a terrible war, and she finds refuge with St. Joseph.

Hillert, Margaret. *The Cookie House.* Modern Curriculum, c1978. 31pp.
A poor woodcutter's two children, lost in the woods, come upon a gingerbread house inhabited by a wicked witch.

Hyman, Trina Schart. *Little Red Riding Hood.* Holiday House, c1983. 32pp.
On her way to deliver a basket of food to her sick grandmother, Elisabeth encounters a sly wolf.

LaMarche, Jim. *The Elves and the Shoemaker.* Chronicle Books, c2003. 26pp.
A poor shoemaker becomes successful with the help of two elves who finish his shoes during the night.

Lesser, Rika. *Hansel and Gretel.* Dutton Children's Books, 1999. 40pp.
A retelling of the well-known tale in which two children are left in the woods but find their way home despite an encounter with a wicked witch.

From Nancy J. Keane, *The Big Book of Children's Reading Lists: 100 Great, Ready-to-Use Book Lists for Educators, Librarians, Parents, and Children.* Westport, CT: Libraries Unlimited, 2006. Copyright © 2006 by Libraries Unlimited.

German

Long, Laurel. ***The Lady & the Lion: A Brothers Grimm Tale.*** Dial Books, c2003. 32pp.
With help from Sun, Moon, and North Wind, a lady travels the world seeking to save her beloved from the evil enchantress who turned him first into a lion, then into a dove.

McCafferty, Catherine. ***Rapunzel.*** McGraw-Hill Children's, c2002. 32pp.
An illustrated retelling of the fairy tale in which a beautiful young woman, hidden away in a tower by a powerful witch, wins the heart of a passing prince, who falls in love with her singing.

Orgel, Doris. ***The Bremen Town Musicians and Other Animal Tales from Grimm.*** Roaring Brook Press, c2004. 46pp.
Presents illustrated retellings of six animal stories by the Grimm brothers, including the title work, in which four aging animals, no longer of any use to their masters, find a new home after outwitting a gang of robbers.

Shulevitz, Uri. ***The Golden Goose.*** Farrar, Straus & Giroux, c1995. 32pp.
Retells the Brothers Grimm's story in which a simpleton gets into a sticky situation with a golden goose and is rewarded for his generosity.

Wells, Rosemary. ***The Fisherman and His Wife: A Brand New Version.*** Dial Books for Young Readers, c1998. 32pp.
The fisherman's greedy wife is never satisfied with the wishes granted her by an enchanted fish.

Zelinsky, Paul O. ***Rumpelstiltskin.*** Dutton Children's Books, c1986. 37pp.
A strange little man helps the miller's daughter spin straw into gold for the king on the condition that she will give him her first-born child.

Books for Children Ages 8–12

Grimm's Fairy Tales. SeaStar Books, c2001. 160pp.
Presents twenty-two fairy tales by the Brothers Grimm based on a 1909 edition of the stories, along with twenty-one full-color paintings and twenty-eight black-and-white drawings by Arthur Rackham. Tales include "Rapunzel," "Red Riding Hood," "Hansel and Gretel," and "The Elves and the Shoemaker."

Norling, Beth. ***Sister Night & Sister Day.*** Allen & Unwin, c2000. 33pp.
A retelling of a Grimm fairy tale in which two sisters, different as night and day, are rewarded according to what they deserve.

From Nancy J. Keane, *The Big Book of Children's Reading Lists: 100 Great, Ready-to-Use Book Lists for Educators, Librarians, Parents, and Children.* Westport, CT: Libraries Unlimited, 2006. Copyright © 2006 by Libraries Unlimited.

Mexican

Books for Children of All Ages

Aardema, Verna. ***Borreguita and the Coyote: A Tale from Ayutla, Mexico.*** Knopf (distributed by Random House), 1998, c1991. 28pp.

A little lamb uses her clever wiles to keep a coyote from eating her up.

Climo, Shirley. ***The Little Red Ant and the Great Big Crumb: A Mexican Fable.*** Clarion Books, c1995. 39pp.

A small red ant finds a crumb in a Mexican cornfield, but she is afraid that she lacks the strength to move it herself and goes off to find an animal that can.

Ehlert, Lois. ***Cuckoo: A Mexican Folktale = Cucu: Un Cuento Folklorico Mexicano.*** Harcourt Brace, c1997. 34pp.

A traditional Mayan tale that reveals how the cuckoo lost her beautiful feathers.

Harper, Jo. ***The Legend of Mexicatl.*** Turtle Books (distributed by Publishers Group West), c1998. 33pp.

When Mexicatl responds to the call of the Great Spirit by leading the people to a better land, his followers express gratitude by naming themselves after him.

Johnston, Tony. ***The Tale of Rabbit and Coyote.*** Putnam & Grosset, 1998, c1994. 32pp.

Rabbit outwits Coyote in this Zapotec tale, which explains why coyotes howl at the moon.

Lewis, Thomas P. ***Hill of Fire.*** HarperCollins, c1971. 63pp.

An easy-to-read account of the birth of Paricutin volcano in the field of a poor Mexican farmer.

Maitland, Katherine. ***Ashes for Gold: A Tale from Mexico.*** Mondo, c1994. 22pp.

Tricked by a clever acquaintance, a poor Mexican still manages to turn ashes into gold.

Ober, Hal. ***How Music Came to the World: An Ancient Mexican Myth.*** Houghton Mifflin, c1994. 32pp.

Retells a Mexican legend in which the sky god and the wind god bring music from Sun's house to the Earth.

Rockwell, Anne F. ***The Boy Who Wouldn't Obey: A Mayan Legend.*** Greenwillow Books, c2000. 24pp.

When Chac, the great lord who makes rain, takes a disobedient boy as his servant, they are both in for trouble.

Rodanas, Kristina. ***Dragonfly's Tale.*** Clarion Books, c1991. 29pp.

After a poor harvest two children regain the Corn Maidens' blessings for their people with the aid of a cornstalk toy, the dragonfly.

From Nancy J. Keane, *The Big Book of Children's Reading Lists: 100 Great, Ready-to-Use Book Lists for Educators, Librarians, Parents, and Children.* Westport, CT: Libraries Unlimited, 2006. Copyright © 2006 by Libraries Unlimited.

Mexican

Wisniewski, David. ***Rain Player.*** Clarion Books, c1991. 32pp.
To bring rain to his thirsty village, Pik challenges the rain god to a game of pok-a-tok.

Books for Children Ages 8–12

Coburn, Jewell Reinhart. ***Domitila: A Cinderella Tale from the Mexican Tradition.*** Shen's Books, c2000. 32pp.
By following her mother's admonition to perform every task with care and love, a poor young Mexican girl wins the devotion of the governor's son.

Dalal, Anita. ***Myths of Pre-Columbian America***. Raintree Steck-Vaughn, c2002. 48pp.
Recounts the myths of pre-Columbian America and explains how they reflect the environment, way of life, and religion of the people who created them.

Endredy, James. ***The Journey of Tunuri and the Blue Deer: A Huichol Indian Story.*** Bear Cub Books, c2003. 32pp.
Retells a traditional Huichol tale in which the young Tunuri learns his place in the natural world when, after being lost in the forest, he meets the magical Blue Deer and follows him on a special journey.

Hayes, Joe. ***La llorona = The Weeping Woman: An Hispanic Legend Told in Spanish and English.*** Cinco Puntos Press, c2004. 28pp.
A retelling, in parallel English and Spanish text, of the traditional tale told in the Southwest and in Mexico of how the beautiful Maria became a ghost.

Kimmel, Eric A. ***The Witch's Face: A Mexican Tale.*** Holiday House, c1993. 32pp.
Don Aurelio falls in love with a witch who has a beautiful face, but he fails to heed her special instructions.

Petersen, Patricia ***Voladores***. P. Bedrick Books, c2002. 32pp.
When Water and Volcano become jealous of the people's devotion to Sun, they cause chaos, which can only be overcome by Wind, but only one small boy is willing to try to reach Wind to ask for his help.

From Nancy J. Keane, *The Big Book of Children's Reading Lists: 100 Great, Ready-to-Use Book Lists for Educators, Librarians, Parents, and Children.* Westport, CT: Libraries Unlimited, 2006. Copyright © 2006 by Libraries Unlimited.

Middle Eastern

Books for Children of All Ages

Climo, Shirley. ***The Persian Cinderella.*** HarperCollins, c1999. 32pp.
A retelling of the traditional Persian tale in which Settareh, neglected and abused by her stepmother and stepsisters, finds her life transformed with the help of a little blue jug. (Iran)

De Paola, Tomie. ***The Legend of the Persian Carpet.*** Putnam, c1993. 32pp.
Tells how the first Persian carpet was created to replace King Balash's lost treasure. (Iran)

Hickox, Rebecca. ***The Golden Sandal: A Middle Eastern Cinderella Story.*** Holiday House, c1998. 32pp.
An Iraqi version of "Cinderella" in which a kind and beautiful girl who is mistreated by her stepmother and stepsister finds a husband with the help of a magic fish. (Iraq)

Kimmel, Eric A. ***The Three Princes: A Tale from the Middle East.*** Holiday House, c1994. 32pp.
Retelling of a tale about a princess who promises to marry the prince who finds the most precious treasure.

Shah, Idries. ***The Man with Bad Manners.*** Hoopoe Books, c2003. 32pp.
A clever boy and other villagers devise a plan to improve the manners of one of their neighbors. Based on a folktale from Afghanistan.

Shah, Idries. ***The Old Woman and the Eagle.*** Hoopoe Books, c2003. 32pp.
A Sufi teaching tale from Afghanistan about an old woman who insists that an eagle must really be a pigeon. (Afghanistan)

Young, Ed. ***What About Me?*** Philomel Books, c2002. 32pp.
A young boy determinedly follows the instructions of the Grand Master in the hope of gaining knowledge, only to be surprised about how he acquires it. Based on a Sufi tale.

Zeman, Ludmila. ***Sindbad's Secret.*** Tundra Books, Tundra Books of Northern New York, c2003. 32pp.
Sinbad the Sailor shares with a porter the story of the trials he endured to gain the greatest prize of all.

Books for Children Ages 8–12

McCaughrean, Geraldine. ***Gilgamesh.*** Eerdmans Books for Young Readers, 2003, c2002. 95pp.
A retelling, based on seventh-century B.C. Assyrian clay tablets, of the wanderings and adventures of the god king Gilgamesh, who ruled in ancient Mesopotamia (now Iraq) in about 2700 B.C., and of his faithful companion, Enkidu.

Pullman, Philip. ***Aladdin and the Enchanted Lamp.*** Arthur A. Levine Books, c2005. 70pp.
Presents an illustrated retelling of the tale of a poor tailor's son who becomes a wealthy prince with the help of a magic lamp he finds in an enchanted cave.

Schwartz, Howard. ***Jerusalem of Gold: Jewish Stories of the Enchanted City.*** Jewish Lights Publishing, c2003. 56pp.
Jewish stories set in Jerusalem, adapted from the Talmud and Midrash, Hasidic sources, and oral tradition, with origins in the Middle East, Eastern Europe, Spain, Italy, and Greece.

Zeman, Ludmila. ***Sindbad: From the Tales of the Thousand and One Nights.*** Tundra Books, c1999. 34pp.
Follows the adventures of Sindbad, the legendary sailor.

From Nancy J. Keane, *The Big Book of Children's Reading Lists: 100 Great, Ready-to-Use Book Lists for Educators, Librarians, Parents, and Children.* Westport, CT: Libraries Unlimited, 2006. Copyright © 2006 by Libraries Unlimited.

Scandinavian

Books for Children of All Ages

Asbjornsen, Peter Christen. ***The Three Billy Goats Gruff.*** Clarion, c1973. 31pp.
Three clever billy goats outwit a big, ugly troll that lives under the bridge they must cross on their way up the mountain. (Norway)

Batt, Tanya Robyn. ***The Princess and the White Bear King.*** Barefoot Books, c2004. 40pp.
A girl travels east of the sun and west of the moon to free her beloved prince from a magic spell. (Norway)

Hooks, William H. ***The Gruff Brothers.*** Gareth Stevens, 1997, c1990. 32pp.
A retelling, in rebus format, of the traditional tale in which three clever billy goats outwit a big, ugly troll. (Norway)

Kimmel, Eric A. ***Boots and His Brothers: A Norwegian Tale.*** Holiday House, c1992
A young man's kindness to an old beggar woman earns him his weight in gold and half a kingdom. (Norway)

Kimmel, Eric A. ***Easy Work!: An Old Tale.*** Holiday House, c1998. 32pp.
Thinking his work in the fields is harder than his wife's work in the house, Mr. McTeague trades places with her for one day. (Norway)

Lunge-Larsen, Lise. ***The Race of the Birkebeiners.*** Houghton Mifflin, c2001. 33pp.
Tells how the infant Prince Hakon is rescued by men fiercely loyal to his dead father. They ski across the rugged mountains in blizzard conditions to save him from his enemies, the Baglers. (Norway)

MacDonald, Margaret Read. ***Fat Cat: A Danish Folktale.*** August House Littlefolk, c2001. 32pp.
A retelling of a Danish folktale in which a greedy cat grows enormous as he eats everything in sight, including his friends and neighbors who call him fat. (Denmark)

Shepard, Aaron. ***The Princess Mouse: A Tale of Finland.*** Atheneum Books for Young Readers, c2003. 32pp.
A retelling of a Finnish folk tale about a young man who plans to marry his mouse sweetheart. (Finland)

From Nancy J. Keane, *The Big Book of Children's Reading Lists: 100 Great, Ready-to-Use Book Lists for Educators, Librarians, Parents, and Children.* Westport, CT: Libraries Unlimited, 2006. Copyright © 2006 by Libraries Unlimited.

Scandinavian

Books for Children Ages 8–12

Dasent, George Webbe. ***East O' the Sun and West O' the Moon.*** Candlewick Press, 1992
A girl travels east of the sun and west of the moon to free her beloved prince from a magic spell. (Norway)

DeSpain, Pleasant. ***Tales of Enchantment***. August House, c2003. 71pp.
A collection of nine traditional tales of leprechauns, dwarfs, shape shifters and other enchanted creatures from various countries, including Russia, Norway, and Germany.

Lunge Larsen, Lise. ***The Troll with No Heart in His Body and Other Tales of Trolls from Norway.*** Houghton Mifflin, c1999. 92pp.
A collection of Norwegian folktales all featuring trolls: The Three Billy Goats Gruff, The Boy Who Became a Lion, a Falcon, and an Ant, Butterball, The Boy and the North Wind, The White Cat in the Dovre Mountain, The Sailors and the Troll, The Eating Competition, and The Troll with No Heart in His Body. (Norway)

Swedish Folk Tales. Floris Books, 2004. 235pp.
Contains a collection of twenty nine Swedish folk tales, illustrated by artist John Bauer, and includes stories by Elsa Beskow, Anna Wahlenberg, and Alfred Smedberg. (Sweden)

From Nancy J. Keane, *The Big Book of Children's Reading Lists: 100 Great, Ready-to-Use Book Lists for Educators, Librarians, Parents, and Children.* Westport, CT: Libraries Unlimited, 2006. Copyright © 2006 by Libraries Unlimited.

Slavic

Books for Children of All Ages

Arnold, Katya. ***That Apple Is Mine!*** Holiday House, c2000. 32pp.
In this retelling of a Russian folktale, Rabbit, Crow, and Hedgehog fight over ownership of an apple, until Bear persuades them to share. (Russia)

Brett, Jan. ***The Mitten: A Ukrainian Folktale.*** Putnam, c1989. 32pp.
Several animals sleep snugly in Nicki's lost mitten, until the bear sneezes. (Ukraine)

Cole, Joanna. ***Bony-legs.*** Scholastic, c1983. 47pp.
When a terrible witch vows to eat her for supper, a little girl escapes with the help of a mirror and comb given to her by the witch's cat and dog. ((Russia)

Gag, Wanda. ***Gone Is Gone, Or, the Story of a Man Who Wanted to Do Housework.*** University of Minnesota Press, 2003. 64pp.
Mr. Fritzl, the farmer, thought it would be so much fun to keep house and do housework. He soon finds that plowing fields is easier and simpler. (Czech)

Ginsburg, Mirra. ***Clay Boy: Adapted from a Russian Folk Tale.*** Greenwillow Books, c1997. 32pp.
Wanting a son, an old man and woman make a clay boy, who comes to life and begins eating everything in sight, until he meets a clever goat. (Russia)

Kimmel, Eric A. ***The Birds' Gift: A Ukrainian Easter Story.*** Holiday House, c1999. 32pp.
Villagers take in a flock of golden birds nearly frozen by an early snow and are rewarded with beautifully decorated eggs the next spring. (Ukraine)

Kimmel, Eric A. ***The Castle of the Cats.*** Holiday House, c2004. 32pp.
Presents a retelling of an Eastern European folktale about Ivan, a kind but simple young man who is urged by his father to compete with his brothers for the family farm, and who meets with success in a very unlikely place. (Ukraine)

Martin, Rafe. ***The Language of Birds.*** Putnam, c2000. 32pp.
A retelling of the Russian tale about a wealthy merchant's younger son who proves his worth in an unusual way. (Russia)

Martin, Rafe. ***The Twelve Months.*** Stoddart Kids (distributed in the United States by General Distribution Services), 2001, c2000. 32pp.
A retelling of a Slavic Cinderella tale in which a young girl is given impossible tasks to perform by her cruel aunt and cousin. By virtue of her sweet nature she is helped and rewarded by the twelve months. (Czech)

McCaughrean, Geraldine. ***Grandma Chickenlegs.*** Carolrhoda Books, c2000. 29pp.
In this variation of the traditional "Baba Yaga" story, a young girl must rely on the advice of her dead mother and her special doll when her wicked stepmother sends her to get a needle from Grandma Chickenlegs. (Russia)

From Nancy J. Keane, *The Big Book of Children's Reading Lists: 100 Great, Ready-to-Use Book Lists for Educators, Librarians, Parents, and Children.* Westport, CT: Libraries Unlimited, 2006. Copyright © 2006 by Libraries Unlimited.

Slavic

Peck, Jan. ***The Giant Carrot.*** Dial Books for Young Readers, c1998. 32pp.
Little Isabelle surprises her family with her unique way of helping a carrot seed grow and of getting the huge vegetable from the ground. Includes a recipe for carrot pudding. (Russia)

Polacco, Patricia. ***Babushka Baba Yaga.*** Philomel Books, c1993. 32pp.
The villagers are afraid of her, so the legendary Baba Yaga disguises herself as an old woman in order to know the joys of being a grandmother. (Russia)

Polacco, Patricia. ***Luba and the Wren.*** Philomel Books, c1999. 34pp.
In this variation on "The Fisherman and His Wife," a young Ukrainian girl must repeatedly return to the wren she has rescued to relay her parents' increasingly greedy demands. (Ukraine)

Pollock, Yevonne. ***The Old Man's Mitten: A Traditional Tale.*** Mondo, 1994, c1986. 24pp.
A mouse, a frog, a rabbit, a fox, a wolf, and a bear all squeeze into a lost mitten until its owner comes back to reclaim it. (Ukraine)

Ransome, Arthur. ***The Fool of the World and the Flying Ship: A Russian Tale.*** Farrar, Straus & Giroux, c1987. 48pp.
When the Czar proclaims that he will marry his daughter to the man who brings him a flying ship, the Fool of the World sets out to try his luck and meets some unusual companions on the way. (Russia)

Shepard, Aaron. ***The Sea King's Daughter: A Russian Legend.*** Atheneum Books for Young Readers, c1997. 28pp.
A talented musician from Novgorod plays so well that the Sea King wants him to marry one of his daughters. (Russia)

Soldier and Tsar in the Forest: A Russian Tale. Farrar, Straus & Giroux, c1972. 32pp.
Not knowing the man he meets in the forest is the tsar, a young soldier discloses that he has deserted. (Russia)

Spirin, Gennadii. ***The Tale of the Firebird.*** Philomel Books, c2002. 32pp.
When Prince Ivan sets out to find the Firebird for his father, the tsar, he must complete a series of tasks before obtaining the Firebird and winning the hand of a beautiful princess. (Russia)

Tolstoy, Graf Aleksey Konstantinovich. ***The Enormous Turnip.*** Harcourt, c2003. 20pp.
A cumulative tale in which the turnip planted by an old man grows so enormous that everyone must help to pull it up. (Russia)

Weninger, Brigitte. ***The Elf's Hat.*** North-South Books, c2000. 36pp.
A retelling of a Russian cumulative tale in which a number of animals crowd into a lost hat to make their home, until a tiny flea comes along. (Russia)

Wisniewski, David. ***Golem.*** Clarion Books, c1996. 32pp.
A saintly rabbi miraculously brings to life a clay giant, who helps him watch over the Jews of sixteenth-century Prague. (Czech)

From Nancy J. Keane, *The Big Book of Children's Reading Lists: 100 Great, Ready-to-Use Book Lists for Educators, Librarians, Parents, and Children.* Westport, CT: Libraries Unlimited, 2006. Copyright © 2006 by Libraries Unlimited.

Slavic

Yep, Laurence. ***The Khan's Daughter: A Mongolian Folktale.*** Scholastic, 2002, c1997. 32pp.
In this retelling of a Mongolian folktale, a simple shepherd must pass three tests to marry the Khan's beautiful daughter. (Mongolia)

Yolen, Jane. ***The Firebird.*** HarperCollins, c2002. 32pp.
A retelling of the Russian folktale in which Prince Ivan encounters the magical Firebird, who helps him defeat the evil Kostchei. (Russia)

Yolen, Jane. ***The Flying Witch.*** HarperCollins, c2003. 32pp.
Relates how a turnip farmer's daughter outwits the fearsome witch Baba Yaga. (Russia)

Yolen, Jane. ***The Sea King.*** Crocodile Books, USA, c2003. 32pp.
A tale, based on themes from Russian folklore, about a man who makes a promise to the Sea King but fails to keep it. (Russia)

Ziefert, Harriet. ***The Snow Child.*** Puffin Books, c2000. 32pp.
An elderly couple who long for a child build a snow child which comes to life and makes them very happy—until the coming of spring when the days become too warm for her to stay. (Russia)

Books for Children Ages 8–12

Barber, Antonia. ***Hidden Tales from Eastern Europe.*** Frances Lincoln Children's Books, 2003, c2002. 45pp.
Presents a collection of seven Eastern European folktales from Russia, Slovenia, Poland, Slovakia, Croatia, Serbia, and Romania about the people and culture of the region.

Keding, Dan. ***Stories of Hope and Spirit: Folktales from Eastern Europe.*** August House, c2004. 77pp.
Presents a collection of twelve folktales of hope and spirit from the Baltic regions of Eastern Europe, including stories from Croatia, Serbia, Russia, Estonia, Chechnia, Georgia, Slovakia, Moldavia, and Latvia.

Kimmel, Eric A. ***Bearhead: A Russian Folktale.*** Holiday House, c1991. 32pp.
Bearhead succeeds in outwitting the witch Madame Hexaba and a frog-headed goblin.

Kimmel, Eric A. ***I Know Not What, I Know Not Where: A Russian Tale.*** Holiday House, c1994. 63pp.
A retelling of a Russian fairy tale in which an archer assigned many dangerous quests by the greedy, cruel tsar wins a crown and the woman of his dreams.

Mayer, Marianna. ***Baba Yaga and Vasilisa the Brave.*** Morrow Junior Books, c1994. 40pp.
A retelling of the old Russian fairy tale, in which beautiful Vasilisa uses the help of her doll to escape from the clutches of the witch Baba Yaga, who sets in motion the events that lead to the marriage of Vasilisa to the tsar.

From Nancy J. Keane, *The Big Book of Children's Reading Lists: 100 Great, Ready-to-Use Book Lists for Educators, Librarians, Parents, and Children.* Westport, CT: Libraries Unlimited, 2006. Copyright © 2006 by Libraries Unlimited.

Fractured Fairy Tales

Books for Children of All Ages

Ada, Alma Flor. *Dear Peter Rabbit.* Atheneum Books for Young Readers, c1994. 32pp.
Presents letters between such fairy tale characters as Goldilocks, Baby Bear, Peter Rabbit, and the Three Pigs.

Ada, Alma Flor. *With Love, Little Red Hen.* Atheneum Books for Young Readers, c2001. 34pp.
A series of letters describing the actions of Goldilocks, Peter Rabbit, the Three Pigs, Little Red Hen, and other storybook characters when Little Red Hen and her chicks become the target of the unsavory Wolf and his cousin, Fer O'Cious.

Ada, Alma Flor. *Yours Truly, Goldilocks.* Atheneum Books for Young Readers, c1998. 32pp.
Presents the correspondence of Goldilocks, the Three Pigs, Baby Bear, Peter Rabbit, and Little Red Riding Hood as they plan to attend a housewarming party for the pigs and avoid the evil wolves in the forest.

Calmenson, Stephanie. *The Principal's New Clothes.* Scholastic, c1989. 40pp.
In this version of the Andersen tale, the vain principal of P.S. 88 is persuaded by two tailors that they will make him an amazing, one-of-a-kind suit that will be visible only to intelligent people who are good at their jobs.

Cole, Babette. *Prince Cinders.* Putnam, 1997, c1987. 32pp.
A fairy grants a small, skinny prince a change in appearance and the chance to go to the Palace Disco.

Edwards, Pamela Duncan. *Dinorella: A Prehistoric Fairy Tale.* Hyperion Books for Children, c1997. 32pp.
In this story, loosely based on "Cinderella" but featuring dinosaurs, the Duke falls in love with Dinorella when she rescues him from the dreaded deinonychus at the Dinosaur Dance.

Ernst, Lisa Campbell. *Goldilocks Returns.* Simon & Schuster Books for Young Readers, c2000. 34pp.
Thirty years after Goldilocks first met the three bears, she returns to fix up their cottage and soothe her guilty conscience.

Goode, Diane. *Dinosaur's New Clothes.* Scholastic, c1999. 33pp.
In this retelling of the familiar story about two rascals who sell a vain emperor an invisible suit of clothes, the characters are presented as dinosaurs.

Granowsky, Alvin. *That Awful Cinderella.* Raintree Steck-Vaughn, c1993. 25pp.
Contains the classic fairy tale about Cinderella, entitled "Cinderella—A Classic Tale," along with a retelling, entitled "That Awful Cinderella," which is written from the point of view of one of Cinderella's stepsisters.

From Nancy J. Keane, *The Big Book of Children's Reading Lists: 100 Great, Ready-to-Use Book Lists for Educators, Librarians, Parents, and Children.* Westport, CT: Libraries Unlimited, 2006. Copyright © 2006 by Libraries Unlimited.

Fractured Fairy Tales

Granowsky, Alvin. ***The Unfairest of Them All.*** Raintree Steck-Vaughn, c1999. 25pp.
Presents the classic story about Snow White, a young woman whose beauty drives her stepmother to attempt to kill her; and includes an additional tale in which the stepmother gets to tell her side of the story.

Harris, Jim. ***The Three Little Dinosaurs.*** Pelican, c1999. 30pp.
In this variation on "The Three Little Pigs," three young dinosaurs set out on their own, only to be hassled by a Tyrannosaurus rex, who gets a big surprise in the end.

Jackson, Ellen B. ***Cinder Edna.*** Lothrop, Lee & Shepard, c1994. 32pp.
Cinderella and Cinder Edna, who live next door to each other, each with a cruel stepmother and stepsisters, have different approaches to life. Although both end up with the princes of their dreams, one is a great deal happier than the other.

Johnston, Tony. ***The Cowboy and the Black-Eyed Pea.*** Putnam & Grosset , c1996. 32pp.
In this adaptation of "The Princess and the Pea," the wealthy daughter of a Texas rancher devises a plan to find a real cowboy among her many suitors.

Ketteman, Helen. ***Bubba the Cowboy Prince: A Fractured Texas Tale.*** Scholastic, 1997. 32pp.
Loosely based on "Cinderella," this story is set in Texas; the fairy godmother is a cow; and the hero, named Bubba, is the stepson of a wicked rancher.

Lasky, Kathryn. ***The Emperor's Old Clothes.*** Harcourt, 2002, c1999. 32pp.
A continuation of "The Emperor's New Clothes," in which a simple farmer finds the emperor's old clothes on his way home from the market and decides to put them on.

Meddaugh, Susan. ***Cinderella's Rat.*** Houghton Mifflin, c1997. 32pp.
One of the rats that was turned into a coachman by Cinderella's fairy godmother tells his story.

Minters, Frances. ***Cinder-Elly.*** Puffin Books, 1997, c1994. 32pp.
In this rap version of the traditional fairy tale, the overworked younger sister gets to go to a basketball game and meets a star player, Prince Charming.

Osborne, Mary Pope. ***Kate and the Beanstalk.*** Atheneum Books for Young Readers, c2000. 35pp.
In this version of the classic tale, a girl climbs to the top of a giant beanstalk, where she uses her quick wits to outsmart a giant and make her and her mother's fortune.

Palatini, Margie. ***Piggie Pie!*** Clarion Books, c1995. 32pp.
Gritch the Witch flies to Old MacDonald's farm for some pigs to make a piggie pie, but when she arrives she can't find a single porker.

From Nancy J. Keane, *The Big Book of Children's Reading Lists: 100 Great, Ready-to-Use Book Lists for Educators, Librarians, Parents, and Children.* Westport, CT: Libraries Unlimited, 2006. Copyright © 2006 by Libraries Unlimited.

Fractured Fairy Tales

Palatini, Margie. ***Zoom Broom.*** Hyperion Paperbacks for Children, c2000. 32pp.
When her broom breaks down, Gritch the Witch visits a foxy salesman in search of a new Zoom Broom but ends up with something unexpected.

Perlman, Janet. ***Cinderella Penguin, or, the Little Glass Flipper.*** Puffin Books, 1995, c1992. 32pp.
A retelling of the classic "Cinderella," with penguins as the characters.

Pratchett, Terry. ***The Amazing Maurice and His Educated Rodents.*** HarperCollins, c2001. 241pp.
A talking cat, intelligent rats, and a strange boy cooperate in a Pied Piper scam, until they try to con the wrong town and are confronted by a deadly, evil rat king.

Pullman, Philip. ***I Was a Rat!*** Knopf (distributed by Random House), 2000, c1999. 164pp.
A little boy turns life in London upside down when he appears at the house of a lonely old couple and insists he was a rat.

Scieszka, Jon. ***The Frog Prince, Continued.*** Viking Press, c1991. 32pp.
After the frog turns into a prince, he and the Princess do not live happily ever after, and the Prince decides to look for a witch to help him remedy the situation.

Scieszka, Jon. ***The Stinky Cheese Man and Other Fairly Stupid Tales.*** Viking Press, c1992. 51pp.
Madcap revisions of familiar fairy tales.

Stanley, Diane. ***Rumpelstiltskin's Daughter.*** Morrow Junior Books, c1997. 32pp.
Rumpelstiltskin's daughter may not be able to spin straw into gold, but she is more than a match for a monarch whose greed has blighted an entire kingdom.

Trivizas, Eugenios. ***The Three Little Wolves and the Big Bad Pig.*** Margaret K. McElderry Books, c1993. 32pp.
An altered retelling of the traditional tale about the conflict between pig and wolf—with a surprise ending.

Vande Velde, Vivian. ***The Rumpelstiltskin Problem.*** Houghton Mifflin, c2000. 116pp.
A collection of variations on the familiar story of a boastful miller and the daughter he claims can spin straw into gold.

Vande Velde, Vivian. ***Tales from the Brothers Grimm and the Sisters Weird.*** Harcourt Brace, c1995. 128pp.
Presents thirteen twisted versions of such familiar fairy tales as "Little Red Riding Hood," "Jack and the Beanstalk," "Hansel and Gretel," and "The Three Billy Goats Gruff."

A Wolf at the Door: And Other Retold Fairy Tales. Simon & Schuster Books for Young Readers, c2000. 166pp.
Presents thirteen short fantasy stories based on classic fairy tales, written by a variety of authors, including Jane Yolen, Neil Gaiman, and Tanith Lee.

From Nancy J. Keane, *The Big Book of Children's Reading Lists: 100 Great, Ready-to-Use Book Lists for Educators, Librarians, Parents, and Children.* Westport, CT: Libraries Unlimited, 2006. Copyright © 2006 by Libraries Unlimited.

How a Book Is Made

Books for Children of All Ages

Aliki. ***How a Book Is Made.*** HarperTrophy, 1988, c1986. 32pp. (NF)
Describes the stages involved in making a book, starting with the writing of the manuscript and the drawing of the pictures, and explaining all the technical processes leading to printed and bound copies.

Bunting, Eve. ***Once Upon a Time.*** R.C. Owen Publishers, c1995. 32pp. (NF)
Author Eve Bunting tells about her life and her writing.

Burkholder, Kelly. ***Stories.*** Rourke Press, c2001. 24pp.
Discusses different kinds of writing, how to get ideas, practicing writing, and editing and revising.

Christelow, Eileen. ***What Do Authors Do?*** Clarion Books, c1995. 32pp. (NF)
Text and cartoon illustrations describe the process of writing, illustrating, and publishing a children's book, including generating ideas, revising text, and promoting the finished product.

Christelow, Eileen. ***What Do Illustrators Do?*** Clarion Books, c1999. 40pp. (NF)
Provides two illustrators going through all the steps involved in creating new picture books of "Jack and the Beanstalk," including layout, scale, and point of view.

Howe, James. ***Playing with Words.*** R. C. Owen, c1994. 32pp. (NF)
The author of the Bunnicula books, the Pinky and Rex series, the Sebastian Barth mysteries, and other books for children describes his life and his approach to his writing.

Leedy, Loreen. ***Look at My Book: How Kids Can Write & Illustrate Terrific Books.*** Holiday House, c2004. 32pp. (NF)
Provides ideas and simple directions for writing, illustrating, designing, and binding books.

Lester, Helen. ***Author: A True Story.*** Houghton Mifflin, c1997. 32pp. (NF)
Children's author Helen Lester describes her life from age three to adulthood and discusses how she writes.

Royston, Angela. ***How Is a Book Made?*** Heinemann Library, c2005. 32pp. (NF)
Traces in text and photos the process by which wood, glue, and ink are brought together to make books, covering such aspects as cover design, printing, page trimming, and binding.

Stevens, Janet. ***From Pictures to Words: A Book About Making a Book.*** Holiday House, c1995. (NF)
Illustrator Janet Stevens introduces the processes involved in making a book, from manuscript to finished book.

From Nancy J. Keane, *The Big Book of Children's Reading Lists: 100 Great, Ready-to-Use Book Lists for Educators, Librarians, Parents, and Children.* Westport, CT: Libraries Unlimited, 2006. Copyright © 2006 by Libraries Unlimited.

African

Books for Children of All Ages

Angelou, Maya. ***Kofi and His Magic.*** Crown, 2003. 42pp. (NF)
A young Ashanti boy describes some of the wonders of his life in and around the West African village Bonwire.

Dahl, Michael. ***South Africa.*** Bridgestone Books, c1998. 24pp. (NF)
Discusses the history, landscape, people, animals, food, sports, and culture of South Africa.

Davis, Lucile. ***Ghana.*** Bridgestone Books, c1999. 24pp. (NF)
An introduction to the geography, history, natural resources, culture, and people of the west African country Ghana.

Feelings, Muriel L. ***Moja Means One: Swahili Counting Book.*** Puffin Books, 1976, c1971. 30pp. (NF)
The numbers 1 through 10 in Swahili accompany two-page illustrations of various aspects of East African life.

Feelings, Muriel L. ***Zamani Goes to Market.*** Africa World Press, c1990. 44pp.
Zamani's unselfishness is rewarded when he spends the first money he earns on a gift for Mother.

Haskins, James. ***Count Your Way Through Africa.*** Carolrhoda Books, c1989. 24pp. (NF)
Uses the Swahili words for the numbers from 1 to 10 to introduce the land, history, and culture of Africa.

Hetfield, Jamie. ***The Maasai of East Africa.*** PowerKids Press, c1996. 24pp. (NF)
Describes the customs, traditions, food, clothes, and homes of the Maasai people, who live in the grasslands of eastern Africa.

Murphy, Patricia J. ***Tanzania.*** Bridgestone Books, c2003. 24pp. (NF)
Describes the geography, people, social life and customs, education, basic facts, animals, and sports of the East African country Tanzania. Includes a list of words in Kiswahili and instructions for playing the game *bao*.

Nicolotti, Muriel. ***Kuntai: A Masai Child.*** Blackbirch Press, Thompson/Gale, c2005. 24pp. (NF)
Provides a description of a young Masai boy, Kuntai, and includes information about the country, region, and culture he is from, as well as a discussion of different aspects of his school and family life.

Oluonye, Mary N. ***South Africa.*** Carolrhoda Books, c1999. 48pp. (NF)
Describes the people, government, geography, religion, language, customs, lifestyle, and culture of South Africa.

Onyefulu, Ifeoma. ***Emeka's Gift: An African Counting Story.*** Puffin Books, 1999, c1995. 22pp. (NF)
Emeka is going to visit his grandmother and wishes to take her a present. As he passes through the market, he sees lots of things she would like, but with no money, he cannot buy anything. Would Granny understand? The story is illustrated with photographs taken in Emeka's village in Nigeria.

From Nancy J. Keane, *The Big Book of Children's Reading Lists: 100 Great, Ready-to-Use Book Lists for Educators, Librarians, Parents, and Children.* Westport, CT: Libraries Unlimited, 2006. Copyright © 2006 by Libraries Unlimited.

African

Onyefulu, Ifeoma. *Here Comes Our Bride!: An African Wedding Story.* Frances Lincoln Children's Books, (distributed by Publishers Group West), c2004. 26pp. (NF)

A colorful picture book depicting a traditional Nigerian wedding as well as the second, religious service.

Onyefulu, Ifeoma. *Welcome Dede!: An African Naming Ceremony.* Frances Lincoln Children's Books, c2003. 26pp. (NF)

Amarlai has a new baby cousin, and he helps his family prepare for the traditional African naming ceremony.

Peffer-Engels, John. *The Benin Kingdom of West Africa.* PowerKids Press, c1996. 24pp. (NF)

Describes the history and customs of the Edo of Benin, who live in the rain forest of Nigeria and are known for their ivory and brass art.

Books for Children Ages 8–12

Brownlie, Alison. *West Africa.* Raintree Steck-Vaughn, c1999. 32pp. (NF)

Describes the West African culture of food, including the kinds of food grown and eaten, and various feast days like Ramadan, Easter, naming ceremonies, and yam festivals.

Clark, Domini. *South Africa: The Culture.* Crabtree Publishing, c2000. 32pp. (NF)

Portrays the mix of people and cultures that make up South Africa today, including a special section on traditional beliefs and customs.

Giles, Bridget. *Myths of West Africa.* Raintree Steck-Vaughn, c2002. 48pp.

Recounts the myths of West Africa, explaining how the myths reflect the environment, way of life, and religion of the region's people.

Knight, Margy Burns. *Africa Is Not a Country.* Millbrook Press, c2000. 39pp. (NF)

Demonstrates the diversity of the African continent by describing daily life in some of its fifty-three nations.

Murphy, Patricia J. *South Africa.* Benchmark Books, c2004. 48pp. (NF)

An introduction to the history, geography, language, schools, and social life and customs of South Africa.

Musgrove, Margaret. *Ashanti to Zulu: African Traditions.* Dial Books for Young Readers, c1976. 32pp. (NF)

Explains some traditions and customs of twenty-six African tribes beginning with letters from A to Z.

Nicholson, Robert. *The Zulus.* Chelsea Juniors, 1994. 32pp. (NF)

Presents the history and culture of the Zulu people through an exploration of their artifacts, customs, beliefs, and daily routines.

From Nancy J. Keane, *The Big Book of Children's Reading Lists: 100 Great, Ready-to-Use Book Lists for Educators, Librarians, Parents, and Children.* Westport, CT: Libraries Unlimited, 2006. Copyright © 2006 by Libraries Unlimited.

Asian

Compiled by Pooja Makhijani, essayist, journalist, and writer of children's literature; editor of *Under Her Skin: How Girls Experience Race in America* and author of *Mama's Saris,* a picture book (www.poojamakhijani.com).

Books for Children of All Ages

Atkins, Jeannine. *Aani and the Tree Huggers.* Lee & Low Books, c1995. 32pp.
Based on true events in India in the 1970s. Young Aani and the other women in her village defend their forest from developers by wrapping their arms around the trees, making it impossible to cut them down.

Bond, Ruskin. *Binya's Blue Umbrella.* Boyds Mills Press, c1995. 68pp.
A young girl receives a bright blue umbrella in exchange for a necklace. The umbrella brings a smile to everyone's face except one man, who wants it for himself.

Bond, Ruskin. *Cherry Tree.* Boyds Mills Press, 1996, c1991. 31pp.
A story from India in which a little girl plants a cherry seed and cares for the cherry tree through its difficult life. A story about life and growing older

Gavin, Jamila. *Fine Feathered Friend.* Crabtree, 2002, c1996. 44pp.
In India, Raju is angry about spending two months on his aunt and uncle's farm while his family attends a wedding in England, but things looks much brighter after he becomes mother to a newly hatched chick.

Gavin, Jamila. *Grandpa Chatterji.* Egmont Children's Books, c1994. 30pp.
Neeta and Sanjay discover their loving and surprising Indian grandfather.

Gavin, Jamila. *Grandpa's Indian Summer.* Egmont Children's Books, c1996. 30pp.
Neeta and Sanjay visit their grandfather in Calcutta.

Gilmore, Rachna. *A Gift for Gita.* Tilbury House, c2002. 24pp.
During a visit from her beloved grandmother, Gita realizes that her memories of India have faded and that America is her true home.

Gilmore, Rachna. *Lights for Gita.* Tilbury House, c1994. 24pp.
Just moved from India, Gita looks forward to her favorite holiday, Divali, but things are so different in her new home that she wonders if she will ever adjust.

Gilmore, Rachna. *Roses for Gita.* Tilbury House, 2001, c1996. 24pp.
Although Gita misses her grandmother and her grandmother's garden in India, she discovers a new friend and a new garden at her next-door neighbor's house.

Heine, Theresa. *Elephant Dance.* Barefoot Books, c2004. 44pp.
Grandfather tells many stories about his native India in answer to Ravi and Anjali's questions, such as the tale of a procession of elephants on the feast of Divaali when he was a boy. Includes facts about life in India, a list of cooking spices, and descriptions of Indian animals.

From Nancy J. Keane, *The Big Book of Children's Reading Lists: 100 Great, Ready-to-Use Book Lists for Educators, Librarians, Parents, and Children.* Westport, CT: Libraries Unlimited, 2006. Copyright © 2006 by Libraries Unlimited.

Asian

Jaffrey, Madhur. ***Robi Dobi: The Marvelous Adventure of an Indian Elephant.*** Dial Books for Young Readers, c1997. 76pp.
An Indian elephant befriends a mouse, a butterfly, and a parrot, and together they have many adventures.

Jeyaveeran, Ruth. ***The Road to Mumbai.*** Houghton Mifflin, c2004. 32pp.
Shoba and her pet monkey, Fuzzy Patel, set out overnight by flying bed to attend Fuzzy's cousin's wonderful wedding in Mumbai, India.

Kalman, Maira. ***Swami on Rye: Max in India.*** Viking Press, c1995. 34pp.
Max, the famous dog-poet and Hollywood director, faces fatherhood and searches for the meaning of life in exotic India.

Khan, Rukhsana. ***Ruler of the Courtyard.*** Viking Press, c2003. 34pp.
After confronting what she believes to be a snake in the bath house, Saba finds the courage to overcome her fear of the chickens in the courtyard.

Khan, Rukhsana. ***Silly Chicken.*** Viking Press, c2005. 36pp.
In Pakistan, Rani believes that her mother loves their pet chicken Bibi more than she cares for her, until the day that a fluffy chick appears and steals Rani's own affections.

Krishnaswami, Uma. ***Chachaji's Cup.*** Children's Book Press, (distributed by Publishers Group West), c2003. 31pp.
Through stories told over a beloved old teacup, a boy learns about his family history and the Partition of India from his great uncle.

Krishnaswami, Uma. ***Monsoon.*** Farrar, Straus & Giroux, c2003. 32pp.
A child describes waiting for the monsoon rains to arrive and the worry that they will not come.

McDonald, Megan. ***Baya, Baya, Lulla-by-A.*** Atheneum Books for Young Readers, c2003. 32pp.
As a mother in rural India sings to her baby, a weaverbird builds a nest for its young.

Parkison, Jami. ***Amazing Mallika.*** MarshMedia, c1997. 30pp.
A tiger cub who lives in India's Ranthambhore Park wildlife preserve learns some ways to control her quick temper. Endpapers give factual information about India.

Ravishankar, Anushka. ***Tiger on a Tree.*** Farrar, Straus & Giroux, 2004, c1997. 40pp.
After trapping a tiger in a tree, a group of men must decide what to do with it.

Smith, Jeremy. ***Lily's Garden of India.*** Gingham Dog Press, c2003. 36pp.
Lily, wandering in her mother's garden, is summoned by the plants in the Indian Garden, who tell her of the culture, festivals, food, and drink of India.

Wettasinghe, Sybil. ***The Umbrella Thief.*** Kane/Miller Book Publishers, c1987. 24pp.
When each of the umbrellas he brings back to his village disappears, Kiri Mama devises a plan to track down the thief.

Yamate, Sandra S. ***Ashok by Any Other Name.*** Polychrome Publishing, c1992. 32pp.
Ashok is an Indian American boy who wishes he had a more "American" name. In a series of mishaps, he searches for the perfect name for himself.

From Nancy J. Keane, *The Big Book of Children's Reading Lists: 100 Great, Ready-to-Use Book Lists for Educators, Librarians, Parents, and Children.* Westport, CT: Libraries Unlimited, 2006. Copyright © 2006 by Libraries Unlimited.

Caribbean

Books for Children of All Ages

Brownlie, Alison. ***Jamaica.*** Waterbird Books, 2003. 32pp. (NF)
Introduces the Caribbean island nation of Jamaica, describing how people live, eat, play, and earn their living in the countryside and in various cities.

A Caribbean Counting Book. Houghton Mifflin Company, 1996. 24pp. (NF)
A collection of rhymes from various Caribbean countries that are chanted as songs and in games.

Lessac, Frane ***My Little Island.*** HarperCollins, 1984. 38pp.
A young boy goes with his best friend to visit the little Caribbean island where he was born.

Books for Children Ages 8–12

Hernandez, Roger E. ***Cuba.*** Mason Crest Publishers, c2004. 64pp. (NF)
Presents the geography, history, economy, cities and communities, and people and culture of Cuba. Includes recipes, related projects, and a calendar of festivals.

Hernandez, Romel. ***Puerto Rico.*** Mason Crest Publishers, c2004. 63pp. (NF)
Presents the geography, history, economy, cities and communities, and people and culture of Puerto Rico. Includes recipes, related projects, and a calendar of festivals.

Hernandez, Romel. ***Trinidad & Tobago.*** Mason Crest Publishers, c2004 63pp. (NF)
Presents the geography, history, economy, cities and communities, and people and culture of Trinidad and Tobago. Includes recipes, related projects, and a calendar of festivals.

Kozleski, Lisa. ***Leeward Islands: Anguilla, St Martin, St. Barts, St. Eustatius, Guadeloupe, St. Kitts and Nevis, Antigua and Barbuda, and Montserrat.*** Mason Crest Publishers, c2004. 63pp. (NF)
Presents the geography, history, economy, cities and communities, and people and culture of the Leeward Islands. Includes recipes, related projects, and a calendar of festivals.

Temko, Florence. ***Traditional Crafts from the Caribbean.*** Lerner, c2001. 64pp. (NF)
Provides instructions on how to make traditional Caribbean Island handicrafts such as Jamaican woven fish, Puerto Rican *vejigante* masks, and tap tap trucks.

Temple, Bob. ***Dominican Republic.*** Mason Crest Publishers, c2004. 63pp. (NF)
Presents the geography, history, economy, cities and communities, and people and culture of the Dominican Republic. Includes recipes, related projects, and a calendar of festivals.

Temple, Bob. ***Haiti.*** Mason Crest Publishers, c2004. 63pp. (NF)
Presents the geography, history, economy, cities and communities, and people and culture of Haiti. Includes recipes, related projects, and a calendar of festivals.

From Nancy J. Keane, *The Big Book of Children's Reading Lists: 100 Great, Ready-to-Use Book Lists for Educators, Librarians, Parents, and Children.* Westport, CT: Libraries Unlimited, 2006. Copyright © 2006 by Libraries Unlimited.

Hispanic

Books for Children of All Ages

Arroz Con Leche: Popular Songs and Rhymes from Latin America. Scholastic, c1989. 32pp. (NF)
A collection of traditional Latin American songs and rhymes, in Spanish and English, with the music included.

Dorros, Arthur. *Abuela.* Dutton Children's Books, c1991. 40pp.
While riding on a bus with her grandmother, a little girl imagines that they are carried up into the sky and fly over the sights of New York City.

Elya, Susan Middleton. *Say Hola to Spanish at the Circus.* Lee & Low Books, c2000. 32pp. (NF)
Simple text and pictures of circus scenes help young readers build their Spanish vocabularies.

Mora, Pat. *A Birthday Basket for Tia.* Aladdin Paperbacks, 1997, c1992. 32pp.
With the help and interference of her cat Chica, Cecilia prepares a surprise gift for her great-aunt's ninetieth birthday.

Saenz, Benjamin Alire. *Grandma Fina and Her Wonderful Umbrellas = La Abuelita Finay y Sus Sombrillas Maravillosas.* Cinco Puntos Press, c1999. 31pp.
After her friends and family all notice that her favorite yellow umbrella is torn, Grandma Fina gets quite a surprise on her birthday.

Soto, Gary. *Big Bushy Mustache.* Knopf, (distributed by Random House), c1998. 30pp.
Wanting to look more like his father, Ricky borrows a mustache from a school costume, but when he loses it on the way home, his father comes up with a replacement.

Soto, Gary. *Chato and the Party Animals.* Putnam, c2000. 32pp.
Chato decides to throw a *pachanga* for his friend Novio Boy, who has never had a birthday party.

Stevens, Jan Romero. *Carlos and the Squash Plant.* Northland, c1993. 34pp.
Having ignored his mother's warnings about what will happen if he doesn't bathe after working on his family's New Mexican farm, Carlos awakens one morning to find a squash growing out of his ear.

Stevens, Jan Romero. *Carlos Digs to China.* Rising Moon, c2004. 34pp.
A children's story written in both English and Spanish about a boy named Carlos, who digs a hole to China, where he can eat egg rolls, chow mein, and fortune cookies, because he is tired of the food on his side of the world.

From Nancy J. Keane, *The Big Book of Children's Reading Lists: 100 Great, Ready-to-Use Book Lists for Educators, Librarians, Parents, and Children.* Westport, CT: Libraries Unlimited, 2006. Copyright © 2006 by Libraries Unlimited.

Hispanic

Tenorio-Coscarelli, Jane. ***The Tamale Quilt Story.*** 1/4 Inch Designs, c1998. 47pp.
Rosa, sick for the holidays, is warmed by her grandmother's story of how she and her mother, father, and brother made tamales, and by the quilt her grandmother made to commemorate those happy occasions.

Torres, Leyla. ***Saturday Sancocho.*** Farrar, Straus & Giroux, 1999, c1995. 32pp.
Maria Lili and her grandmother barter a dozen eggs at the market square to get the ingredients to cook their traditional Saturday chicken *sancocho*. Includes recipe.

Books for Children Ages 8–12

Kent, Deborah. ***The Changing Face of America: Hispanic Roots, Hispanic Pride.*** Child's World, c2004. 40pp. (NF)
Introduces the Hispanic American culture: its origins, history, variety, and impact on American society.

Nickles, Greg. ***The Hispanics.*** Crabtree, c2001. 32pp. (NF)
Text and photographs provide information about the experiences of Hispanics in the United States and Canada, discussing why people left Spain and Latin America, their journeys to North America, early settlements, neighborhoods, culture and traditions, fiestas, and other topics.

Turck, Mary. ***Mexico & Central America: A Fiesta of Culture, Crafts, and Activities for Ages 8–12.*** Chicago Review Press, c2004. 147pp. (NF)
An introduction to Mexico and the countries of Central America, with illustrated maps and notes on the Spanish language; features forty projects and three plays based on the Mexican and Central American cultures.

From Nancy J. Keane, *The Big Book of Children's Reading Lists: 100 Great, Ready-to-Use Book Lists for Educators, Librarians, Parents, and Children.* Westport, CT: Libraries Unlimited, 2006. Copyright © 2006 by Libraries Unlimited.

Jewish

Books for Children of All Ages

Emerman, Ellen. ***Is It Shabbos Yet?*** HaChai, c2001. 32pp.
Young Malkie helps her mother get ready for the Jewish Sabbath, taking part in cleaning, shopping, and cooking.

Hest, Amy. ***The Friday Nights of Nana.*** Candlewick Press, c2001. 26pp.
Jennie helps her grandmother prepare for a family Sabbath celebration.

Kimmelman, Leslie. ***Dance, Sing, Remember: A Celebration of Jewish Holidays.*** HarperCollins, c2000. 34pp. (NF)
Explains eleven major Jewish holidays and how they are celebrated.

Oberman, Sheldon. ***The Always Prayer Shawl.*** Boyds Mills Press, c1994. 34pp.
A prayer shawl is handed down from grandfather to grandson in this story of Jewish tradition and the passage of generations.

Podwal, Mark H. ***A Sweet Year: A Taste of the Jewish Holidays.*** Doubleday Books for Young Readers, c2003. 32pp. (NF)
Pictures and easy-to-read text introduce Jewish holidays, focusing on the foods associated with each.

Polacco, Patricia. ***The Keeping Quilt.*** Simon & Schuster Books for Young Readers, c1998. 41pp.
A homemade quilt ties together the lives of four generations of an immigrant Jewish family, remaining a symbol of their enduring love and faith.

Zucker, Jonny. ***Apples and Honey: A Rosh Hashanah Story.*** Barron's, c2002. 24pp. (NF)
A Jewish family celebrates Rosh Hashanah, the Jewish New Year. Includes information about the meaning and customs associated with the holiday.

Books for Children Ages 8–12

Ferro, Jennifer. ***Jewish Foods & Culture.*** Rourke Press, c1999. 48pp. (NF)
Discusses some of the foods enjoyed by Jews and describes special foods that are part of such specific celebrations as the Passover seder. Includes recipes.

Ganeri, Anita. ***Jewish Festivals Throughout the Year.*** Smart Apple Media, 2004, c2003. 30pp. (NF)
Introduces the main Jewish festivals, from Rosh Hashanah to Shavuot, tells the story behind each festival, and describes how each is celebrated around the world today.

Wood, Angela. ***Jewish Synagogue.*** Gareth Stevens, 2000. 32pp. (NF)
Introduces the reader to the Jewish religion and describes what goes on in a synagogue.

From Nancy J. Keane, *The Big Book of Children's Reading Lists: 100 Great, Ready-to-Use Book Lists for Educators, Librarians, Parents, and Children.* Westport, CT: Libraries Unlimited, 2006. Copyright © 2006 by Libraries Unlimited.

Middle Eastern

Books for Children of All Ages

Haskins, James. ***Count Your Way Through the Arab World.*** Carolrhoda Books, c1987. 24pp. (NF)
Uses Arabic numerals from 1 to 10 to introduce concepts about Arab countries and Arab culture.

Johnson, Julia. ***A Is for Arabia.*** Stacey International, c2002. 29pp. (NF)
A rhyming, alphabet book that takes the reader on a trip across the lands of Arabia, showing it customs, its people, and its animals, from A to Z.

Matze, Claire Sidhom. ***The Stars in My Geddoh's Sky.*** Whitman, c1999. 32pp.
Alex's Arabic-speaking grandfather comes to visit the United States, and Alex learns about his grandfather's Middle Eastern homeland.

Segal, Sheila F. ***Joshua's Dream: A Journey to the Land of Israel.*** UAHC Press, c1992. 26pp.
Joshua's dream of taking part in the transformation of Israel's desert land finally comes true.

Books for Children Ages 8–12

Cane, Graeme. ***Welcome to Saudi Arabia.*** Gareth Stevens, c2002. 48pp (NF)
Presents information on the geography, history, government and economy, arts, people, and social life and customs of Saudi Arabia, the largest country in the Middle East.

Khan, Rukhsana. ***Muslim Child: Understanding Islam Through Stories and Poems.*** Whitman, 2002, c1999. 104pp.
A collection of stories and poems about Muslim children from a variety of backgrounds, focusing on the celebration of holidays and practices of Islam.

Wolf, Bernard. ***Coming to America: A Muslim Family's Story.*** Lee & Low Books, c2003. 50pp. (NF)
Depicts the joys and hardships experienced by a Muslim family that immigrates to New York City from Alexandria, Egypt, in the hope of making a better life for themselves.

From Nancy J. Keane, *The Big Book of Children's Reading Lists: 100 Great, Ready-to-Use Book Lists for Educators, Librarians, Parents, and Children.* Westport, CT: Libraries Unlimited, 2006. Copyright © 2006 by Libraries Unlimited.

Native American

Books for Children of All Ages

Abbink, Emily. ***Colors of the Navajo.*** Carolrhoda Books, c1998. 24pp. (NF)
Uses colors to focus on the history, culture, and physical surroundings of the Navajo Indians.

Lassieur, Allison. ***The Cheyenne.*** Bridgestone Books, c2001. 24pp. (NF)
A brief introduction to the people, culture, history, and lifestyle of the Cheyenne Indians.

Lassieur, Allison. ***The Choctaw Nation.*** Bridgestone Books, c2001. 24pp. (NF)
A brief introduction to the people, geography, culture, and lifestyle of the Choctaw Indians.

Lassieur, Allison. ***The Creek Nation.*** Bridgestone Books, c2002. 24pp. (NF)
A description of the history, culture, society, religion, and government of the Creek Indians.

Mattern, Joanne. ***The Shawnee Indians.*** Bridgestone Books, c2001. 24pp. (NF)
A brief introduction to the history, culture, and lifestyle of the Shawnee Indians.

Mattern, Joanne. ***The Shoshone People.*** Bridgestone Books, c2001. 24pp. (NF)
A brief introduction to the people, history, culture, and lifestyle of the Shoshone Indians.

Press, Petra. ***The Apache.*** Compass Point Books, c2002. 48pp. (NF)
Photographs and simple text give young readers an introduction to Apache history and culture.

Press, Petra. ***The Blackfeet.*** **Compass** Point Books, c2001. 48pp. (NF)
Text and illustrations chronicle the history of the Blackfeet Indians.

Press, Petra. ***The Cherokee.*** Compass Point Books, c2002. 48pp. (NF)
An introduction to the culture and history of the Cherokee people, discussing their lifestyle, economy, ceremonies and festivals, and wars, and looking at the lives of modern-day Cherokees.

Press, Petra. ***The Iroquois.*** Compass Point Books, c2001. 48pp. (NF)
Text and illustrations introduce the history and culture of the Iroquois people.

Press, Petra. ***The Nez Perce.*** Compass Point Books, c2002. 48pp. (NF)
An illustrated introduction to the culture and history of the Nez Perce people, a Native American group that originated in the northwestern United States.

Press, Petra. ***The Pueblo.*** Compass Point Books, c2001. 48pp. (NF)
An illustrated introduction to the culture and history of the Pueblo people.

From Nancy J. Keane, *The Big Book of Children's Reading Lists: 100 Great, Ready-to-Use Book Lists for Educators, Librarians, Parents, and Children.* Westport, CT: Libraries Unlimited, 2006. Copyright © 2006 by Libraries Unlimited.

Native American

Press, Petra. *The Seminole.* Compass Point Books, c2002. 48pp. (NF)
Photographs and simple text introduce young readers to the history and culture of the Seminole Indians.

Press, Petra. *The Shawnee.* Compass Point Books, c2002. 48pp. (NF)
An illustrated introduction to the culture and history of the Shawnee people, a Native American group that originated in the northeastern United States.

Press, Petra. *The Zuni.* Compass Point Books, c2002. 48pp. (NF)
An illustrated introduction to the culture and history of the Zuni people, a Native American group that originated in the southwestern United States.

Rosinsky, Natalie M. *The Algonquin.* Compass Point Books, c2005. 47pp. (NF)
A children's history of the Algonquin people: who they are and where they live, their culture, religion, and family life, the effects of French traders, soldiers, and missionaries, as well as the broken promises made by the British.

Rosinsky, Natalie M. *The Hopi.* Compass Point Books, c2005. 48pp. (NF)
A children's history of the Hopi people: who they are and where they live, their culture, religion, and family life, the effects of the Spanish conquest, explorers, and government interference, as well as information on forced assimilation and resistance.

Books for Children Ages 8–12

Hoyt Goldsmith, Diane. *Potlatch: A Tsimshian Celebration.* Holiday House, c1997. 32pp. (NF)
Describes the traditions of the Tsimshian Indians living in Metlakatla, Alaska, and in particular, those connected with a potlatch they hold to celebrate their heritage.

Hoyt Goldsmith, Diane. *Pueblo Storyteller.* Holiday House, c1991. 26pp. (NF)
A young Cochiti Indian girl living with her grandparents in the Cochiti Pueblo near Santa Fe, New Mexico, describes her home and family and the day-to-day life and customs of her people.

Smith, Cynthia Leitich. *Jingle Dancer.* Morrow Junior Books, c2000. 32pp. (NF)
Jenna, a member of the Muscogee, or Creek Nation, borrows jingles from the dresses of several friends and relatives so that she can perform the jingle dance at the powwow; also includes a note about the jingle dance tradition and its regalia.

Sneve, Virginia Driving Hawk. *The Cheyennes.* Holiday House, c1996. 32pp. (NF)
Provides an overview of the social life and customs and history of the Cheyenne Indians.

Sneve, Virginia Driving Hawk. *The Seminoles.* Holiday House, c1994. 32pp. (NF)
Discusses the history, lifestyle, customs, and current situation of the Seminoles.

From Nancy J. Keane, *The Big Book of Children's Reading Lists: 100 Great, Ready-to-Use Book Lists for Educators, Librarians, Parents, and Children.* Westport, CT: Libraries Unlimited, 2006. Copyright © 2006 by Libraries Unlimited.

Sense of Community

Books for Children of All Ages

Blos, Joan W. ***Old Henry.*** Mulberry Paperback Book, 1990, c1987. 32pp.
Henry's neighbors are scandalized that he ignores them and lets his property get run down, until they drive him away and find themselves missing him.

Bunting, Eve. ***Rudi's Pond.*** Clarion Books, c1999. 32pp.
When a sick boy dies, his friends and classmates build a schoolyard pond in his memory.

Bunting, Eve. ***Smoky Night.*** Harcourt Brace, c1994. 36pp.
When the Los Angeles riots break out in the streets of their neighborhood, a young boy and his mother learn the value of getting along with others no matter what their background or nationality.

Bunting, Eve. ***The Wednesday Surprise.*** Clarion Books, c1989. 32pp.
On Wednesday nights when Grandma stays with Anna, everyone thinks she is teaching Anna to read.

Collier, Bryan. ***Uptown.*** H. Holt, c2000. 32pp.
A tour of the sights of Harlem, including the Metro-North Train, brownstones, shopping on 125th Street, a barber shop, summer basketball, the Boy's Choir, and sunset over the Harlem River.

Crew, Gary. ***Memorial.*** Simply Read Books, c2004. 32pp.
A young boy, concerned over the city's plans to cut down a memorial tree planted after World War I, learns about the tree's significance from his great-grandfather, grandfather, and father—all war veterans.

DiSalvo-Ryan, DyAnne. ***A Castle On Viola Street.*** HarperCollins, c2001. 32pp.
A hard-working family gets their own house at last by joining a community program that restores old houses.

DiSalvo-Ryan, DyAnne. ***City Green.*** Morrow Junior Books, c1994. 32pp.
Marcy and Miss Rosa start a campaign to clean up an empty lot and turn it into a community garden.

Fleischman, Paul. ***Weslandia.*** Candlewick Press, c1999. 34pp.
Wesley's garden produces a crop of huge, strange plants, which provide him with clothing, shelter, food, and drink, thus helping him create his own civilization and changing his life.

From Nancy J. Keane, *The Big Book of Children's Reading Lists: 100 Great, Ready-to-Use Book Lists for Educators, Librarians, Parents, and Children.* Westport, CT: Libraries Unlimited, 2006. Copyright © 2006 by Libraries Unlimited.

Sense of Community

Grifalconi, Ann. ***The Village of Round and Square Houses.*** Little, Brown, c1986. 32pp.
A grandmother explains to her listeners why, in their village on the side of a volcano, the men live in square houses and the women in round ones.

Jennings, Sharon. ***Franklin's Neighborhood.*** Kids Can Press, c1999. 32pp.
Franklin has to decide what he likes best about his neighborhood.

Lester, Helen. ***Hooway for Wodney Wat.*** Houghton Mifflin, c1999. 32pp.
All his classmates make fun of Rodney because he can't pronounce his name, but it is Rodney's speech impediment that drives away the class bully.

Muth, Jon J. ***Stone Soup.*** Scholastic Press, c2003. 32pp.
Three hungry men charm a poor village into making enough soup to feed them all.

Singer, Marilyn. ***Block Party Today!*** Knopf, (distributed by Random House), c2004. 30pp.
Three friends resolve their differences and enjoy their neighborhood's block party.

Smith, Cynthia Leitich. ***Jingle Dancer.*** Morrow Junior Books, c2000. 32pp.
Jenna, a member of the Muscogee, or Creek Nation, borrows jingles from the dresses of several friends and relatives so that she can perform the jingle dance at the powwow; also includes a note about the jingle dance tradition and its regalia.

Spinelli, Eileen. ***Somebody Loves You, Mr. Hatch.*** Aladdin Paperbacks, 1996, c1991. 32pp.
An anonymous valentine changes the life of the unsociable Mr. Hatch, turning him into a laughing friend who helps and appreciates all his neighbors.

Books for Children Ages 8–12

Blume, Judy. ***Iggie's House.*** Atheneum Books for Young Readers, 2001, c1970. 117pp.
When an African American family with three children moves into a white neighborhood, eleven-year-old Winnie learns the difference between being a good neighbor and being a good friend.

Bonners, Susan. ***Edwina Victorious.*** Farrar, Straus & Giroux, c2000. 131pp.
Edwina follows in the footsteps of her namesake great aunt when she begins to write letters to the mayor about community problems and poses as Edwina the elder.

From Nancy J. Keane, *The Big Book of Children's Reading Lists: 100 Great, Ready-to-Use Book Lists for Educators, Librarians, Parents, and Children.* Westport, CT: Libraries Unlimited, 2006. Copyright © 2006 by Libraries Unlimited.

Sense of Community

Fogelin, Adrian. ***Anna Casey's Place in the World.*** Peachtree, c2001. 207pp.
Anna, a twelve-year-old girl with strong survival instincts, tries to adjust to life in a Florida foster home in a strange neighborhood with an overly tidy single woman and Eb, another foster child who is not at all sure he wants to stay there.

Haugaard, Kay. ***No Place.*** Milkweed Editions, (distributed by Publishers Group West), c1998. 187pp.
Having no place to play in their run-down, inner-city Los Angeles neighborhood, twelve-year-old Arturo and the other students in his sixth-grade class raise money and build a park, in the process learning about hard work, creativity, and teamwork.

Lowry, Lois. ***See You Around, Sam!*** Houghton Mifflin, c1996. 113pp.
Sam Krupnik, mad at his mother because she won't let him wear his new plastic fangs in the house, decides to run away to Alaska.

Moses, Will. ***Silent Night.*** Philomel Books, c1997. 40pp.
One snowy Christmas Eve a Vermont community makes preparations for the holiday as well as for the arrival of another Christmas miracle.

Pellegrino, Marjorie White. ***My Grandma's the Mayor.*** Magination Press, c2000. 31pp.
Annie is unhappy that she has to share her grandmother, the mayor, with so many people, but when she helps out during a town emergency, Annie appreciates all that her grandmother does in the community.

Quattlebaum, Mary. ***Jackson Jones and Mission Greentop.*** Delacorte Press, c2004. 101pp.
His plot in a community garden brings ten-year-old Jackson Jones more zucchini than he cares to see and the unwanted attention of a bully, but when a company plans to destroy the garden, Jackson turns his attention to trying to save it.

Rylant, Cynthia. ***Some Good News.*** Aladdin Paperbacks, 2001, c1999. 55pp.
Nine-year-old cousins Rosie, Lily, and Tess create a neighborhood newspaper celebrating all their friends on Cobble Street.

Whelan, Gloria. ***A Haunted House in Starvation Lake.*** Random House, c2003. 71pp.
The community of Starvation Lake helps fourth-grader Dawn Zonder clean and repair an old house, hoping that her family will find the money to be able to move in.

From Nancy J. Keane, *The Big Book of Children's Reading Lists: 100 Great, Ready-to-Use Book Lists for Educators, Librarians, Parents, and Children.* Westport, CT: Libraries Unlimited, 2006. Copyright © 2006 by Libraries Unlimited.

War

Books for Children of All Ages

Balgassi, Haemi. ***Peacebound Trains.*** Clarion Books, c1996. 47pp.
Sumi's grandmother tells the story of her family's escape from Seoul during the Korean War, while they watch the trains which will eventually bring her mother back from army service.

Benchley, Nathaniel. ***Sam, The Minuteman.*** HarperCollins, c1969. 62pp.
An easy-to-read account of Sam and his father fighting as minutemen against the British in the Battle of Lexington.

Borden, Louise. ***The Little Ships: The Heroic Rescue at Dunkirk In World War II.*** Aladdin Paperback, 2003, c1997. 32pp.
A young English girl and her father take their sturdy fishing boat and join the scores of other civilian vessels crossing the English Channel in a daring attempt to rescue Allied and British troops trapped by Nazi soldiers at Dunkirk.

Bunting, Eve. ***The Wall.*** Clarion Books, c1990. 32pp.
A boy and his father come from far away to visit the Vietnam War Memorial in Washington, D.C., and find the name of the boy's grandfather, who was killed in the conflict.

Cutler, Jane. ***The Cello of Mr. O.*** Dutton Children's Books, c1999. 32pp.
When a concert cellist plays in the square for his neighbors in a war-besieged city, his priceless instrument is destroyed by a mortar shell, but he finds the courage to return the next day.

Fleming, Candace. ***Boxes for Katje.*** Farrar, Straus & Giroux, c2003. 34pp.
After a young Dutch girl writes to her new American friend thanking her for the care package sent after World War II, she begins to receive increasingly larger boxes.

Fox, Mem. ***Feathers and Fools.*** Harcourt Brace, c1996. 34pp.
A modern fable about some peacocks and swans who allow the fear of their differences to become so great that they end up destroying each other.

Heide, Florence Parry. ***Sami and the Time of the Troubles.*** Clarion Books, c1992. 33pp.
A ten-year-old Lebanese boy goes to school, helps his mother with chores, plays with his friends, and lives with his family in a basement shelter when bombings occur and fighting begins on his street.

From Nancy J. Keane, *The Big Book of Children's Reading Lists: 100 Great, Ready-to-Use Book Lists for Educators, Librarians, Parents, and Children.* Westport, CT: Libraries Unlimited, 2006. Copyright © 2006 by Libraries Unlimited.

War

Houston, Gloria. ***The Year of the Perfect Christmas Tree: An Appalachian Story.*** Dial Books for Young Readers, c1988. 32pp.

Ruthie and her mother wonder how they will fulfill their obligation of getting the perfect Christmas tree to the town for the holiday celebration, since Papa has left the Appalachian area to go to war.

Oppenheim, Shulamith Levey. ***The Lily Cupboard.*** HarperCollins, c1992. 29pp.

Miriam, a young Jewish girl, is forced to leave her parents and hide with strangers in the country during the German occupation of Holland.

Polacco, Patricia. ***The Butterfly.*** Philomel Books, c2000. 50pp.

During the Nazi occupation of France, Monique's mother hides a Jewish family in her basement and tries to help them escape to freedom.

Say, Allen. ***Grandfather's Journey.*** Houghton Mifflin, c1993. 32pp.

A Japanese American man recounts his grandfather's journey to America, which he later also undertakes, and the feelings of being torn by love for two different countries.

Seuss, Dr. ***The Butter Battle Book.*** Random House, c1984. 48pp.

Engaged in a long-running battle, the Yooks and the Zooks develop more and more sophisticated weaponry as they attempt to outdo each other.

Turner, Ann Warren. ***The Drummer Boy: Marching to the Civil War.*** HarperCollins, c1998. 32pp.

A thirteen-year-old soldier, coming of age during the American Civil War, beats his drum to raise tunes and spirits and muffle the sounds of the dying.

Turner, Ann Warren. ***Katie's Trunk.*** Aladdin Paperbacks, 1997, c1992. 32pp.

Katie, whose family is not sympathetic to the rebel soldiers during the American Revolution, hides under the clothes in her mother's wedding trunk when they invade her home.

Uchida, Yoshiko. ***The Bracelet.*** Philomel Books, c1993. 32pp.

Emi, a Japanese American in the second grade, is sent with her family to an internment camp during World War II. Although she loses the bracelet her best friend has given her, she finds that she does not need a physical reminder of that friendship.

Books for Children Ages 8–12

Abells, Chana Byers. ***The Children We Remember.*** Greenwillow Books, c1986. 50pp. (NF)

Text and photographs briefly describe the fate of Jewish children in World War II Europe after the Nazis took over.

From Nancy J. Keane, *The Big Book of Children's Reading Lists: 100 Great, Ready-to-Use Book Lists for Educators, Librarians, Parents, and Children.* Westport, CT: Libraries Unlimited, 2006. Copyright © 2006 by Libraries Unlimited.

War

Borden, Louise. ***Sleds on Boston Common: A Story from the American Revolution.*** Margaret K. McElderry Books, c2000. 40pp.

Henry complains to the royal governor, General Gage, after his plan to sled down the steep hill at Boston Common is thwarted by the masses of British troops camped there.

Dabba Smith, Frank. ***My Secret Camera: Life in the Lodz Ghetto.*** Harcourt, c2000. 42pp. (NF)

Photographs taken secretly by a young Jewish man document the fear, hardship, generosity, and humanity woven through the daily life of the Jews forced to live in the Lodz ghetto during the Holocaust.

Granfield, Linda. ***In Flanders Fields: The Story of the Poem by John Mccrae.*** Stoddart Kids, 1996, c1995. 32pp.

Presents the context for the writing of the famous poem by the Canadian medical officer who attended injured soldiers in Flanders during the First World War.

Kirkpatrick, Katherine. ***Redcoats and Petticoats.*** Holiday House, c1999. 32pp.

Members of a family in the village of Setauket on Long Island are displaced by the Redcoats and serve as spies for the Revolutionary Army of George Washington.

Lee, Milly. ***Nim and the War Effort.*** Farrar, Straus & Giroux, c1997. 40pp.

In her determination to prove that an Asian American can win the contest for the war effort, Nim does something that leaves her Chinese grandfather both bewildered and proud.

Maruki, Toshi. ***Hiroshima No Pika.*** Lothrop, Lee & Shepard, c1980. 48pp. (NF)

A retelling of a mother's account of what happened to her family during the "flash" that destroyed Hiroshima in 1945.

Mochizuki, Ken. ***Baseball Saved Us.*** Lee & Low Books, c1993. 32pp.

A Japanese American boy learns to play baseball when he and his family are forced to live in an internment camp during World War II, and his ability to play helps him after the war is over.

Rubin, Susan Goldman. ***Fireflies in the Dark: The Story of Friedl Dicker-Brandeis and the Children of Terezin.*** Holiday House, c2000. 47pp. (NF)

Covers the years during which Friedl Dicker, a Jewish woman from Czechoslovakia, taught art to children at the Terezin Concentration Camp. Includes art created by the teacher and students, excerpts from diaries, and interviews with camp survivors.

From Nancy J. Keane, *The Big Book of Children's Reading Lists: 100 Great, Ready-to-Use Book Lists for Educators, Librarians, Parents, and Children.* Westport, CT: Libraries Unlimited, 2006. Copyright © 2006 by Libraries Unlimited.

Airplanes

Books for Children of All Ages

Bingham, Caroline. ***Airplane.*** DK Publishing, c2003. 30pp. (NF)
Introduces assorted airplanes and other flying machines, including gliders, helicopters, and space shuttles.

Bingham, Caroline. ***DK Big Book of Airplanes.*** DK Publishing, c2001. 32pp. (NF)
Profiles fourteen fast or unusual types of aircraft, with color photos and descriptions that explain what makes them unique. Covers such craft as the Gee Bee, the ultralight, the Concorde, and the F-16.

Crews, Donald. ***Flying.*** Greenwillow Books, c1986. 32pp. (NF)
An airplane takes off, flies, and lands after having passed over cities, country areas, lakes, and more.

Gutman, Anne. ***Lisa's Airplane Trip.*** Knopf, (distributed by Random House), c2001. 28pp.
Lisa takes an exciting airplane ride all by herself from Paris to New York.

Simon, Seymour. ***Amazing Aircraft.*** SeaStar Books, c2002. 32pp. (NF)
An easy-to-read overview of the history of aircraft.

Sturges, Philemon. ***I Love Planes!*** HarperCollins, c2003. 25pp.
A child celebrates his love of planes by naming his favorite kinds and their notable characteristics.

Books for Children Ages 8–12

Grant, R. G. ***Flight: The Trials and Triumphs of Air Pioneers.*** DK Publishing, c2003. 96pp. (NF)
Photos, illustrations, and text describe a wide variety of aircraft and the pilots who have flown them.

Roza, Greg. ***The Incredible Story of Aircraft Carriers.*** PowerKids Press, c2004. 24pp.
A children's guide to the history of aircraft carriers; includes information on the first carriers and early aircraft, the USS *Enterprise*, supercarriers, and the flight deck and catapult.

Simon, Seymour. ***From Paper Airplanes to Outer Space.*** R.C. Owen Publishers, c2000. 32pp. (NF)
The children's book author describes his life, his daily activities, and his creative process, showing how all are intertwined.

Sinclair, Julie L. ***The Airplane.*** Capstone Press, c2004. 32pp. (NF)
An account of the history of the airplane, including how the airplanes of the past evolved into today's aircraft.

Stille, Darlene R. ***Airplanes.*** Children's Press, c1997. 47pp. (NF)
An introduction to airplanes, describing their parts, various uses, and the science behind how they fly.

Weitzman, David. ***Jenny: The Airplane That Taught America to Fly.*** Roaring Brook Press, c2002. 32pp. (NF)
Presents the development and history of the JN 4D airplane, commonly called the Jenny, and portrays a woman pilot who trained army air cadets for World War I and later carried airmail.

From Nancy J. Keane, *The Big Book of Children's Reading Lists: 100 Great, Ready-to-Use Book Lists for Educators, Librarians, Parents, and Children.* Westport, CT: Libraries Unlimited, 2006. Copyright © 2006 by Libraries Unlimited.

Boats

Books for Children of All Ages

Barton, Byron. *Boats.* Crowell, c1986. 32pp. (NF)
Depicts several kinds of boats and ships.

Burningham, John. *Mr. Gumpy's Outing.* H. Holt, 1990, c1970. 32pp.
Mr. Gumpy accepts more and more riders on his boat, until the inevitable occurs.

Collicutt, Paul. *This Boat.* Farrar, Straus & Giroux, c2001. 26pp. (NF)
Depicts many different types of boats and ships, with short descriptions of their various characteristics.

Crews, Donald. *Harbor.* Mulberry Books, 1987, c1982. 32pp. (NF)
Presents various kinds of boats that come and go in a busy harbor.

Crews, Donald. *Sail Away.* HarperTrophy, 2000, c1995. 32pp.
A family takes an enjoyable trip in their sailboat and watches the weather change throughout the day.

Gibbons, Gail. *Boat Book.* Holiday House, c1983. 32pp. (NF)
Introduces many kinds of boats and ships, including rowboats, canoes, sailboats, speedboats, cruise ships, submarines, tugboats, and tankers.

Gutman, Anne. *Gaspard on Vacation.* A. Knopf, (distributed by Random House), c2001. 24pp.
While on vacation with his family in Venice, Gaspard gets tired of visiting museums, so he takes off by himself for a boating adventure on the canals.

Martin, Jacqueline Briggs. *On Sand Island.* Houghton Mifflin, c2003. 32pp.
In 1916 on an island in Lake Superior, Carl builds himself a boat by bartering with the other islanders for parts and labor.

Paulsen, Gary. *Canoe Days.* Dragonfly Books, 2001, c1999. 32pp.
A canoe ride on a northern lake during a summer day reveals the quiet beauty and wonder of nature in and around the peaceful water.

Rotner, Shelley. *Boats Afloat.* Orchard Books, c1998. 32pp. (NF)
Photographs and simple text describe all kinds of large and small boats and their functions.

From Nancy J. Keane, *The Big Book of Children's Reading Lists: 100 Great, Ready-to-Use Book Lists for Educators, Librarians, Parents, and Children.* Westport, CT: Libraries Unlimited, 2006. Copyright © 2006 by Libraries Unlimited.

Boats

Books for Children Ages 8–12

Beyer, Mark. ***Boats of the Past.*** PowerKids Press, c2002. 24pp. (NF)
Describes boats throughout history, including dugout canoes, steamboats, and steel hulls.

Frederick, Dawn. ***How It Happens at the Boat Factory.*** Clara House Books, c2002. 32pp. (NF)
Photographs and text describe how aluminum boats are made.

Graham, Ian. ***Superboats.*** Heinemann Library, c2003. 32pp. (NF)
Describes the specifications, safety equipment, and uses of a variety of fast, powerful, and luxurious powerboats, including ski boats, motor yachts, one-person hydroplanes, and 2,000-horsepower offshore racing powerboats.

Loves, June. ***Ships.*** Chelsea House, c2002. 32pp. (NF)
An illustrated guide to ships, presented in the form of computer screen pictures, covering the history, types, parts, movement, and uses of the water vessels.

Peterson, Tiffany. ***Watercraft.*** Heinemann Library, c2003. 32pp. (NF)
Presents instructions for drawing various boats, ship, and other watercraft, including a jet ski, a tall ship, and a riverboat.

Rossi, Renzo. ***A History of Powered Ships.*** Blackbirch Press, c2005. 48pp. (NF)
Covers the history of powered boats from the first steamers to the modern pleasure boats.

Rossi, Renzo. ***A History of Water Travel.*** Blackbirch Press, Thomson/Gale, c2005. 48pp. (NF)
Chronicles the history of water travel technology, from the first rafts to modern racing yachts, profiling the evolution of such craft as canoes, gondolas, fishing boats, large sailing ships, and lifeboats.

Wilkinson, Philip. ***Ships.*** Kingfisher, c2000. 63pp. (NF)
Text and illustrations describe how ships and boats have been used throughout history, from the earliest trading vessels to modern luxury liners.

From Nancy J. Keane, *The Big Book of Children's Reading Lists: 100 Great, Ready-to-Use Book Lists for Educators, Librarians, Parents, and Children.* Westport, CT: Libraries Unlimited, 2006. Copyright © 2006 by Libraries Unlimited.

Buses

Books for Children of All Ages

Cazet, Denys. ***Minnie and Moo Go to Paris.*** DK Pub. 1999. 48pp.
Two cow friends, Minnie and Moo, find a bus and try to drive to Paris to see the Eiffel Tower.

Ellis, Sarah. ***Next Stop!*** Fitzhenry & Whiteside, 2000. 32pp.
While riding the bus, Claire helps the driver, her father, and meets her mother during the trip.

Kovalski, Maryann. ***The Wheels on the Bus.*** Little Brown, c1987. 32pp.
While a grandmother and grandchildren wait for the bus, they sing the title song with such gusto they miss their bus.

Pulver, Robin. ***Axle Annie.*** Dial Books for Young Readers, c1999. 32pp.
The schools in Burskyville never close for snow because Axle Annie is always able to make it up the steepest hill in town, until Shifty Rhodes and Hale Snow set out to stop her.

From Nancy J. Keane, *The Big Book of Children's Reading Lists: 100 Great, Ready-to-Use Book Lists for Educators, Librarians, Parents, and Children.* Westport, CT: Libraries Unlimited, 2006. Copyright © 2006 by Libraries Unlimited.

Trains

Books for Children of All Ages

Chall, Marsha Wilson. ***Prairie Train.*** HarperCollins, c2003. 34pp.
A young girl experiences the thrill of her first train ride when she takes the Great Northern from the country to visit her grandmother in the city.

Collicutt, Paul. ***This Train.*** Farrar, Straus & Giroux, 2001, c1999. 24pp. (NF)
Simple text and illustrations depict different kinds of trains going uphill and downhill, crossing bridges and tunnels, using electricity or steam, carrying passengers or freight, even when it snows.

Crews, Donald. ***Freight Train.*** Greenwillow Books, c1978. 24pp.
Brief text and illustrations trace the journey of a colorful train as it goes through tunnels, past cities, and over trestles.

Gibbons, Gail. ***Trains.*** Holiday House, c1987. 32pp. (NF)
Examines different kinds of trains, past and present, describing their features and functions.

Lewis, Kevin. ***Chugga-Chugga Choo-Choo.*** Hyperion Books for Children, c1999. 27pp.
A rhyming story about a freight train's day, from loading freight in the morning to retiring to the roundhouse after the day's work is done.

Mills, Claudia. ***Gus and Grandpa Ride the Train.*** Farrar, Straus & Giroux, 2000, c1998. 47pp.
Gus waves at the train near his grandfather's house, sets up a toy train, and eventually gets to ride on the train with his grandfather.

Newman, Patricia. ***Jingle the Brass.*** Farrar, Straus & Giroux, c2004. 32pp.
On a train trip, an engineer teaches a boy the expressions used by railroad workers as he describes the different kinds of cars, freight, and people they see.

Panahi, H. L. ***Bebop Express.*** Laura Geringer Books/Amistad, c2005. 32pp.
A rollicking, rhythmic express train takes passengers on a ride through the history of American jazz.

Ray, Mary Lyn. ***All Aboard!*** Little, Brown, c2002. 32pp.
Mr. Barnes goes on a train trip and enjoys all the sights and sounds of the ride.

Simon, Seymour. ***Seymour Simon's Book of Trains.*** HarperCollins, c2002. 34pp. (NF)
Explores the various types of trains and their uses.

From Nancy J. Keane, *The Big Book of Children's Reading Lists: 100 Great, Ready-to-Use Book Lists for Educators, Librarians, Parents, and Children.* Westport, CT: Libraries Unlimited, 2006. Copyright © 2006 by Libraries Unlimited.

Trains

Sturges, Philemon. ***I Love Trains!*** HarperCollins, c2001. 28pp.
A boy expresses his love of trains, describing many kinds of train cars and their special jobs.

Wilcoxen, Chuck. ***Niccolini's Song.*** Dutton Children's Books, c2004. 34pp.
A gentle night watchman at the railroad yard lulls anxious train engines to sleep by singing just the right song.

Books for Children Ages 8–12

Beyer, Mark. ***Trains of the Past.*** PowerKids Press, c2002. 24pp. (NF)
Illustrations and simple text provide a brief introduction to the history of trains, discussing when they were first invented, how they have been used throughout the years, and the role they played in the development of the United States.

Loves, June. ***Trains.*** Chelsea House, c2002. 32pp. (NF)
An illustrated guide to trains, presented in the form of computer screen pictures, covering the history, types, parts, movement, and uses of railway vehicles.

Roza, Greg. ***The Incredible Story of Trains.*** PowerKids Press, 2004. 24pp. (NF)
Explores the history of trains, focusing on how developments in technology have affected train engines, brakes, speed, design, and performance.

Stille, Darlene R. ***Trains.*** Children's Press, c1997. 47pp. (NF)
Presents information in simple text about different types of trains and how they work.

Stone, Lynn M. ***Diesel Locomotives.*** Rourke Press, c1999. 24pp. (NF)
Describes the history and uses of diesel locomotives, the different types, and some famous models.

Stone, Lynn M. ***Passenger Trains.*** Rourke Press,. c1999. 24pp. (NF)
Describes the history and uses of passenger trains, the different types, and some famous ones.

Weitzman, David. ***The John Bull: A British Locomotive Comes to America.*** Farrar, Straus & Giroux, c2004. 34pp. (NF)
Describes how John Bull, a steam locomotive, was built in England, brought to the United States in 1831. assembled, put to work, and modified over time, leading the way for modern rail transportation.

From Nancy J. Keane, *The Big Book of Children's Reading Lists: 100 Great, Ready-to-Use Book Lists for Educators, Librarians, Parents, and Children.* Westport, CT: Libraries Unlimited, 2006. Copyright © 2006 by Libraries Unlimited.

Trucks

Books for Children of All Ages

Crews, Donald. ***Truck.*** Greenwillow Books, c1980. 32pp.
Follows the journey of a truck from loading to unloading.

Hewitt, Sally. ***Cars and Trucks.*** Chrysalis Education, c2003. 24pp. (NF)
Provides information about different types of cars and trucks, how they work, and how they are used.

McNaught, Harry. ***The Truck Book.*** Random House, c1978. 32pp. (NF)
Text and illustrations describe a variety of trucks and their functions.

Mitton, Tony. ***Dazzling Diggers.*** Kingfisher, c2000. 24pp. (NF)
Rhyming text and illustrations explain how digging machines scoop, lift, move rubble, squish through mud, and help buildings tower up tall.

Ransom, Candice F. ***Big Rigs.*** Lerner, c2005. 32pp. (NF)
Looks at different types of big rig trucks and the cargoes they carry. Includes a diagram that identifies the parts of a big rig.

Simon, Seymour. ***Seymour Simon's Book of Trucks.*** HarperCollins, c2000. 36pp. (NF)
Describes various kinds of trucks and their functions, including a log truck, cement mixer truck, and sanitation truck.

Books for Children Ages 8–12

Graham, Ian. ***Off Road Vehicles.*** Heinemann Library, c2003. 32pp. (NF)
Describes cars, trucks, and other vehicles that are designed to be driven on all sorts of surfaces, from dirt to mud or snow and ice.

Mitchell, Joyce Slayton. ***Tractor Trailer Trucker: A Powerful Truck Book.*** Tricycle Press, c2000. 40pp. (NF)
Introduces the various parts of a tractor trailer and their functions as a truck driver prepares to take his "big rig" on the road.

Molzahn, Arlene Bourgeois. ***Trucks and Big Rigs.*** Enslow, c2003. 48pp. (NF)
Discusses different types of trucks, from light pickup trucks to the massive crawler transporters that move space shuttles to the launch pad at the Kennedy Space Center in Cape Canaveral, Florida.

Sessler, Peter C. ***Stock Trucks.*** Rourke Press, c1999. 24pp. (NF)
Describes NASCAR pickup truck racing, its rules, how the trucks are equipped, and how fast they travel.

Stille, Darlene R. ***Trucks.*** Children's Press, c1997. 47pp. (NF)
Describes different kinds of trucks, including tractor trailers and tank trucks, pickups, tow trucks, fire trucks, garbage trucks, vans, and recreational vehicles.

From Nancy J. Keane, *The Big Book of Children's Reading Lists: 100 Great, Ready-to-Use Book Lists for Educators, Librarians, Parents, and Children.* Westport, CT: Libraries Unlimited, 2006. Copyright © 2006 by Libraries Unlimited.

Habitats

Books for Children of All Ages

Aloian, Molly. ***Many Kinds of Animals.*** Crabtree Pub. c2005. 32pp. (NF)
Presents a children's study of animals such as fish, mollusks, amphibians, arthropods, birds, reptiles, and mammals, and discusses their habitats, what they look like, how they move, what they eat, and how they protect themselves from predators.

Amos, Janine. ***Animals.*** Two-Can, c2000. 48pp. (NF)
An introduction to the animal kingdom, discussing animal groupings, habitats, communication, feeding, and development.

Chessen, Betsey. ***Animal Homes.*** Scholastic, c1998. 16pp. (NF)
Photographs and simple text describe the habitats of different animals.

Ehlert, Lois. ***Nuts to You!*** Harcourt Brace, c1993. 34pp.
A rascally squirrel has an indoor adventure in a city apartment.

Eugene, Toni. ***Hide and Seek.*** National Geographic Society, 1998. 12pp. (NF)
Describes how various animals use camouflage to protect against predators. Features pop-up and movable illustrations.

George, Lindsay Barrett. ***In the Woods: Who's Been Here?*** Greenwillow Books, c1995. 41pp.
A boy and girl in the autumn woods find an empty nest, a cocoon, gnawed bark, and other signs of unseen animals and their activities.

Gregoire, Elizabeth. ***Whose House Is This?: A Look at Animal Homes-Webs, Nests, and Shells.*** Picture Window Books, c2005. 24pp.
Contains picture riddles and facts about the different types of homes in which animals live, and includes a glossary, and resources for further study. (NF)

Hoberman, Mary Ann. ***A House Is a House for Me.*** Viking Press, 1978. 48pp.
Lists in rhyme the dwellings of various animals and things.

Jenkins, Steve. ***I See a Kookaburra!: Discovering Animal Habitats Around the World.*** Houghton Mifflin, 2005. 32pp. (NF)
Presents a colorful children's book that describes the various animals and, insects, and sea life that inhabit various environments.

Kalman, Bobbie. ***Animals Called Mammals.*** Crabtree Pub. c2005. 32pp. (NF)
Presents a children's study of mammals such as horses, lions, gorillas, whales, and others, and discusses they habitats, what they look like and how they move, how whales breathe, how they care for their young, and how they protect themselves.

From Nancy J. Keane, *The Big Book of Children's Reading Lists: 100 Great, Ready-to-Use Book Lists for Educators, Librarians, Parents, and Children.* Westport, CT: Libraries Unlimited, 2006. Copyright © 2006 by Libraries Unlimited.

Habitats

Nathan, Emma. ***What Do You Call a Termite Home?: And Other Animal Homes.*** Blackbirch Press, c2000. 24pp. (NF)

Explains the terms used for homes built by different animals and provides information on how such animals as beavers, termites, eagles, and rabbits build their homes.

Relf, Patricia. ***The Magic School Bus Hops Home: A Book about Animal Habitats.*** Scholastic, c1995. 32pp.

Ms. Frizzle's class learns about the kinds of homes and living conditions that various animals require.

Slater, Teddy. ***Animal Hide-and-Seek.*** G. Stevens, 2005, c1997. 32pp. (NF)

Examines how and why certain birds, insects, and mammals disappear by blending in with their backgrounds.

Tuxworth, Nicola. ***A First Book about Animal Homes.*** G. Stevens, 1999. 24pp. (NF)

Photographs and simple text describe where such animals as chickens, cows, rabbits, fish, bees, hamsters, and dogs are kept.

Books for Children Ages 8–12

Burnie, David. ***The Kingfisher Illustrated Animal Encyclopedia.*** Kingfisher, 2000. 319pp. (NF)

An illustrated encyclopedia describing the physical characteristics, behavior, and habitats of a variety of animals.

Cole, Melissa S. ***Forests.*** Blackbirch Press, Thomson/Gale, c2003. 24pp. (NF)

Photographs and easy to follow text describe forests and the food chains, food webs, animal survival techniques, and other aspects of life that make them distinct.

The Dictionary of the Environment and Its Biomes. Franklin Watts, c2001. 128pp. (NF)

Contains two hundred alphabetically arranged entries that provide information about the climate, precipitation, seasons, and dominant plant and animal life found in each of the Earth's twelve major biomes and examines related topics such as environmental issues, habitats, and species.

Kaner, Etta. ***Animals Migrating: How, When, Where and Why Animals Migrate.*** Kids Can Press, c2005. 40pp. (NF)

Presents an illustrated guide to animal migration, and includes information on how and why animals move to new habitats, with descriptions of mammals, birds, insects, and sea life that migrate.

Nadeau, Isaac. ***Food Chains in a Meadow Habitat.*** PowerKids Press, 2002. 24pp. (NF)

Photographs and simple text explain the food chain which is found in meadow habitats, discussing how each insect, plant, and animal fits into the process.

From Nancy J. Keane, *The Big Book of Children's Reading Lists: 100 Great, Ready-to-Use Book Lists for Educators, Librarians, Parents, and Children.* Westport, CT: Libraries Unlimited, 2006. Copyright © 2006 by Libraries Unlimited.

Bats

Books for Children of All Ages

Appelt, Kathi. ***Bat Jamboree.*** HarperCollins, c1996. 24pp.
At an abandoned outdoor movie theater, fifty-five bats perform in a toe-tapping, wing-flapping revue—and await the grand finale.

Appelt, Kathi. ***Bats Around the Clock.*** HarperCollins, c2000. 32pp.
Click Dark hosts a special twelve-hour program of American Bat Stand, at which the bats rock and roll until the midnight hour ends.

Cannon, Annie. ***The Bat in the Boot.*** Orchard Books, c1996. 32pp.
A family finds a baby bat in their mudroom and takes care of him until his mother comes back for him.

Cannon, Janell. ***Stellaluna.*** Harcourt, c1993. 48pp.
After she falls headfirst into a bird's nest, a baby bat is raised like a bird, until she is reunited with her mother.

Davies, Nicola. ***Bat Loves the Night.*** Candlewick Press, 2004, c2001. 28pp.
Bat wakes up, flies into the night, uses the echoes of her voice to navigate, hunts for her supper, and returns to her roost to feed her baby.

Earle, Ann. ***Zipping, Zapping, Zooming Bats.*** HarperCollins, c1995. 32pp. (NF)
Provides basic facts about the behavior of bats and describes how they benefit the environment.

Foster, Kelli C. ***Bat's Surprise.*** Barron's, c1993. 32pp.
Bat manages to get his friends' cooperation in making something for the art show without them even knowing.

Gibbons, Gail. ***Bats***. Holiday House, c1999. 30pp. (NF)
Describes different kinds of bats, their physical characteristics, habits and behavior, and efforts to protect them.

Krulik, Nancy E. ***The Magic School Bus Going Batty: A Book About Bats.*** Scholastic, c1996. 32pp.
Ms. Frizzle's class learn lessons about bats when they accidentally transform the Magic School Bus and then themselves into creatures of the night while trying to find out what their teacher has done with their parents.

From Nancy J. Keane, *The Big Book of Children's Reading Lists: 100 Great, Ready-to-Use Book Lists for Educators, Librarians, Parents, and Children.* Westport, CT: Libraries Unlimited, 2006. Copyright © 2006 by Libraries Unlimited.

Bats

Markle, Sandra. ***Outside and Inside Bats.*** Walker, 2004, c1997. 40pp. (NF)
Describes the inner and outer workings of bats, discussing their diet, anatomy, and reproduction.

Mayr, Diane. ***Littlebat's Halloween Story.*** Whitman, c2001. 31pp.
Littlebat loves to listen to the stories being told below the attic where he sleeps, but he has to wait until just the right time to get close enough to hear them better.

McNulty, Faith. ***When I Lived With Bats.*** Scholastic, c1998. 48pp.
A girl describes how she spent a summer observing the bats around and inside her house, and what she discovered about their characteristics and behavior.

Mitchard, Jacquelyn. ***Baby Bat's Lullaby.*** HarperCollins, c2004. 32pp.
With loving words, a mother bat lulls her baby to sleep.

Pringle, Laurence P. ***Bats!: Strange and Wonderful.*** Boyds Mills Press, c2000. 32pp. (NF)
An introduction to the life and behavior of bats.

Books for Children Ages 8–12

Kovacs, Deborah. ***Noises in the Night: The Habits of Bats.*** Raintree Steck-Vaughn, c2001. 48pp. (NF)
Describes the work of researchers on Barro Colorado Island in Panama, who are studying the behavior of the various species of bats living in the rain forests there.

Markle, Sandra. ***Outside and Inside Bats.*** Walker, 2004, c1997. 40pp. (NF)
Describes the inner and outer workings of bats, discussing their diet, anatomy, and reproduction.

Mason, Adrienne. ***Bats.*** Kids Can Press, c2003. 32pp. (NF)
Describes the bodies, movements, foods, life cycle, and defenses of large and small bats.

Stuart, Dee. ***Bats: Mysterious Flyers of the Night.*** Carolrhoda Books, c1994. 47pp. (NF)
In words and photographs discusses bats, their characteristics, their system of navigation, and how they live.

Swanson, Diane. ***Bats.*** Gareth Stevens, c2003. 32pp. (NF)
Describes the physical characteristics, behavior, habitat, and life cycle of the only mammal with wings.

From Nancy J. Keane, *The Big Book of Children's Reading Lists: 100 Great, Ready-to-Use Book Lists for Educators, Librarians, Parents, and Children.* Westport, CT: Libraries Unlimited, 2006. Copyright © 2006 by Libraries Unlimited.

Bugs

Books for Children of All Ages

Barner, Bob. ***Bug Safari.*** Holiday House, c2004. 32pp.
Tells how the author, as a young boy, followed a trail of ants and came across various other insects and small creatures, then briefly provides facts about each creature encountered.

Bernard, Robin. ***Insects.*** National Geographic Society, 2001, c1999. 16pp. (NF)
Introduces the body parts and other characteristics that are common to many kinds of insects.

Dussling, Jennifer. ***Bugs! Bugs! Bugs!*** DK Publishing, 1998. 32pp. (NF)
Describes the hunting activities of various bugs, including the praying mantis, wood ant, and dragonfly.

Fowler, Allan. ***Spiders Are Not Insects.*** Children's Press, c1996. 31pp. (NF)
An introduction to the spider, an eight-legged creature, not to be confused with the six-legged insect.

Graham, Margaret Bloy. ***Be Nice to Spiders.*** Harper & Row, c1967. 32pp.
The zoo animals become happy and peaceful when Helen the spider spins webs and catches the flies that had made them miserable.

Green, Jen. ***Under a Stone.*** Crabtree, c1999. 32pp. (NF)
Presents information on the various creatures and critters, mainly insects, that live under rocks, on the ground, and in the topsoil, including spiders, bees, groundhogs, slugs, ants, and badgers.

Harvey, Bev. ***Arthropods.*** Chelsea Clubhouse, c2003. 32pp. (NF)
Introduces the physical characteristics and habits of various types of arthropods, including insects and spiders as well as lobsters, crabs, and shrimp.

Holland, Gay W. ***Look Closer: An Introduction to Bug-Watching.*** Millbrook Press, c2003. 32pp. (NF)
Describes a variety of insects and how they can be observed in a garden, in open fields, in the woods, in water, and elsewhere.

Holmes, Anita. ***Insect Detector.*** Benchmark Books, 2000, c2001. 32pp. (NF)
Simple information allows the reader to "detect" which of a variety of creatures are actually insects.

Llewellyn, Claire. ***The Best Book of Bugs.*** Kingfisher, c1998. 33pp. (NF)
Describes the habits and life cycles of various insects and provides clues for identifying them in their natural habitats.

Markle, Sandra. ***Creepy, Crawly Baby Bugs.*** Walker, 2003, c1996. 32pp. (NF)
Offers a close look at baby insects, tracking the development of caterpillars, wasps, gnats, and other bugs.

From Nancy J. Keane, *The Big Book of Children's Reading Lists: 100 Great, Ready-to-Use Book Lists for Educators, Librarians, Parents, and Children.* Westport, CT: Libraries Unlimited, 2006. Copyright © 2006 by Libraries Unlimited.

Bugs

Murphy, Stuart J. ***The Best Bug Parade.*** HarperCollins, c1996. 33pp. (NF)
A variety of different bugs compare their relative sizes while going on parade.

Rockwell, Anne F. ***Bugs Are Insects.*** HarperCollins, c2001. 33pp. (NF)
Introduces common backyard insects and explains the basic characteristics of these creatures.

Singer, Marilyn. ***A Pair of Wings.*** Holiday House, c2001. 32pp. (NF)
Text and pictures describe the great variety of wings insects and animals have and show how these wings are used.

Slater, Teddy. ***Animal Hide-and-Seek.*** Gareth Stevens, 2005, c1997. 32pp. (NF)
Examines how and why certain birds, insects, and mammals disappear by blending in with their backgrounds.

Tagliaferro, Linda. ***Spiders and Their Webs.*** Capstone Press, c2004. 24pp. (NF)
Provides descriptions of how spiders spin their webs with strings of silk made in their bodies, explains how they use webs to catch insects to eat, and looks at how female spiders use silk to make egg sacs. Includes photographs of different types of spiders and webs.

Weber, Rebecca. ***Tricky Insects: And Other Fun Creatures.*** Compass Point Books, c2003. 24pp. (NF)
Provides directions for simple activities to learn more about various common insects, snails, and worms.

Books for Children Ages 8–12

Bailey, Jill. ***Bugs A-Z.*** Blackbirch Press, Thomson/Gale, c2002. 64pp. (NF)
Provides brief informational entries on insects and spiders, arranged alphabetically from "Ant" to "Zygaenid."

Facklam, Margery. ***The Big Bug Book.*** Little, Brown, c1994. 32pp. (NF)
Describes thirteen of the world's largest insects, including the birdwing butterfly and the Goliath beetle.

Hickman, Pamela M. ***Bug Book.*** Kids Can Press, 1999, c1996. 32pp. (NF)
A simplified introduction to a variety of insects, with tips on how to observe them.

Johnson, Jinny. ***Simon & Schuster Children's Guide to Insects and Spiders.*** Simon & Schuster Books for Young Readers, 1996. 80pp. (NF)
Provides an introduction to more than 100 insects and arachnids, giving general information about family characteristics and habits, and more specific facts about some species.

From Nancy J. Keane, *The Big Book of Children's Reading Lists: 100 Great, Ready-to-Use Book Lists for Educators, Librarians, Parents, and Children.* Westport, CT: Libraries Unlimited, 2006. Copyright © 2006 by Libraries Unlimited.

Bugs

Maynard, Christopher. ***Bugs: A Close up View of the Insect World.*** DK Publishing, 2001. 96pp. (NF)
Explores the world of insects, discussing what they eat, how they are born, their development and reproduction, and other interesting facets of their lives.

Montgomery, Sy. ***The Tarantula Scientist.*** Houghton Mifflin, c2004. 80pp. (NF)
Describes the research that Samuel Marshall and his students are doing on tarantulas, including the largest spider on earth, the Goliath bird-eating tarantula.

Murray, Peter. ***Insects.*** Child's World, c2005. 32pp. (NF)
Presents an introduction to insects, describing their shared characteristics, discussing the process of metamorphosis, and looking at the behaviors of different groups of insects. Includes a glossary.

Nathan, Emma. ***What Do You Call a Baby Scorpion?: And Other Baby Spiders and Insects.*** Blackbirch Press, c1999. 24pp. (NF)
Provides the special names for such baby insects and arachnids as the grub, maggot, and spiderling, describing their physical characteristics and behavior.

O'Neil, Amanda. ***I Wonder Why Spiders Spin Webs and Other Questions About Creepy Crawlies.*** Kingfisher, c1998. 32pp. (NF)
Provides the answers to forty questions about mosquitoes, bees, grasshoppers, and other insects, plus spiders.

Reinhart, Matthew. ***Insect-lo-pedia: Young Naturalist's Handbook.*** Hyperion Books for Children, c2003. 47pp. (NF)
Illustrations and easy-to-follow text introduce young readers to different types of bugs, their physical characteristics, defense systems, eating habits, and more.

Solway, Andrew. ***Classifying Insects.*** Heinemann Library, c2003. 32pp. (NF)
Explains what insects are and how they differ from other animals, with an overview of the life cycle of a variety of insects, including ants, bees, cockroaches, grasshoppers, dragonflies, and butterflies.

Stewart, Melissa. ***Maggots, Grubs, and More: The Secret Lives of Young Insects.*** Millbrook Press, c2003. 63pp. (NF)
Describes the life cycles of a variety of insects.

Wechsler, Doug. ***Bizarre Bugs.*** Boyds Mills Press, c2003, c1995. 35pp. (NF)
An introduction to the world of insects through text and photographs.

Winner, Cherie. ***Everything Bug: What Kids Really Want to Know About Insects and Spiders.*** NorthWord Press, c2004. 63pp. (NF)
Presents twenty-five questions and answers about insects and spiders, including why bugs are important, how long they've existed, and whether spiders make noise.

From Nancy J. Keane, *The Big Book of Children's Reading Lists: 100 Great, Ready-to-Use Book Lists for Educators, Librarians, Parents, and Children.* Westport, CT: Libraries Unlimited, 2006. Copyright © 2006 by Libraries Unlimited.

Dinosaurs

Books for Children of All Ages

Alphin, Elaine Marie. *Dinosaur Hunter.* HarperCollins, c2003. 48pp.
In Wyoming in the 1880s, a young boy fulfills his dream of finding a dinosaur skeleton on his father's ranch, outwits a man who would cheat him, and sells his find to a team of fossil hunters.

Ashby, Ruth. *My Favorite Dinosaurs.* Milk & Cookies Press, (distributed by Simon & Schuster), c2005. 32pp. (NF)
Presents a full-color, illustrated children's study of ancient dinosaurs and describes what they looked like, what they ate, and how they hunted.

Barner, Bob. *Dinosaur Bones.* Chronicle Books, c2001. 30pp.
Presents a poem about dinosaur bones with paper collage illustrations, and includes facts about dinosaurs on each page.

Bilgrami, Shaheen. *Amazing Dinosaur Discovery.* Sterling/Pinwheel Book, c2002. 14pp.
A dinosaur-crazy boy goes on a trip to a dinosaur museum with his dad, where he sees real skeletons of the various creatures in his scrapbook. Includes fast facts on various dinosaurs, as well as pull-tab illustrations that show each one as a skeleton and as a live animal.

Carr, Karen. *Dinosaur Hunt: Texas, 115 Million Years Ago.* HarperCollins, c2002. 48pp.
Describes a prehistoric battle between two dinosaurs, based on fossil footprints found near the Paluxy River in Texas.

Cohen, Daniel. *Allosaurus.* Bridgestone Books, c2003. 24pp. (NF)
Briefly describes how this dinosaur looked, what it ate, where it lived, and how scientists learned about it.

Cohen, Daniel. *Pteranodon.* Bridgestone Books, 2000, c2001. 24pp. (NF)
Discusses the physical characteristics, habitat, food, relatives, and extinction of this flying reptile that lived on the earth during the age of dinosaurs.

Cohen, Daniel. *Stegosaurus.* Bridgestone Books, 2000, c2001. 24pp. (NF)
Discusses the physical characteristics, food, habitat, relatives, and extinction of this slow-moving vegetarian dinosaur.

Dahl, Michael. *Long-neck: The Adventure of Apatosaurus.* Picture Window Books, c2004. 24pp. (NF)
Explains how scientists learn about dinosaurs and what their discoveries have revealed about apatosaurus.

Dahl, Michael. *Swift thief: The Adventure of Velociraptor.* Picture Window Books, c2004. 24pp. (NF)
Explains how scientists learn about dinosaurs and what their discoveries have revealed about velociraptor.

Dahl, Michael. *T. Rex: The Adventure of Tyrannosaurus Rex.* Picture Window Books, c2004. 24pp. (NF)
Explains how scientists learn about dinosaurs and what their discoveries have revealed about *Tyrannosaurus rex.*

From Nancy J. Keane, *The Big Book of Children's Reading Lists: 100 Great, Ready-to-Use Book Lists for Educators, Librarians, Parents, and Children.* Westport, CT: Libraries Unlimited, 2006. Copyright © 2006 by Libraries Unlimited.

Dinosaurs

Dahl, Michael. ***Three-horn: The Adventure of Triceratops.*** Picture Window Books, c2004. 24pp. (NF)
Explains how scientists learn about dinosaurs and what their discoveries have revealed about triceratops.

Dahl, Michael. ***Winged and Toothless: The Adventure of Pteranodon.*** Picture Window Books, c2004. 24pp. (NF)
Explains how scientists learn about dinosaurs and what their discoveries have revealed about pteranodon.

Davis, Kenneth C. ***Don't Know Much About Dinosaurs.*** HarperCollins, c2004. 48pp. (NF)
Questions and answers provide information about dinosaurs, including the different species, what they ate, how they lived, and why they may have become extinct.

Dixon, Dougal. ***Ankylosaurus and Other Mountain Dinosaurs.*** Picture Window Books, c2005. 24pp. (NF)
Examines the ankylosaurus and other prehistoric dinosaurs that lived in the mountainous regions of the world, including the stegoceras, eoraptor, and scelidosaurus, and discusses how they lived and survived.

Dixon, Dougal. ***Deltadromeus and Other Shoreline Dinosaurs.*** Picture Window Books, c2005. 24pp. (NF)
Examines the deltadromeus and other prehistoric dinosaurs that lived near the shoreline, including paralititan, suchomimus, and pelecanimimus, and discusses how they lived and survived.

Dixon, Dougal. ***Triceratops and Other Forest Dinosaurs.*** Picture Window Books, c2005. 24pp. (NF)
Presents a study of the triceratops and other dinosaurs that once lived in forested areas, including the parasaurolophus, stygimoloch, and tyrannosaur.

French, Vivian. ***T. Rex.*** Candlewick Press, c2004. 29pp. (NF)
Presents facts about the life of *Tyrannosaurus rex* within the framework of a visit to a museum by a boy and his grandfather.

Geraghty, Paul. ***Dinosaur in Danger.*** Barron's, c2004. 32pp.
When a fiery blast issues from a great volcano, a young dinosaur is separated from its family and must struggle to survive on its own.

Harrison, Carol. ***Dinosaurs Everywhere!*** Scholastic, c1998. 38pp. (NF)
Discusses the probable structure and behavior of dinosaurs and describes such individual species as the tyrannosaur, maiasaura, and seismosaurus.

Heidbreder, Robert. ***Drumheller Dinosaur Dance.*** Kids Can Press, c2004. 32pp.
A boy dreams that at night, the bones of the dinosaurs in Drumheller, Alberta, come alive and dance.

MacLeod, Elizabeth. ***What Did Dinosaurs Eat?: And Other Things You Want to Know About Dinosaurs.*** Kids Can Press, c2001. 32pp. (NF)
Provides answers to questions about dinosaurs, explaining what dinosaurs are, and discussing their size, eating habits, intelligence, speed, colors, physical abilities, and other topics.

From Nancy J. Keane, *The Big Book of Children's Reading Lists: 100 Great, Ready-to-Use Book Lists for Educators, Librarians, Parents, and Children.* Westport, CT: Libraries Unlimited, 2006. Copyright © 2006 by Libraries Unlimited.

Dinosaurs

McCarty, Peter. ***T Is for Terrible.*** H. Holt, c2004. 32pp.
A tyrannosaurus rex explains that he cannot help it that he is enormous and hungry and is not a vegetarian.

O'Brien, Patrick. ***Gigantic!: How Big Were the Dinosaurs?*** H. Holt, 2002, c1999. 32pp. (NF)
Explains the names of fourteen dinosaurs, from Stegosaurus to Compsognathus, and describes their physical characteristics, size, and probable behavior.

O'Malley, Kevin. ***Captain Raptor and the Moon Mystery.*** Walker, c2005. 26pp.
Captain Raptor and his spaceship crew rush to investigate when an unidentified object lands on one of the moons of the planet Jurassica.

Penner, Lucille Recht. ***Dinosaur Babies.*** Random House, 2003, c1991. 32pp. (NF)
Describes the characteristics and behavior of baby dinosaurs.

Redmond, Shirley-Raye. ***The Dog That Dug for Dinosaurs: A True Story.*** Aladdin Paperbacks, c2004. 32pp. (NF)
Relates the true story of a dog who helped his owner, twelve-year-old Mary Ann Anning, find dinosaur bones in Lyme Regis, England, including an ichthyosaurus, a plesiosaur, and the first pterodactyl.

Stickland, Paul. ***Dinosaur Roar!*** Puffin Books, 2001, c1994. 29pp.
Illustrations and rhyming text present all kinds of dinosaurs, including ones that are sweet, grumpy, spiky, or lumpy.

Tanaka, Shelley. ***New Dinos: The Latest Finds! The Coolest Dinosaur Discoveries!*** Atheneum Book for Young Readers, c2002. 48pp. (NF)
Describes some of the newly discovered dinosaurs and what paleontologists have learned about these prehistoric creatures in recent years.

Wallace, Karen. ***I Am a Tyrannosaurus.*** Atheneum Books for Young Readers, c2003. 26pp.
A hungry Tyrannosaurus rex prowls through the forest.

Williams, Judith. ***Discovering Dinosaurs with a Fossil Hunter.*** Enslow, c2004. 24pp. (NF)
Briefly explains the work of paleontologists, scientists who learn about dinosaurs by studying fossils.

Zimmerman, Howard. ***Dinosaurs! The Biggest, Baddest, Strangest, Fastest.*** Atheneum Books for Young Readers, c2000. 63pp. (NF)
Presents facts about and illustrations of dinosaurs, grouped by size, speed, eating habits, and appearance.

Zoehfeld, Kathleen Weidner. ***Did Dinosaurs Have Feathers?*** HarperCollins, c2004. 33pp. (NF)
Discusses the discovery and analysis of Archaeopteryx, a feathered dinosaur that may have been an ancestor of modern birds.

Zoehfeld, Kathleen Weidner. ***Dinosaurs Big and Small.*** HarperCollins, c2002. 33pp. (NF)
Introduces several different dinosaurs, looks at how they varied in size and weight, and explains how scientists have learned about these prehistoric creatures.

From Nancy J. Keane, *The Big Book of Children's Reading Lists: 100 Great, Ready-to-Use Book Lists for Educators, Librarians, Parents, and Children.* Westport, CT: Libraries Unlimited, 2006. Copyright © 2006 by Libraries Unlimited.

Dinosaurs

Books for Children Ages 8–12

Bailey, Jacqui. ***Monster Bones: The Story of a Dinosaur Fossil.*** Picture Window Books, 2004, c2003. 31pp. (NF)

Describes how the bones of a dinosaur became fossilized, were discovered by a paleontologist, and were ultimately displayed in a museum.

Bishop, Nic. ***Digging for Bird Dinosaurs: An Expedition to Madagascar.*** Houghton Mifflin, c2000. 48pp. (NF)

The story of Cathy Forster's experiences as a member of a team of paleontologists who went on an expedition to the island of Madagascar in 1998 to search for fossil birds.

Bonner, Hannah. ***When Bugs Were Big, Plants Were Strange, and Tetrapods Stalked the Earth: A Cartoon Prehistory of Life Before Dinosaurs.*** National Geographic, c2003. 44pp. (NF)

Takes a tour of the earth 320 million years ago, during the Paleozoic Era, and investigates the plants and animals found there.

Halls, Kelly Milner. ***Dinosaur Mummies: Beyond Bare Bone Fossils.*** Darby Creek Publishing, c2003. 48pp. (NF)

Photographs, illustrations, and simple text describe Leonardo, the most complete dinosaur mummy ever found.

Helm, Charles. ***Daniel's Dinosaurs: A True Story of Discovery.*** Maple Tree Press, (distributed by Publishers Group West), c2004. 32pp. (NF)

Presents a study of dinosaur tracks and follows two young boys in their search for fossils, along with paleontologist Philip Currie, in the Tumbler Ridge area of British Columbia.

Lambert, David. ***Dinosaur Encyclopedia: From Dinosaurs to the Dawn of Man.*** DK Publishing, c2001. 376pp. (NF)

Provides an overview of fossils, evolution, and prehistoric life and investigates four major groups of prehistoric animals.

Lessem, Don. ***Armored Dinosaurs.*** Lerner, c2005. 48pp. (NF)

Describes how armor helped dinosaurs such as Albertosaurus and Edmontonia to survive attack, as well as how scientists have learned about armored dinosaurs through studying fossils.

Markle, Sandra. ***Outside and Inside Dinosaurs.*** Atheneum Books for Young Readers, c2000. 40pp. (NF)

Describes the inner and outer workings of dinosaurs, discussing what has been learned from fossils about their anatomy, diet, and behavior.

Nye, Bill. ***Bill Nye the Science Guy's Great Big Dinosaur Dig.*** Hyperion Books for Children, c2002. 48pp. (NF)

Describes over thirty species of dinosaurs and includes "12 prehistoric experiments."

Zoehfeld, Kathleen Weidner. ***Dinosaur Parents, Dinosaur Young: Uncovering the Mystery of Dinosaur Families.*** Clarion Books, c2001. 58pp. (NF)

Describes the relationship between adult dinosaurs and their young.

From Nancy J. Keane, *The Big Book of Children's Reading Lists: 100 Great, Ready-to-Use Book Lists for Educators, Librarians, Parents, and Children.* Westport, CT: Libraries Unlimited, 2006. Copyright © 2006 by Libraries Unlimited.

Ecology

Books for Children of All Ages

Arnosky, Jim. ***Beachcombing: Exploring the Seashore.*** Dutton Children's Books, c2004. 26pp. (NF)
Illustrations and text describe some of the many things that can be found on a walk along a beach, including coconuts, shark teeth, jellyfish, crabs, and different kinds of shells.

Asch, Frank. ***The Earth and I.*** Gulliver Books, c1994. 32pp.
A child explains how he and the earth dance and sing together and take turns listening to each other.

Berger, Barbara. ***Grandfather Twilight.*** Philomel Books, c1984. 28pp.
At the day's end, Grandfather Twilight walks in the forest to perform his evening task, bringing the miracle of night to the world.

Cherry, Lynne. ***The Great Kapok Tree: A Tale of the Amazon Rain Forest.*** Harcourt Brace, c1990. 33pp.
The many different animals that live in a great kapok tree in the Brazilian rain forest try to convince a man with an ax of the importance of not cutting down their home.

Cherry, Lynne. ***The Sea, The Storm, and the Mangrove Tangle.*** Farrar, Straus & Giroux, c2004. 36pp.
A seed from a mangrove tree floats on the sea until it comes to rest on the shore of a faraway lagoon, where, over time, it becomes a mangrove island that shelters many birds and animals, even during a hurricane.

Cuomo, Mario Matthew. ***The Blue Spruce.*** Sleeping Bear Press, c1999. 48pp.
When a storm knocks down the blue spruce tree in a boy's yard, he and his father work with all their might to right the tree again.

Faundez, Anne. ***Animals in Danger.*** QEB Publishing, c2004. 24pp. (NF)
Photographs and easy-to-follow text teach beginning readers about endangered animals, their habitat, physical characteristics, behavior, and lifestyle.

Foster, Leila Merrell. ***Antarctica.*** Heinemann Library, c2001. 32pp. (NF)
Photographs, maps, and text provide information about the weather, animals, people, and other special features of the continent of Antarctica.

Fowler, Allan. ***Life in a Tide Pool.*** Children's Press, c1996. 31pp. (NF)
Explains how tidal pools form and the types of plants and animals that inhabit them.

Gaff, Jackie. ***I Wonder Why Pine Trees Have Needles and Other Questions About Forests.*** Kingfisher, c2005. 32pp. (NF)
A colorful question and answer book for children about forests and the plants and animals that inhabit them.

Galko, Francine. ***Cave Animals.*** Heinemann Library, c2003. 32pp. (NF)
Describes caves, the different kinds of animals that can be found in them, and their ecological importance.

From Nancy J. Keane, *The Big Book of Children's Reading Lists: 100 Great, Ready-to-Use Book Lists for Educators, Librarians, Parents, and Children.* Westport, CT: Libraries Unlimited, 2006. Copyright © 2006 by Libraries Unlimited.

Ecology

Galko, Francine. *Coral Reef Animals.* Heinemann Library, c2003. 32pp. (NF)
Describes coral reefs, the different kinds of animals that can be found in them, and their ecological importance.

Galko, Francine. *Desert Animals.* Heinemann Library, c2003. 32pp. (NF)
Describes deserts, the different kinds of animals that can be found in them, and their ecological importance.

Galko, Francine. *Wetland Animals.* Heinemann Library, c2003. 32pp.
Describes wetlands, the different kinds of animals that can be found in them, and their ecological importance.

Gibbons, Gail. *Deserts.* Holiday House, c1996. 32pp. (NF)
An introduction to the characteristics of deserts and the plants and animals that inhabit them.

Gray, Susan Heinrichs. *Grasslands.* Compass Point Books, 2000, c2001. 48pp. (NF)
Briefly describes different types of grasslands, their plant and animal life, and environmental threats.

Green, Jen. *A Dead Log.* Crabtree, c1999. 32pp. (NF)
Describes the various creatures and plants that live in, on, or under a dead log.

Guiberson, Brenda Z. *Rain, Rain, Rain Forest.* H. Holt, c2004. 32pp. (NF)
Takes a journey through a rain forest, investigating the plants and animals that dwell there.

Himmelman, John. *Frog in a Bog.* Charlesbridge, c2004. 32pp. (NF)
Introduces the bog ecosystem by chronicling a complex chain of events set off by the simple jump of a frog into some moss.

Himmelman, John. *Mouse in a Meadow.* Charlesbridge, c2005. 32pp. (NF)
The author provides full-color, detailed nature illustrations depicting the various species of mice, insects, snakes, spiders, and beetles that inhabit a typical North American meadow.

Lauber, Patricia. *Be a Friend to Trees.* HarperCollins, c1994. 32pp. (NF)
Discusses the importance of trees as sources of food, oxygen, and other essential things.

Lock, Deborah. *Forest.* DK Publishing, c2004. 48pp. (NF)
Introduces characteristics of different kinds of forests found around the world, the plants and animals that populate them, and how they are endangered.

MacGill-Callahan, Sheila. *And Still the Turtle Watched.* Puffin Books, 1996, c1991. 32pp.
A turtle carved in rock on a bluff over the Hudson River by Indians long ago watches with sadness the changes humans brings over the years.

Oliver, Clare. *Life in a Pond.* Raintree Steck-Vaughn, c2002. 32pp. (NF)
Describes the plant and animal life in ponds and the threats to pond ecology.

Pascoe, Elaine. *Pond.* Blackbirch Press, Thomson/Gale, c2005. 24pp. (NF)
Discusses some of the plant and animal life that inhabit ponds, such as lily pads and water lilies, algae, dragonflies, water bugs, snails and turtles, and frogs, and includes color photographs and fun projects to do.

Pyers, Greg. *Desert Explorer.* Raintree, c2004. 32pp. (NF)
Takes an in-depth look at desert habitats and the animals, organisms, and plants that dwell there, as observed during an imaginary journey across the Sahara Desert.

From Nancy J. Keane, *The Big Book of Children's Reading Lists: 100 Great, Ready-to-Use Book Lists for Educators, Librarians, Parents, and Children.* Westport, CT: Libraries Unlimited, 2006. Copyright © 2006 by Libraries Unlimited.

Ecology

Pyers, Greg. ***Forest Explorer.*** Raintree, c2004. 32pp. (NF)
Takes an in-depth look at forest habitats and the animals, organisms, and plants that dwell there, as observed during an imaginary journey through a temperate forest.

Pyers, Greg. ***Mountain Explorer.*** Raintree, c2005. 32pp. (NF)
Simple text and pictures introduce mountain habitats, plants, and animals especially in the Swiss Alps.

Pyers, Greg. ***Ocean Explorer.*** Raintree, c2005. 32pp. (NF)
Simple text and pictures introduce the ocean habitat, plants, and animals.

Pyers, Greg. ***River Explorer.*** Raintree, c2004. 32pp. (NF)
Takes an in-depth look at river habitats and the animals, organisms, and plants that dwell there, as observed during an imaginary journey down the Ganges River.

Rosinsky, Natalie M. ***Dirt: The Scoop on Soil.*** Picture Window Books, c2003. 24pp. (NF)
Discusses the nature, uses, and importance of soil and the many forms of life that it supports.

Stone, Lynn M. ***Animal Life in the Desert.*** Rourke Press, c1997. 24pp. (NF)
Describes the lives and interactions of animals and plants in the desert.

Suzuki, David T. ***Salmon Forest.*** GreyStone Books (distributed in the United States by Publishers Group West), c2003. 32pp.
During a walk in the woods with her father, Kate learns about the life cycle of the sockeye salmon, as well as its place in the larger circle of life.

Books for Children Ages 8–12

Doris, Ellen. ***Life at the Top: Discoveries in a Tropical Forest Canopy.*** Raintree Steck-Vaughn, 2000, c2001. 47pp. (NF)
Photographs and text provide information about the work being done by scientists with the Smithsonian Tropical Research Institute in Panama's Metropolitan Natural Park to learn about the biodiversity of the forest's canopy.

Johansson, Philip. ***The Frozen Tundra: A Web of Life.*** Enslow, c2004. 48pp. (NF)
Provides a description of the arctic tundra, discussing the weather, landscape, and plant and animal communities that live in the northern biome.

Knight, Tim. ***Fantastic Feeders.*** Heinemann Library, c2003. 32pp. (NF)
Explores different kinds of food eaten by certain animals and the special teeth or other tools they have for eating that food, as well as some of the ways plants avoid being eaten.

Littlefield, Cindy A. ***Awesome Ocean Science!: Investigating the Secrets of the Underwater World.*** Williamson, c2003. 120pp. (NF)
Explores the wonders of the ocean, its floor, and the plants and animals that dwell in it; teaches how to protect these resources; and provides hands-on activities for further investigation.

Morris, Neil. ***Earth's Changing Coasts.*** Raintree, c2004. 32pp. (NF)
Looks at the geography and people that make up coastal regions throughout the world, focusing on the changing characteristics of both.

From Nancy J. Keane, *The Big Book of Children's Reading Lists: 100 Great, Ready-to-Use Book Lists for Educators, Librarians, Parents, and Children.* Westport, CT: Libraries Unlimited, 2006. Copyright © 2006 by Libraries Unlimited.

Ecology

Morris, Neil. ***Earth's Changing Continents.*** Raintree, c2004. 32pp. (NF)
Looks at the geography and people that characterize the continents of the earth, focusing on the changing characteristics of each.

Morris, Neil. ***Earth's Changing Deserts.*** Raintree, c2004. 32pp. (NF)
Examines how deserts are formed and how they are constantly changing, what animals and plants live there, and ways in which humans live in and change deserts.

Morris, Neil. ***Earth's Changing Islands.*** Raintree, c2004. 32pp. (NF)
Looks at the geography and people that make up island regions throughout the world, focusing on the changing characteristics of both.

Morris, Neil. ***Earth's Changing Mountains.*** Raintree, c2004. 32pp. (NF)
Looks at the geography and people that make up mountain regions throughout the world, focusing on the changing characteristics of both.

Morris, Neil. ***Earth's Changing Rivers.*** Raintree, c2004. 32pp. (NF)
Looks at the geography and people that make up river regions throughout the world, focusing on the changing characteristics of both.

Pascoe, Elaine. ***The Ecosystem of a Fallen Tree.*** PowerKids Press, c2003. 32pp. (NF)
Describes the plant and animal life associated with a fallen tree, all of which create a miniature, codependent ecosystem.

Pascoe, Elaine. ***The Ecosystem of a Milkweed Patch.*** PowerKids Press, c2003. 32pp. (NF)
Describes the interdependence of some of the plants and animals that can be found in a milkweed patch.

Pascoe, Elaine. ***The Ecosystem of an Apple Tree.*** PowerKids Press, c2003. 32pp. (NF)
Describes the plant and animal life associated with an apple tree, all of which create a miniature, codependent ecosystem.

Patent, Dorothy Hinshaw. ***Colorful Captivating Coral Reefs.*** Walker, c2003. 40pp. (NF)
Provides an overview of coral reefs as ecosystems, describing different types of corals and how they reproduce, and discussing the variety of fishes and other animals that depend on coral reefs to sustain them.

Patent, Dorothy Hinshaw. ***Garden of the Spirit Bear: Life in the Great Northern Rainforest.*** Clarion Books, c2004. 40pp. (NF)
An introduction to the Great Bear Rainforest along the Pacific Coast of British Columbia, Canada. It discusses the lives of the black bears that live in the region, as well as old growth trees, First Nations people, salmon, and other plants and animals, and looks at the threat posed to the forest by logging interests.

Reid, Greg. ***Deserts.*** Chelsea Clubhouse, 2004. 32pp. (NF)
An introduction to deserts; explains what they are and their characteristics; looks at the different types of deserts and the life they support; provides information about indigenous people in these environments; and discusses desert resources, the threats they face, and protection efforts.

From Nancy J. Keane, *The Big Book of Children's Reading Lists: 100 Great, Ready-to-Use Book Lists for Educators, Librarians, Parents, and Children.* Westport, CT: Libraries Unlimited, 2006. Copyright © 2006 by Libraries Unlimited.

Seasons—General

Books for Children of All Ages

Brown, Margaret Wise. ***The Little Island.*** Doubleday Book for Young Readers, 2003, c1946. 46pp.
Depicts the changes that occur on a small island as the seasons come and go, as day changes to night, and as a storm approaches.

Deady, Kathleen W. ***All Year Long.*** Carolrhoda Books, c2004. 32pp.
A rhyming celebration of the cycles of the seasons and the beauty of the natural world.

Eckart, Edana. ***Watching the Seasons.*** Children's Press, c2004. 24pp. (NF)
Simple text introduces facts about the four seasons.

Ganeri, Anita. ***Season to Season.*** Heinemann Library, c2005. 32pp. (NF)
Explains why seasons occur and looks at some of the patterns in nature that are repeated every year with the changing of the seasons.

Gibbons, Gail. ***The Reasons for Seasons.*** Holiday House, c1995. 32pp. (NF)
Explains how the position of Earth causes seasons and the wonderful things that each season brings.

Gibbons, Gail. ***The Seasons of Arnold's Apple Tree.*** Harcourt Brace, c1984. 32pp.
As the seasons pass, Arnold enjoys a variety of activities as a result of his apple tree. Includes a recipe for apple pie and a description of how an apple cider press works.

Hall, Donald. ***Ox-cart Man.*** Viking Press, c1979. 40pp.
Describes the day-to-day life throughout the changing seasons of a New England family in the early nineteenth century.

Hansen, Ann Larkin. ***Seasons on the Farm.*** Abdo, c1996. 32pp. (NF)
Describes how each season of the year affects farmers and the work they do.

Hubbell, Will. ***Apples Here!*** Whitman, c2002. 32pp. (NF)
Shows how apples grow through the seasons, from buds, to blossoms, to fruit, and become part of people's lives and celebrations.

Iverson, Diane. ***Discover the Seasons.*** Dawn Publications, c1996. 48pp. (NF)
Looks at the seasons, giving each a theme, exploring through hands-on activities that adults and children can share. Includes recipes.

Kalman, Bobbie. ***Changing Seasons.*** Crabtree, c2005. 32pp. (NF)
An introduction to the four seasons—summer, spring, winter, autumn—including information on how the earth moves around the sun and how it tilts on its axis, and provides descriptions of each of the seasons, explaining what happens to plant and animal life, in simple text with photographs.

Kinsey-Warnock, Natalie. ***From Dawn Till Dusk.*** Houghton Mifflin, c2002. 40pp.
A woman fondly reminisces about the experiences she shared with her family throughout the various seasons on their Vermont farm.

From Nancy J. Keane, *The Big Book of Children's Reading Lists: 100 Great, Ready-to-Use Book Lists for Educators, Librarians, Parents, and Children.* Westport, CT: Libraries Unlimited, 2006. Copyright © 2006 by Libraries Unlimited.

Seasons—General

Martin, Bill. ***The Turning of the Year.*** Harcourt Brace, c1998. 28pp.
Describes the characteristics of each month in rhyming text and illustrations.

Quiri, Patricia Ryon. ***Seasons.*** Compass Point Books, 2000, c2001. 32pp. (NF)
Briefly explains why we have seasons and how they affect people and other living things.

Riley, Peter D. ***Seasons.*** Gareth Stevens, c2004. 31pp. (NF)
An introduction to some of the characteristics of the four seasons.

Rockwell, Anne F. ***Four Seasons Make a Year.*** Walker, 2004. 32pp. (NF)
Describes the passing of the seasons through the changes in plants and animals that occur on a farm.

Siddals, Mary McKenna. ***Tell Me a Season.*** Clarion Books, c1997. 26pp.
Nature displays different colors to announce the seasons of the year and the time of day.

Tudor, Tasha. ***Around the Year.*** Simon & Schuster Books for Young Readers, 2001, c1957. 58pp. (NF)
Brief rhymes and drawings of activities popular in the nineteenth century portray events brought about by each month of the year.

Updike, John. ***A Child's Calendar: Poems.*** Holiday House, c1999. 29pp.
A collection of twelve poems describing the activities in a child's life and the changes in the weather as the year moves from January to December.

Van Laan, Nancy. ***Busy, Busy Moose.*** Houghton Mifflin, c2003. 48pp.
Moose helps his little animal friends in many ways during the four seasons.

Books for Children Ages 8–12

Bruchac, Joseph. ***Thirteen Moons on Turtle's Back: A Native American Year of Moons.*** Philomel Books, c1992. 32pp.
Celebrates the seasons of the year through poems from the legends of such Native American tribes as the Cherokee, Cree, and Sioux.

Ehrlich, Gretel. ***A Blizzard Year: Timmy's Almanac of the Seasons.*** Hyperion Paperbacks for Children, 2001, c1999. 122pp.
For one year, thirteen-year-old Timmy records in her journal the changes she sees in the natural world and her family's activities on their Wyoming ranch as they fight to save it from financial ruin.

Splear, Elsie Lee. ***Growing Seasons.*** Putnam, c2000. 36pp. (NF).
Born into an Illinois farm family in 1906. Elsie Lee Splear describes how she, her parents, and her sisters lived in the early years of the twentieth century and how the changing seasons shaped their existence.

Strudwick, Leslie. ***The Science of Seasons.*** Gareth Stevens, c2001. 32pp. (NF)
Text and photos explain the scientific changes that affect the natural world during each season of the year.

From Nancy J. Keane, *The Big Book of Children's Reading Lists: 100 Great, Ready-to-Use Book Lists for Educators, Librarians, Parents, and Children.* Westport, CT: Libraries Unlimited, 2006. Copyright © 2006 by Libraries Unlimited.

Autumn

Books for Children of All Ages

Arnosky, Jim. ***Every Autumn Comes the Bear.*** Putnam & Grosset, 1996, c1993. 32pp.
Every autumn a bear shows up behind the farm and goes through a series of routines before finding a den among the hilltop boulders, where he sleeps all winter long.

DeGezelle, Terri. ***Autumn.*** Bridgestone Books, c2003. 24pp. (NF)
Explains why seasons change and describes the ways trees, animals, and people react to autumn.

Finnegan, Mary Pat. ***Autumn: Signs of the Season Around North America.*** Picture Window Books, c2003. 24pp. (NF)
Examines how autumn brings observable changes in weather, nature, and people.

Florian, Douglas. ***Autumnblings: Poems & Paintings.*** Greenwillow Books, c2003. 48pp.
A collection of poems that portray the essence of the season between summer and winter.

Fowler, Allan. ***How Do You Know It's Fall?*** Children's Press, 1992. 31pp. (NF)
Presents the many signs of fall, including geese flying south, squirrels hiding acorns, and people playing football.

Glaser, Linda. ***It's Fall!*** Millbrook Press, c2001. 32pp.
A child observes the many changes that occur in nature with the coming of the fall season. Includes suggested activities.

Hall, Zoe. ***Fall Leaves Fall!*** Scholastic, c2000. 32pp.
When fall comes, two brothers enjoy catching the falling leaves, stomping on them, kicking them, jumping in piles of them, and using them to make pictures. Includes a description of how leaves change throughout the year.

Kelley, Marty. ***Fall Is Not Easy.*** Zino Press Children's Books, c1998. 32pp.
A tree tells why, out of all four seasons, autumn is the hardest.

Lenski, Lois. ***Now It's Fall.*** Random House, 2000, c1948. 49pp.
A poem and illustrations celebrating aspects of fall—raking leaves, collecting nuts, returning to school, and celebrating Halloween.

From Nancy J. Keane, *The Big Book of Children's Reading Lists: 100 Great, Ready-to-Use Book Lists for Educators, Librarians, Parents, and Children.* Westport, CT: Libraries Unlimited, 2006. Copyright © 2006 by Libraries Unlimited.

Autumn

Nidey, Kelly. ***When Autumn Falls.*** Whitman, c2004. 32pp.
Observes the aptly named fall season, characterized by falling leaves, falling apples, falling players on the football field, and falling temperatures.

Saunders-Smith, Gail. ***Animals in the Fall.*** Pebble Books, c1998. 24pp. (NF)
Simple text and photographs present the behavioral changes of animals as winter approaches, such as growing thicker fur, migrating, and hibernating.

Spinelli, Eileen. ***I Know It's Autumn.*** HarperCollins, c2004. 32pp.
A rhyming celebration of the sights, smells, and sounds of autumn, such as pumpkin muffins, turkey stickers on spelling papers, and piles of raked leaves.

Stille, Darlene R. ***Fall.*** Compass Point Books, c2001. 32pp. (NF)
Explores the science of seasons, focusing on fall, discussing the signs of fall, fall colors, harvest, and other topics; and includes a glossary, references, an index, and photographs.

Van Allsburg, Chris. ***The Stranger.*** Houghton Mifflin, c1986. 32pp.
The enigmatic origins of the stranger Farmer Bailey whom hits with his truck and brings home to recuperate seem to have a mysterious relation to the changing season.

Books for Children Ages 8–12

Gogerly, Liz. ***Autumn: September, October, and November.*** Rourke Press, c2005. 32pp. (NF)
Examines the important religious and secular holidays that are celebrated around the world in the autumn, including Rosh Hashanah and Yom Kippur, Harvest Festival and Thanksgiving, Halloween, Days of the Dead, Veteran's Day, and Ramadan.

Leaf by Leaf: Autumn Poems. Scholastic, c2001. 38pp.
A collection of poems about the autumn, illustrated with photographs of the outdoors in this season.

From Nancy J. Keane, *The Big Book of Children's Reading Lists: 100 Great, Ready-to-Use Book Lists for Educators, Librarians, Parents, and Children.* Westport, CT: Libraries Unlimited, 2006. Copyright © 2006 by Libraries Unlimited.

Spring

Books for Children of All Ages

Arden, Carolyn. ***Goose Moon.*** Boyds Mills Press, c2004. 32pp.
A young girl anxiously awaits the arrival of spring to see the Goose Moon, a sign that spring is on its way.

Brett, Jan. ***Annie and the Wild Animals.*** Houghton Mifflin, c1985. 32pp.
When Annie's cat disappears, she attempts to form friendships with a variety of unsuitable woodland animals, but with the emergence of spring, everything comes right.

Carney, Margaret. ***At Grandpa's Sugar Bush.*** Kids Can Press, 1998, c1997. 32pp.
A young boy spends his spring vacation helping his grandpa with the annual ritual of tapping the trees, collecting the sap, and making sweet, sticky maple syrup.

Curry, Don L. ***In My Backyard.*** Children's Press, c2004. 23pp.
A girl sees many signs of spring in her backyard, including a frog and a bird.

De Coteau Orie, Sandra. ***Did You Hear Wind Sing Your Name?: An Oneida Song of Spring.*** Walker, 1996, c1995. 32pp.
Pictures and free verse pay homage to the Oneida Indians' view of the cycle of spring.

DeGezelle, Terri. ***Spring.*** Bridgestone Books, c2003. 24pp. (NF)
Explains why seasons change and describes the ways trees, animals, and people react to spring.

Ernst, Lisa Campbell. ***Wake Up, It's Spring!*** HarperCollins, c2004. 36pp.
Word of the arrival of spring spreads from earth to worm to seed to ladybug and on through the natural world to a sleeping family, until everyone is dancing in celebration.

Fowler, Allan. ***How Do You Know It's Spring?*** Children's Press, c1991. 31pp. (NF)
A simple description of the characteristics of spring.

Glaser, Linda. ***It's Spring!*** Millbrook Press, c2002. 32pp.
A child observes the arrival of spring and its effects on plants and animals. Includes suggestions for nature study projects.

Kinsey-Warnock, Natalie. ***When Spring Comes.*** Dutton Children's Books, c1993. 32pp.
A child, living on a farm in the early 1900s, describes some of the activities that mark the approach of spring.

From Nancy J. Keane, *The Big Book of Children's Reading Lists: 100 Great, Ready-to-Use Book Lists for Educators, Librarians, Parents, and Children.* Westport, CT: Libraries Unlimited, 2006. Copyright © 2006 by Libraries Unlimited.

Spring

Peters, Lisa Westberg. ***Cold Little Duck, Duck, Duck.*** Greenwillow Books, c2000. 32pp.
Early one spring a little duck arrives at her pond and finds it still frozen, but not for long.

Plourde, Lynn. ***Spring's Sprung.*** Simon & Schuster Books for Young Readers, c2002. 32pp.
Mother Nature rouses her squabbling daughters, March, April, and May, so they can awaken the world and welcome spring.

Ray, Mary Lyn. ***Mud.*** Harcourt Brace, c1996. 33pp.
As winter melts into spring, the frozen earth turns into magnificent mud.

Rylant, Cynthia. ***Poppleton in Spring.*** Scholastic, c1999. 48pp.
Poppleton the pig does some spring cleaning, tries to buy a bicycle, and stays up all night in a tent in his backyard.

Schnur, Steven. ***Spring Thaw.*** Viking, c2000. 32pp.
Describes spring's gradual arrival on a farm.

Seuling, Barbara. ***Spring Song.*** Gulliver Books, c2001. 32pp.
When new leaves sprout, buds appear, cocoons burst open, and other signs announce the coming of spring, various animals, from bears to bullfrogs, respond to the warmth of the season.

Thayer, Tanya. ***Spring.*** Lerner, c2002. 23pp.c(NF)
Photographs and simple text describe the spring season.

Books for Children Ages 8–12

Burton, Jane. ***The Nature and Science of Spring.*** Gareth Stevens, c1999. 32pp. (NF)
Explains why the season of spring happens and how it manifests itself in the weather and changes in plants and animals.

Jackson, Ellen B. ***The Spring Equinox: Celebrating the Greening of the Earth.*** Millbrook Press, c2002. 32pp. (NF)
Pictures and text describe how the arrival of spring has been celebrated by various cultures throughout history.

Taylor, C. J. ***The Messenger of Spring.*** Tundra Books, Tundra Books of Northern New York, c1997. 24pp.
New Dawn comes to bring Iceman a message, and as he delivers that message, he melts the winter ice and snow Iceman has left, bringing to life the joy of spring.

From Nancy J. Keane, *The Big Book of Children's Reading Lists: 100 Great, Ready-to-Use Book Lists for Educators, Librarians, Parents, and Children.* Westport, CT: Libraries Unlimited, 2006. Copyright © 2006 by Libraries Unlimited.

Summer

Books for Children of All Ages

Andrews, Jan. ***The Twelve Days of Summer.*** Groundwood Books, (distributed by Publishers Group West), c2005. 32pp.
A counting book where a child finds a sparrow's nest and groups of animals come to visit the nest.

Burke, Jennifer S. ***Hot Days.*** Children's Press, c2000. 24pp.
A child describes ways to keep cool when the weather is hot.

Crews, Nina. ***One Hot Summer Day.*** Greenwillow Books, c1995. 24pp.
Relates a child's activities in the heat of a summer day punctuated by a thunderstorm.

DeGezelle, Terri. ***Summer.*** Bridgestone Books, c2003. 24pp. (NF)
Explains why seasons change and describes the ways trees, animals, and people react to summer.

Dotlich, Rebecca Kai. ***Lemonade Sun: And Other Summer Poems.*** Wordsong/Boyds Mills Press, c1998. 32pp.
A collection of poems celebrating summer sights and sounds.

Fowler, Allan. ***How Do You Know It's Summer?*** Children's Press, c1992. 31pp. (NF)
Presents such signs of summer as heat, playtime, thunderstorms, growing, and fun.

Glaser, Linda. ***It's Summer!*** Millbrook Press, c2003. 32pp.
A child observes the coming of summer and its effects on the weather, animals, and plants. Includes suggestions for summertime activities to enjoy alone or with a parent.

Hesse, Karen. ***Come On, Rain!*** Scholastic, 1999. 32pp.
A young girl eagerly awaits a coming rainstorm to bring relief from the oppressive summer heat.

Kelley, Marty. ***Summer Stinks: "An Alphabetical Lexicon for the Estivally Dispirited."*** Zino Press, c2001. 31pp.
In this rhyming alphabet book, a boy lists all his reasons for disliking summer, from the ants that ate his snack to the zapper he touched by mistake.

Paulsen, Gary. ***Canoe Days.*** Dragonfly Books, 2001, c1999. 32pp.
A canoe ride on a northern lake during a summer day reveals the quiet beauty and wonder of nature in and around the peaceful water.

From Nancy J. Keane, *The Big Book of Children's Reading Lists: 100 Great, Ready-to-Use Book Lists for Educators, Librarians, Parents, and Children.* Westport, CT: Libraries Unlimited, 2006. Copyright © 2006 by Libraries Unlimited.

Summer

Payne, Nina. ***Summertime Waltz.*** Farrar, Straus & Giroux, c2005. 32pp.
Illustrations and rhythmic text describe the delights of a summer evening.

Santucci, Barbara. ***Loon Summer.*** Eerdmans Books for Young Readers, c2001. 32pp.
While spending the summer with her father, Rainie wishes her parents would stay together, just like the family of loons she sees on the lake.

Scott, Evelyn. ***The Fourteen Bears: Summer and Winter.*** Random House Children's Books, 2005. 62pp.
A bear family amuses itself with summer and winter activities such as walking, swimming, making snowmen, and decorating trees.

Stille, Darlene R. ***Summer.*** Compass Point Books, c2001. 32pp. (NF)
Explores the science of seasons, focusing on summer, discussing summer sun, why summer occurs, deserts and tropics, and other topics; includes a glossary, references, an index, and photographs.

Thayer, Tanya. ***Summer.*** Lerner, c2002. 23pp. (NF)
Photographs and simple text describe the summer season.

Books for Children Ages 8–12

Bloom, Valerie. ***Hot Like Fire: Poems.*** Bloomsbury Children's Books, 2002. 87pp.
A collection of poems by Valerie Bloom that capture the joys of summer.

Burton, Jane. ***The Nature and Science of Summer.*** Gareth Stevens, c1999. 32pp. (NF)
Explains why the season of summer happens and how it manifests itself in the weather and changes in plants and animals.

Jackson, Ellen B. ***The Summer Solstice.*** Millbrook Press, c2001. 30pp. (NF)
Describes how different civilizations have celebrated the day of the summer solstice.

Senker, Cath. ***Summer: June, July, and August.*** Rourke Press, c2005. 32pp. (NF)
Examines the important religious and secular holidays that are celebrated around the world in the summer, including Shavuot and Pentecost, Flag Day and Independence Day, Dharma Day, and Midsummer's Day.

From Nancy J. Keane, *The Big Book of Children's Reading Lists: 100 Great, Ready-to-Use Book Lists for Educators, Librarians, Parents, and Children.* Westport, CT: Libraries Unlimited, 2006. Copyright © 2006 by Libraries Unlimited.

Winter

Books for Children of All Ages

Baird, Audrey B. ***A Cold Snap!: Frosty Poems.*** Wordsong/Boyds Mills Press, c2002. 32pp.
Poems depicting the weather in late fall and approaching winter.

Brett, Jan. ***Jan Brett's Christmas Treasury.*** Putnam, 2001, c2000. 254pp.
Vivid color illustrations fill this collection of stories by Jan Brett, which also presents the song "The Twelve Days of Christmas" and the poem "The Night Before Christmas."

Burke, Jennifer S. ***Cold Days.*** Children's Press, c2000. 24pp.
A young girl describes how she dresses, what she does, and how she feels on a cold, wintry day.

Carr, Jan. ***Frozen Noses.*** Holiday House, c1999. 26pp.
Describes the delights of such winter activities as throwing snowballs, making a snowman, and going ice skating.

Christiana, David. ***The First Snow.*** Scholastic, 2001, c1996. 32pp.
Winter seeks acceptance from the young Mother Nature, who hates the season and tries to keep it away by painting the trees bright and wild colors.

DeGezelle, Terri. ***Winter.*** Bridgestone Books, c2003. 24pp. (NF)
Explains why seasons change and describes the ways trees, animals, and people react to winter.

Fleming, Denise. ***Time to Sleep.*** H. Holt, c1997. 32pp.
When Bear notices that winter is nearly here, he hurries to tell Snail, after which each animal tells another, until finally the already sleeping Bear is awakened in his den with the news.

Fowler, Allan. ***How Do You Know It's Winter?*** Children's Press, c1991. 31pp. (NF)
A simple description of the characteristics of winter.

Frost, Robert. ***Stopping by Woods on a Snowy Evening.*** Dutton Children's Books, c2001. 32pp.
Illustrations of wintry scenes accompany each line of the well-known poem, in which a man stops to appreciate the beauty of a snowy afternoon.

Ganeri, Anita. ***Hibernation.*** Heinemann Library, c2005. 32pp. (NF)
Presents a children's study of animal hibernation and discusses where different animals hibernate and for how long, as well as the various animals who sleep through the winter such as bears, marmots, snakes, woodchucks, and others.

George, Jean Craighead. ***Dear Rebecca, Winter Is Here.*** HarperCollins, c1993. 32pp.
A grandmother explains to her granddaughter how the arrival of winter brings changes in nature and the earth's creatures, and how the return of spring and summer will bring more changes.

From Nancy J. Keane, *The Big Book of Children's Reading Lists: 100 Great, Ready-to-Use Book Lists for Educators, Librarians, Parents, and Children.* Westport, CT: Libraries Unlimited, 2006. Copyright © 2006 by Libraries Unlimited.

Winter

Gerber, Carole. *Blizzard.* Whispering Coyote, c2001. 32pp.
A raging winter storm contrasts with the cozy atmosphere of a young boy's home.

Glaser, Linda. *It's Winter!* Millbrook Press, c2002. 32pp.
A child observes the coming of winter and its effects on the weather, animals, and plants. Includes suggestions for wintertime activities.

Hader, Berta. *The Big Snow.* Simon & Schuster Books for Young Readers, c1976. 48pp.
The animals of the meadows and forest prepare themselves for winter by storing food, digging tunnels, and growing thick, furry coats to protect themselves from the snow and cold.

Kelley, Marty. *Winter Woes.* Zino Press Children's Books, c2004. 32pp.
Rhyming lament of a young worrywart who wants to go outside and play in the snow but fears what could happen if he does, from slipping on steps to freezing his brain.

Klingel, Cynthia Fitterer. *Winter.* Child's World, 2000, c2001. 24pp. (NF)
Describes winter, the things that can be seen during that season, and the changes that the earth goes through then.

Lenski, Lois. *I Like Winter.* Random House, 2000, c1950. 49pp.
Begins with a song about winter and then tells a story about children's activities in wintertime.

Moore, Eva. *The Magic School Bus Sleeps for the Winter.* Cartwheel Books, c2003. 28pp.
Introduces vocabulary words through a story about Ms. Frizzle's class field trip, on which the bus turns into a bear.

Pascoe, Elaine. *Animals Prepare for Winter.* Gareth Stevens, 2002, c2000. 24pp. (NF)
Describes some of the ways such different creatures as terns, chipmunks, bears, toads, weasels, and praying mantises survive the winter.

Pfeffer, Wendy. *The Shortest Day: Celebrating the Winter Solstice.* Dutton Children's Books, c2003. 40pp. (NF)
Describes how and why daylight grows shorter as winter approaches, the effect of shorter days on animals and people, and how the winter solstice has been celebrated throughout history. Includes activities.

Plourde, Lynn. *Winter Waits.* Simon & Schuster Books for Young Readers, c2001. 32pp.
Father Time's son, Winter, tries to get his busy father's attention.

Root, Phyllis. *Grandmother Winter.* Houghton Mifflin, c1999. 32pp.
When Grandmother Winter shakes out her feather quilt, birds, bats, bears, and other creatures prepare themselves for the cold.

From Nancy J. Keane, *The Big Book of Children's Reading Lists: 100 Great, Ready-to-Use Book Lists for Educators, Librarians, Parents, and Children.* Westport, CT: Libraries Unlimited, 2006. Copyright © 2006 by Libraries Unlimited.

Winter

Rylant, Cynthia. ***Poppleton in Winter.*** Scholastic, c2001. 48pp.
Poppleton the pig makes a new friend after an icicle accident, creates a bust of Cherry Sue, and gets a wintry birthday surprise from his pals.

Spinelli, Eileen. ***Now It Is Winter.*** Eerdmans Books for Young Readers, c2004. 32pp.
A mouse mother reassures her children that spring and all its delights will come again, while trying to teach them about the joys of winter.

Stojic, Manya. ***Snow.*** Knopf, (distributed by Random House), c2002. 32pp.
As snow approaches and begins to fall, Moose, Bear, Fox, and other forest creatures prepare for winter.

Uhlberg, Myron. ***Flying over Brooklyn.*** Peachtree, c1999. 32pp.
Lifted by the wind, a boy flies over snow-covered Brooklyn and admires its winter beauty. Includes information about the 1947 Brooklyn snowstorm, the greatest in its history.

Van Laan, Nancy. ***When Winter Comes.*** Atheneum Books for Young Readers, c2000. 36pp.
Rhyming text asks what happens to different animals and plants "when winter comes and the cold wind blows."

Whitehouse, Patricia. ***Winter.*** Heinemann Library, c2003. 24pp. (NF)
Describes the different sights, sounds, smells, and tastes children are likely to encounter during the winter season, and includes a winter quiz.

Wilson, Karma. ***Bear Snores On.*** Margaret K. McElderry Books, c2002. 34pp.
On a cold winter night many animals gather to party in the cave of a sleeping bear, who then awakes and protests that he has missed the food and the fun.

Books for Children Ages 8–12

Burton, Jane. ***The Nature and Science of Winter.*** Gareth Stevens, c1999. 32pp. (NF)
Explains why the season of winter happens and how it manifests itself in the weather and changes in plants and animals.

Jackson, Ellen B. ***The Winter Solstice.*** Millbrook Press, c1994. 32pp. (NF)
Presents facts and folklore about the shortest day of the year, a day that has been filled with magic since ancient times.

A Snowflake Fell: Poems About Winter. Barefoot Books, c2003. 40pp.
A collection of poems from various poets that illustrate the beauty of winter and the simple pleasures that can be found in the cold, snowy months.

Yolen, Jane. ***Snow, Snow: Winter Poems for Children.*** Wordsong/Boyds Mills Press, c1998. 32pp.
Features original poems about snow.

From Nancy J. Keane, *The Big Book of Children's Reading Lists: 100 Great, Ready-to-Use Book Lists for Educators, Librarians, Parents, and Children.* Westport, CT: Libraries Unlimited, 2006. Copyright © 2006 by Libraries Unlimited.

The Moon

Books for Children of All Ages

Aldrin, Buzz. ***Reaching for the Moon.*** HarperCollins, c2005. 36pp. (NF)
Presents an illustrated account of astronaut Buzz Aldrin's life and the determination and experiences that led him to be part of the first mission to land men on the moon.

Appelt, Kathi. ***I See the Moon.*** Eerdmans Publishing, c1997. 24pp.
A young girl who dreams she is alone at sea in a tiny boat is gradually brought to the realization that God is always with her.

Arden, Carolyn. ***Goose Moon.*** Boyds Mills Press, c2004. 32pp.
A young girl anxiously waits the arrival of spring to see the Goose Moon, a sign that spring is on its way.

Bess, Clayton. ***The Truth About the Moon.*** Houghton Mifflin, c1983. 48pp.
An African child is told several stories about the moon, but he still feels he has not learned the truth.

Birch, Robin. ***Earth, Sun, and Moon.*** Chelsea Clubhouse, c2003. 32pp. (NF)
Describes various attributes of the earth, the sun, and the moon, and explains the relationships between them.

Branley, Franklyn Mansfield. ***The Moon Seems to Change.*** HarperCollins, c1987. 29pp. (NF)
Explains the phases of the moon—the changes that seem to happen to it as it goes around Earth.

Bredeson, Carmen. ***The Moon.*** Children's Press, c2003. 31pp. (NF)
A simple introduction to the physical features, orbit, and efforts to explore the earth's moon.

Conrad, Donna. ***See You Soon Moon.*** Dell Dragonfly Books, 2003, c2001. 30pp.
The moon seems to follow as a child travels to Grandma's house.

Curtis, Carolyn. ***I Took the Moon for a Walk.*** Barefoot Books, 2004. 32pp.
A boy takes the moon for a walk through his neighborhood.

Fletcher, Ralph J. ***Hello, Harvest Moon.*** Clarion Books, c2003. 32pp.
Poetic prose describes a full autumn moon and the magical effect it has on the earth, plants, animals, and people around it.

Fowler, Allan. ***So That's How the Moon Changes Shape!*** Children's Press, c1991. 31pp. (NF)
A simple explanation of the moon and why it changes shape throughout the month.

Garelick, May. ***Look at the Moon.*** Mondo, 1996. 32pp.
A journey in verse to discover whether the same moon shines on all parts of the world.

Getz, David. ***Moonwalkers.*** Chelsea Clubhouse, 2003. 24pp. (NF)
A brief description of the trips to the moon and what was learned from them.

From Nancy J. Keane, *The Big Book of Children's Reading Lists: 100 Great, Ready-to-Use Book Lists for Educators, Librarians, Parents, and Children.* Westport, CT: Libraries Unlimited, 2006. Copyright © 2006 by Libraries Unlimited.

The Moon

Goldstein, Margaret J. ***The Moon.*** Lerner, c2003. 32pp. (NF)
An introduction to the moon, including its place in the solar system, movement in space, physical characteristics, and exploration by humans.

Gralley, Jean. ***The Moon Came Down on Milk Street.*** H. Holt, c2004. 32pp.
When the moon comes down in pieces, different helpers work to set things right again, including the fire chief, rescue workers, and helper dogs.

Henkes, Kevin. ***Kitten's First Full Moon.*** Greenwillow Books, c2004. 32pp.
When Kitten mistakes the full moon for a bowl of milk, she ends up tired, wet, and hungry trying to reach it.

Honey, Elizabeth. ***The Moon in the Man.*** Allen & Unwin, c2002. 32pp.
An illustrated collection of humorous poems for children written by Australian poet Elizabeth Honey.

Hunter, Anne. ***Possum's Harvest Moon.*** Houghton Mifflin, c1996. 32pp.
Possum awakes one autumn evening and decides to invite his animal friends to a party to celebrate the beautiful harvest moon one last time before the long winter.

London, Jonathan. ***I See the Moon and the Moon Sees Me.*** Puffin Books, c1998. 32pp.
An expansion of the classic nursery rhyme into a text that captures a child's perfect day in the midst of mountains, trees, flowers, and other aspects of nature.

Murray, Marjorie Dennis. ***Little Wolf and the Moon.*** Marshall Cavendish, c2002. 32pp.
Every night, Little Wolf looks up at the moon and wonders why it is the way it is.

Oppenheim, Shulamith Levey. ***What Is the Full Moon Full Of?*** Boyds Mills Press, c1997. 32pp.
In this bedtime story, woodland creatures answer the question posed in the title.

Robertson, M. P. ***The Moon in the Swampland.*** Frances Lincoln Children's Books, (distributed by Publishers Group West), c2004. 32pp.
Thomas, a boy who is saved by the Moon from the bogles that inhabit Swampland, leads a rescue team into the swamp when the Moon's failure to appear leads them to believe she has been captured.

Rylant, Cynthia. ***Long Night Moon.*** Simon & Schuster Books for Young Readers, c2004. 32pp.
Text and illustrations depict the varied seasonal full moons that change and assume personalities of their own throughout the year.

Scillian, Devin. ***Cosmo's Moon.*** Sleeping Bear Press, c2003. 40pp.
After Cosmo's affection for the Moon causes it to leave its orbit and begin to follow him around, he must reassure the Moon that saying goodbye makes the hello even sweeter.

Simon, Seymour. ***The Moon.*** Simon & Schuster Books for Young Readers, c2003. 32pp. (NF)
A basic introduction to Earth's closest neighbor, its composition, and human missions to explore it. Illustrated with photographs of the moon taken in space.

From Nancy J. Keane, *The Big Book of Children's Reading Lists: 100 Great, Ready-to-Use Book Lists for Educators, Librarians, Parents, and Children.* Westport, CT: Libraries Unlimited, 2006. Copyright © 2006 by Libraries Unlimited.

The Moon

Spinelli, Eileen. ***Rise the Moon.*** Dial Books for Young Readers, c2003. 34pp.
The moon lights the night for farmers, mothers and babies, wolves, and more.

Suen, Anastasia. ***Man on the Moon.*** Puffin Books, c2002. 32pp. (NF)
Describes in illustrations and simple text the Apollo 11 mission to the moon, culminating in man's first lunar landing.

The Sun, the Moon, and the Stars. Houghton Mifflin, c2003. 36pp.
A collection of more than thirty poems, some by the compiler, others by Walter de la Mare, Russell Hoban, Frank Asch, Jane Taylor, and others.

Tarpley, Natasha. ***Joe-Joe's First Flight.*** Knopf, (distributed by Random House), c2003. 34pp.
Forbidden to fly because of their color, Joe-Joe and the men who clean and repair airplanes in the 1920s are so discouraged that the moon cannot even shine, until Joe-Joe's determination lures the moon back. Includes a history of African American pilots.

Taylor, Joanne. ***Full Moon Rising.*** Tundra Books, Tundra Books of Northern New York, c2002. 32pp.
As a farm family celebrates the moon's cycles, they describe how the moon changes throughout the seasons.

Whitehouse, Patricia. ***The Moon.*** Heinemann Library, c2004. 32pp. (NF)
Examines the size and makeup of the moon; its craters, seas, and mountains; the phases and changes of the moon; gravity and tides; and other interesting facts about it.

Yolen, Jane. ***Owl Moon.*** Philomel Books, c1987. 32pp.
On a winter's night under a full moon, a father and daughter trek into the woods to see the Great Horned Owl.

Books for Children Ages 8–12

Bourgeois, Paulette. ***The Moon.*** Kids Can Press, 1997, c1995. 40pp. (NF)
Provides information about the moon through a collection of facts, experiments, projects, illustrations, and stories and legends.

Crewe, Sabrina. ***The First Moon Landing.*** Gareth Stevens, c2004. 32pp. (NF)
Examines the history of the U.S. space program, focusing on efforts to land a man on the moon in the 1960s, and looks at advancements that have been made in space exploration since the Apollo moon launches.

Kerrod, Robin. ***The Moon.*** Lerner, c2000. 32pp. (NF)
Introduces the moon, its properties, formation, and exploration.

Peddicord, Jane Ann. ***Night Wonders.*** Charlesbridge, c2005. 32pp. (NF)
Presents full-color images of the moon, sun, stars, and planets along with verse and a short narrative that describes them.

Siy, Alexandra. ***Footprints on the Moon.*** Charlesbridge, c2001. 32pp. (NF)
Photographs and simple text chronicle the history of moon exploration and discuss what the future might hold.

From Nancy J. Keane, *The Big Book of Children's Reading Lists: 100 Great, Ready-to-Use Book Lists for Educators, Librarians, Parents, and Children.* Westport, CT: Libraries Unlimited, 2006. Copyright © 2006 by Libraries Unlimited.

The Sun

Books for Children of All Ages

Asch, Frank. ***The Sun Is My Favorite Star.*** Harcourt, c2000. 32pp.
Celebrates a child's love of the sun and the wondrous ways in which it helps the earth and the life upon it.

Branley, Franklyn Mansfield. ***The Sun, Our Nearest Star.*** HarperCollins, c2002. 25pp. (NF)
Describes the sun and how it provides the light and energy that allow plant and animal life to exist on the earth.

Canizares, Susan. ***Sun.*** Scholastic, c1998. 16pp. (NF)
Photographs and simple text describe how the sun brings light and warmth to all living things from sunrise to sunset.

Fowler, Allan. ***Energy from the Sun.*** Children's Press, c1997. 31pp. (NF)
Defines energy and examines how energy from the sun provides us with heat, light, plants, food, and other things necessary for life on Earth.

Kosek, Jane Kelly. ***What's Inside the Sun?*** PowerKids Press, c1999. 24pp. (NF)
Describes the six layers of the sun as well as the role of this star that is part of the Milky Way.

Nelson, Robin. ***A Sunny Day.*** Lerner, c2002. 23pp. (NF)
Photographs and text provide information about weather conditions and things to do on sunny days. Includes sunny day facts.

Simon, Seymour. ***The Sun.*** Morrow Junior Books, c1996. 32pp. (NF)
Describes the nature of the sun, its origin, source of energy, layers, atmosphere, sunspots, and activity.

Stewart, Melissa. ***Fun with The Sun.*** Compass Point Books, c2004. 32pp. (NF)
Provides step-by-step, illustrated instructions for in-depth experiments designed to teach young children about the sun.

Tesar, Jenny E. ***The Sun.*** Heinemann Interactive Library, c1998. 24pp. (NF)
Introduces the sun, discussing its surface, atmosphere, eclipses, birth, death, and place in the solar system.

From Nancy J. Keane, *The Big Book of Children's Reading Lists: 100 Great, Ready-to-Use Book Lists for Educators, Librarians, Parents, and Children.* Westport, CT: Libraries Unlimited, 2006. Copyright © 2006 by Libraries Unlimited.

The Sun

Books for Children Ages 8–12

Asimov, Isaac. ***The Sun.*** Gareth Stevens, c2002. 32pp. (NF)
A description of the sun, the star of our solar system, which includes information on its origin, physical composition, and characteristics, as well as on studies made of the sun by instruments and satellites.

Bailey, Jacqui. ***Sun Up, Sun Down: The Story of Day and Night.*** Picture Window Books, 2004. c2003. 31pp. (NF)
Follows the sun from dawn to dusk to explain how light rays travel, how shadows are formed, how the moon lights up the night sky, and more.

Berger, Melvin. ***Do Stars Have Points?: Questions and Answers About Stars and Planets.*** Scholastic, 1999, c1998. 48pp. (NF)
Questions and answers explore various aspects of stars and our solar system, including the sun, planets, moons, comets, and asteroids.

Bourgeois, Paulette. ***The Sun.*** Kids Can Press, 1997, c1995. 40pp. (NF)
Provides information about the sun through a collection of facts, experiments, projects, illustrations, and stories and legends.

Burton, Jane. ***The Nature and Science of Sunlight.*** Gareth Stevens, c1997. 32pp. (NF)
Examines the energy and light produced by the sun and their importance to life on Earth.

Furniss, Tim. ***The Sun.*** Raintree Steck-Vaughn, c2001. 32pp. (NF)
Presents an introduction to the sun, in simple text with illustrations, including information on its size and the planets that rotate around it, including their orbit, place in the universe, and environment. Includes glossary.

Kerrod, Robin. ***The Sun.*** Lerner, c2000. 32pp. (NF)
Introduces the sun, our star, its relationship to other stars, its solar system, and the effects it has on Earth.

Nicolson, Cynthia Pratt. ***The Stars.*** Kids Can Press, c1998. 40pp. (NF)
Studies the stars and discusses why they twinkle, how light years are measured, why stars are different from planets, and other related topics; includes projects designed to help children learn more about stars.

Stott, Carole. ***1,001 Facts About Space.*** DK Publishing, c2002. 192pp. (NF)
Learn about the sun, planets, galaxies, and stars.

From Nancy J. Keane, *The Big Book of Children's Reading Lists: 100 Great, Ready-to-Use Book Lists for Educators, Librarians, Parents, and Children.* Westport, CT: Libraries Unlimited, 2006. Copyright © 2006 by Libraries Unlimited.

Stars and Planets

Books for Children of All Ages

Barner, Bob. ***Stars! Stars! Stars!*** Chronicle Books, c2002. 28pp. (NF)
Simple rhyming text describes the stars and planets of the solar system.

Birch, Robin. ***Stars.*** Chelsea Clubhouse, c2003. 32pp. (NF)
An introduction to stars and constellations of the Milky Way, as well as galaxies, star clusters, and other phenomena that can be observed with the help of binoculars, telescopes, or observatories.

Davis, Kenneth C. ***The Solar System.*** HarperCollins, c2001. 47pp. (NF)
Presents a children's study of the solar system and includes facts about the nine planets, more than seventy moons, Halley's Comet, the Milky Way, and shooting stars.

Eckart, Edana. ***Watching the Stars.*** Children's Press, c2004. 24pp. (NF)
Contains photographs and brief text that provide very basic information about stars, telescopes, and constellations.

Goldstein, Margaret J. ***Stars.*** Lerner, c2003. 32pp. (NF)
An introduction to the nature of stars, discussing their composition, size, color, formation, life cycle, constellations, clusters, and galaxies, as well as studying them from Earth.

Mitchell, Melanie. ***Stars.*** Lerner, c2004. 23pp. (NF)
A simple introduction to the characteristics of stars.

Mitton, Jacqueline. ***Once upon a Starry Night: A Book of Constellations.*** National Geographic, c2003. 26pp. (NF)
Presents facts about stars, nebulas, galaxies, and constellations and recounts the Greek myths that provided widely known names for ten constellations, from Andromeda to Pegasus.

Tomecek, Steve. ***Stars.*** National Geographic Society, c2003. 31pp. (NF)
Introduces stars and what they are made of, how they shine, their positions in relation to Earth, and more.

Vogt, Gregory. ***Constellations.*** Bridgestone Books, c2003. 24pp. (NF)
Describes several of the major constellations such as the Big Dipper, Orion, Cygnus, and the zodiac.

Vogt, Gregory. ***The Milky Way.*** Bridgestone Books, c2003. 24pp. (NF)
Describes the objects that reside in the Milky Way galaxy, including stars, nebulas, clusters, and black holes, and explains what astronomers have discovered about other galaxies.

From Nancy J. Keane, *The Big Book of Children's Reading Lists: 100 Great, Ready-to-Use Book Lists for Educators, Librarians, Parents, and Children.* Westport, CT: Libraries Unlimited, 2006. Copyright © 2006 by Libraries Unlimited.

Stars and Planets

Books for Children Ages 8–12

Birch, Robin. ***Stars.*** Chelsea Clubhouse, c2004. 32pp. (NF)
Provides information about stars, explaining what they are and how they form; looks at different types of stars; and discusses star death, constellations, and the study of stars.

Croswell, Ken. ***See the Stars: Your First Guide to the Night Sky.*** Boyds Mills Press, c2000. 32pp. (NF)
A book of twelve star gazing activities, one for each month of the year.

Fredericks, Anthony D. ***Exploring the Universe: Science Activities for Kids.*** Fulcrum Resources, c2000. 120pp. (NF)
Provides information about all aspects of the universe: galaxies, the solar system, stars, asteroids and meteoroids, space exploration, and more. Includes related hands-on activities and projects.

Furniss, Tim. ***The Solar System.*** Raintree Steck-Vaughn, c2001. 32pp. (NF)
Presents an introduction to the solar system, in simple text with illustrations, and includes information on the sun, earth, and various planets, including their rotation, place in the universe, and environment. Includes glossary.

Hinz, Joan. ***Dot to Dot in the Sky: Stories in the Stars.*** Whitecap, c2001. 64pp. (NF)
Profiles fifteen constellations, including Ursa Major and Orion, presenting their background myths, illustrations, and instructions for finding them.

Kerrod, Robin. ***The Solar System.*** Lerner, c2000. 32pp. (NF)
Introduces the solar system, its planets, moons, asteroids, and comets, and its exploration.

Krautwurst, Terry. ***Night Science for Kids: Exploring the World After Dark.*** Lark Books, c2003. 144pp. (NF)
Provides ideas and activities for discovering what changes in the world after dark, including the arrival of moths and owls, fog, and the stars.

Love, Ann. ***The Kids Book of the Night Sky.*** Kids Can Press, c2004. 144pp. (NF)
A guide to the night sky for young stargazers, offering advice on how to best view the night sky, and providing facts, legends, and activities associated with the moon, stars, and planets, as well as a look at seasonal attractions.

Peddicord, Jane Ann. ***Night Wonders.*** Charlesbridge, c2005. 32pp. (NF)
Presents full-color images of the moon, sun, stars, and planets along with verse and a short narrative that describes them.

Scagell, Robin. ***Night Sky Atlas.*** DK Publishing, c2004. 96pp. (NF)
Contains a variety of maps used to identify stars, constellations, nebulas, and planets in the night sky; includes see-through maps and general information on star gazing.

Stott, Carole. ***Astronomy.*** Kingfisher, c2003. 63pp. (NF)
Discusses famous astronomers, the solar system, the stars, and other aspects of astronomy. (NF)

From Nancy J. Keane, *The Big Book of Children's Reading Lists: 100 Great, Ready-to-Use Book Lists for Educators, Librarians, Parents, and Children.* Westport, CT: Libraries Unlimited, 2006. Copyright © 2006 by Libraries Unlimited.

Plants

Books for Children of All Ages

Aliki. ***Corn Is Maize: The Gift of the Indians.*** HarperCollins, c1976. 33pp. (NF)
A simple description of how corn was discovered and used by the Indians and how it came to be an important food throughout the world.

Appelt, Kathi. ***Watermelon Day.*** H. Holt, c1996. 32pp.
Young Jesse waits all summer for her watermelon to ripen.

Blackaby, Susan. ***Ann Plants a Garden.*** Picture Window Books, c2005. 24pp.
Easy-to-read, rhyming text describes the many plants found in Ann's garden, which she takes care of every day.

Blackaby, Susan. ***Buds and Blossoms: A Book About Flowers.*** Picture Window Books, c2003. 24pp. (NF)
Describes flower parts, the different flower shapes, and the pollination process, and provides "fun facts" and words to know.

Blackaby, Susan. ***Green and Growing: A Book About Plants.*** Picture Window Books, c2003. 24pp. (NF)
Describes the similarities and differences between several types of plants, shows the plant life cycle, explains how plants are used by people, and presents "fun facts" and words to know.

Bulla, Clyde Robert. ***A Tree Is a Plant.*** HarperCollins, 2001, c1960. 31pp. (NF)
Introduces the tree as "the biggest plant that grows" and explains the life cycle of an apple tree.

Carle, Eric. ***The Tiny Seed.*** Simon & Schuster Books for Young Readers, c1987. 32pp. (NF)
A simple description of a flowering plant's life cycle through the seasons.

Cole, Henry. ***Jack's Garden.*** Greenwillow Books, c1995. 25pp.
Cumulative text and illustrations depict what happens in Jack's garden after he plants his seeds.

Davis, Aubrey ***The Enormous Potato.*** Kids Can Press, 1998, c1997. 32pp.
A farmer's family helps him dig a large potato out of the ground so they can use it to feed the town.

Fleischman, Paul. ***Weslandia.*** Candlewick Press, c1999. 34pp.
Wesley's garden produces a crop of huge, strange plants that provide him with clothing, shelter, food, and drink, thus helping him create his own civilization and changing his life.

From Nancy J. Keane, *The Big Book of Children's Reading Lists: 100 Great, Ready-to-Use Book Lists for Educators, Librarians, Parents, and Children.* Westport, CT: Libraries Unlimited, 2006. Copyright © 2006 by Libraries Unlimited.

Plants

Fowler, Allan. ***From Seed to Plant.*** Children's Press, c2001. 31pp. (NF)
Describes the development of a seed into a plant by means of pollination, fertilization, and seed dispersal.

Ganeri, Anita. ***Plant Life Cycles.*** Heinemann Library, c2005. 32pp. (NF)
Looks at the life cycle patterns of plants, looking at the patterns followed by plants that start as seeds and as bulbs. Includes an activity.

Garland, Sarah. ***Eddie's Garden and How to Make Things Grow.*** Frances Lincoln Children's Books (distributed in the United States by Publishers Group West), c2004. 36pp.
Eddie learns about how plants grow and the connections between all living things when he, his mother, and his little sister plant a garden.

Gibbons, Gail. ***From Seed to Plant.*** Holiday House, c1991. 32pp. (NF)
Explores the intricate relationship between seeds and the plants they produce.

Giesecke, Ernestine. ***Flowers.*** Heinemann Library, c1999. 24pp. (NF)
Presents a brief introduction to the characteristics of flowers and provides photographs and simple information to help the reader identify such flowers as the dandelion, lily, and rose.

Giesecke, Ernestine. ***Forest Plants.*** Heinemann Library, c1999. 32pp. (NF)
Describes how various plants adapt to living in a forest, including the skunk cabbage, maple tree, and dogwood.

Glover, David. ***How Do Things Grow?*** DK Publishing, c2001. 125pp. (NF)
Shows children how to do science experiments about growth and the life cycles of plants and animals.

Guiberson, Brenda Z. ***Cactus Hotel.*** H. Holt, c1991. 32pp. (NF)
Describes the life cycle of the giant saguaro cactus, with an emphasis on its role as a home for other desert dwellers.

Hall, Zoe. ***It's Pumpkin Time!*** Blue Sky Press, 1999, c1994. 32pp.
A sister and brother plant and tend their own pumpkin patch so they will have jack-o'-lanterns for Halloween.

Hillert, Margaret. ***The Magic Beans.*** Modern Curriculum Press, c1966. 28pp.
An easy-to-read version of "Jack and the Beanstalk," in which the boy's mother chops down the beanstalk so he can escape from the giant.

Hoberman, Mary Ann. ***Whose Garden Is It?*** Harcourt, c2004. 32pp.
When Mrs. McGee walks through a garden wondering whose it is, all of the plants and animals as well as the sun and the gardener claim it as their own.

From Nancy J. Keane, *The Big Book of Children's Reading Lists: 100 Great, Ready-to-Use Book Lists for Educators, Librarians, Parents, and Children.* Westport, CT: Libraries Unlimited, 2006. Copyright © 2006 by Libraries Unlimited.

Plants

Jordan, Helene J. ***How a Seed Grows.*** HarperCollins, c1992. 31pp. (NF)
Uses observations of bean seeds planted in eggshells to demonstrate the growth of seeds into plants.

Keats, Ezra Jack. ***Clementina's Cactus.*** Viking Press, c1999. 34pp.
After a rainstorm, Clementina and her father discover a surprise in the prickly skin of the cactus that they've watched growing in the desert.

Legg, Gerald. ***From Seed to Sunflower.*** Franklin Watts, c1998. 29pp. (NF)
Large illustrations and simple text present the life cycle of a sunflower from seed to flower.

Loves, June. ***Trees.*** Chelsea Clubhouse, c2005. 32pp. (NF)
Presents an introduction to trees, nature's biggest plants, in simple text and illustrations; includes information on how they grow, where they grow, their different parts, and their different varieties, as well as useful tips for gardeners.

McEvoy, Paul. ***Flowers.*** Chelsea Clubhouse, c2003. 24pp. (NF)
A color-photo-filled overview of flowers that describes their parts, types, habitats, and reproduction. (NF)

McEvoy, Paul. ***Plants.*** Chelsea Clubhouse, 2003, c2002. 24pp. (NF)
A color-photo-filled overview of plants that describes their parts, types, habitats, varied uses, and production of oxygen.

Relf, Patricia. ***The Magic School Bus Plants Seeds: A Book About How Living Things Grow.*** Scholastic, c1995. 32pp.
The magic school bus turns into a ladybug to help the class learn about how plants grow.

Robbins, Ken. ***Seeds.*** Atheneum Books for Young Readers, c2005. 32pp. (NF)
From flowers to fruits, everything begins with a tiny seed. Young readers will learn how seeds grow and how they vary in shape, size, and dispersal patterns.

Royston, Angela. ***Flowers, Fruits and Seeds.*** Heinemann Library, c1999. 32pp. (NF)
An introduction to how plants reproduce, discussing buds, flowers, fruits, nuts, pods, pollination, and the dispersal of seeds.

Royston, Angela. ***How Plants Grow.*** Heinemann Library, c1999. 32pp. (NF)
An introduction to plants including descriptions of their flowers and fruit, spores and cones, roots, stems, leaves, and methods for storing food.

Scrace, Carolyn. ***Growing Things.*** Franklin Watts, c2002. 31pp. (NF)
Time-lapse illustrations, a split-page format, and simple text teach young readers about the cycle of life.

From Nancy J. Keane, *The Big Book of Children's Reading Lists: 100 Great, Ready-to-Use Book Lists for Educators, Librarians, Parents, and Children.* Westport, CT: Libraries Unlimited, 2006. Copyright © 2006 by Libraries Unlimited.

Plants

Star, Fleur. ***Plant.*** DK Publishing, c2005. 48pp. (NF)
Studies a number of plants and forests around the world and examines how and where they grow, how photosynthesis works, pollination, how certain species of birds and animals help flowers and trees grow, and the various ways in which people use them.

Stewart, Melissa. ***A Parade of Plants.*** Compass Point Books, c2004. 32pp. (NF)
Introduces the parts of a plant, life cycles, and how they grow.

Wellington, Monica. ***Zinnia's Flower Garden.*** Dutton Children's Books, c2005. 32pp.
Zinnia plants a garden, eagerly waits for the plants to grow, sells the beautiful flowers, then gathers seeds to plant the following year. Includes instructions for growing your own flowers.

Whitehouse, Patricia. ***Plant ABC.*** Heinemann Library, c2002. 24pp. (NF)
Introduces the letters of the alphabet while providing information about various plants. Includes photographs. (NF)

Books for Children Ages 8–12

Collard, Sneed B. ***The Prairie Builders: Reconstructing America's Lost Grasslands.*** Houghton Mifflin, c2005. 66pp. (NF)
Presents a comprehensive examination into the efforts to restore the native tallgrass prairie to an 8,000- acre reserve in central Iowa, and describes the process of reintroducing prairie plants and wildlife, including the Regal Fritillary butterfly.

Hickman, Pamela M. ***Plant Book.*** Kids Can Press, 2000, c1996. 32pp. (NF)
Provides illustrations and information about a wide variety of plants found in the United States.

Knight, Tim. ***Fantastic Feeders.*** Heinemann Library, c2003. 32pp. (NF)
Explores different kinds of food eaten by certain animals and the special teeth or other tools they have for eating that food, as well as some of the ways plants avoid being eaten.

MacLeod, Elizabeth. ***Grow It Again.*** Kids Can Press, c1999. 40pp. (NF)
Provides step-by-step instructions for growing plants indoors. Also includes recipes for cooking them.

Pascoe, Elaine. ***Plants with Seeds.*** PowerKids Press, c2003. 32pp. (NF)
Details the life cycles and characteristics of plants that use seeds to reproduce.

Silver, Donald M. ***Backyard.*** Learning Triangle Press, c1997. 47pp. (NF)
Explains how to observe and explore plants, animals, and their interactions in your own backyard.

From Nancy J. Keane, *The Big Book of Children's Reading Lists: 100 Great, Ready-to-Use Book Lists for Educators, Librarians, Parents, and Children.* Westport, CT: Libraries Unlimited, 2006. Copyright © 2006 by Libraries Unlimited.

Mathematics

Books for Children of All Ages

Adler, David A. ***Fraction Fun.*** Holiday House, c1996. 32pp. (NF)
A basic introduction to the concept of fractions.

Anno, Mitsumasa. ***Anno's Counting Book.*** HarperCollins, 1977,. c1975. 28pp. (NF)
Introduces counting and number systems by showing mathematical relationships in nature.

Appelt, Kathi. ***Bat Jamboree.*** HarperCollins, c1996. 24pp.
At an abandoned outdoor movie theater, fifty-five bats perform in a toe-tapping, wing-flapping revue —and await the grand finale.

Axelrod, Amy. ***Pigs Will Be Pigs: Fun with Math and Money.*** Simon & Schuster Books for Young Readers, c1994. 34pp.
The hungry Pig family learns about money and buying power as they turn the house upside down looking for enough money to buy dinner at the local restaurant.

Burns, Marilyn. ***The Greedy Triangle.*** Scholastic, c1994. 36pp.
Dissatisfied with its shape, a triangle keeps asking the local shapeshifter to add more lines and angles until it doesn't know which side is up.

Burns, Marilyn. ***Spaghetti and Meatballs for All!: A Mathematical Story.*** Scholastic, c1997. 36pp.
The seating for a family reunion gets complicated as people rearrange the tables and chairs to seat additional guests.

Clement, Rod. ***Counting on Frank.*** Gareth Stevens Children's Books, c1991. 32pp.
A boy and his dog present amusing counting, size comparison, and mathematical facts.

Cooney, Barbara. ***Miss Rumphius.*** Viking Press, c1982. 32pp.
After making her girlhood dreams of world travel and living by the sea come true, a retired librarian follows her grandfather's advice of doing something to make the world more beautiful, and then passes that wisdom on to her grandniece.

Cuyler, Margery. ***100th Day Worries.*** Simon & Schuster Books for Young Readers, c2000. 32pp.
Jessica worries about collecting 100 objects to take to class for the one hundredth day of school.

Demi. ***One Grain Of Rice: A Mathematical Folktale.*** Scholastic Press, c1997. 36pp.
A reward of one grain of rice doubles day by day into millions of grains of rice when a selfish raja is outwitted by a clever village girl.

Duke, Kate. ***Twenty Is Too Many.*** Dutton Children's Books, c2000. 48pp.
A tale of twenty adventurous guinea pigs on sea and land illustrates the process of subtraction as their numbers dwindle.

Emberley, Ed. ***Ed Emberley's Picture Pie: A Circle Drawing Book.*** Little, Brown, c1984. 45pp.
Shows how to cut a basic circle into arcs and curves and use the pieces to draw birds, animals, snowmen, fish, and many other objects and designs.

From Nancy J. Keane, *The Big Book of Children's Reading Lists: 100 Great, Ready-to-Use Book Lists for Educators, Librarians, Parents, and Children.* Westport, CT: Libraries Unlimited, 2006. Copyright © 2006 by Libraries Unlimited.

Mathematics

Garland, Sherry. ***The Lotus Seed.*** Harcourt Brace, c1993. 32pp.
A young Vietnamese girl saves a lotus seed and carries it with her everywhere to remember a brave emperor and the homeland that she has to flee.

Hightower, Susan. ***Twelve Snails to One Lizard: A Tale of Mischief and Measurement.*** Simon & Schuster Books for Young Readers, c1997. 32pp.
Bubba the bullfrog helps Milo the beaver build a dam by explaining to him the concepts of inches, feet, and yards.

Hort, Lenny. ***How Many Stars in the Sky?*** Mulberry Books, 1997. c1991. 32pp.
One night when Mama is away, Daddy and child seek a good place to count the stars in the night sky.

Jaffe, Elizabeth Dana. ***Can You Eat a Fraction?*** Yellow Umbrella Books, c2002. 17pp. (NF)
Simple text and photographs introduce the concept of fractions and how they are written.

Jonas, Ann. *Splash!* Greenwillow Books, c1995. 26pp.
A little girl's turtle, fish, frogs, dog, and cat jump in and out of a backyard pond, constantly changing the answer to the question "How many are in my pond?"

Leedy, Loreen. ***Fraction Action.*** Holiday House, c1994. 31pp.
Miss Prime and her animal students explore fractions by finding many examples in the world around them.

Leedy, Loreen. ***Measuring Penny.*** H. Holt, c2000, c1997. 32pp.
Lisa learns about the mathematics of measuring by measuring her dog Penny with all sorts of units, including pounds, inches, dog biscuits, and cotton swabs.

Leedy, Loreen. ***Mission: Addition.*** Holiday House, c1997. 32pp.
Miss Prime and her animal students explore addition by finding many examples in the world around them.

Leedy, Loreen. ***Subtraction Action.*** Holiday House, c2000. 32pp.
Introduces subtraction through the activities of animal students at a school fair; includes problems for the reader to solve.

McGrath, Barbara Barbieri. ***The M&M'S Brand Subtraction Book.*** Charlesbridge, c2005. 27pp. (NF)
A colorful rhyming book that presents the basics of single-digit and double-digit subtraction using M & M chocolate candies.

McKissack, Pat. ***A Million Fish—More or Less.*** Knopf, (distributed by Random House), 1996, c1992. 32pp.
A boy learns that the truth is often stretched on the Bayou Clapateaux, and gets the chance to tell his own version of a bayou tale when he goes fishing.

McMillan, Bruce. ***Eating Fractions.*** Scholastic, c1991. 32pp. (NF)
Food is cut into halves, quarters, and thirds to illustrate how parts make a whole. Simple recipes included.

Murphy, Stuart J. *Give Me Half!* HarperCollins, c1996. 34pp.
Introduces the concept of halves using a simple rhyming story about a brother and sister who do not want to share their food.

From Nancy J. Keane, *The Big Book of Children's Reading Lists: 100 Great, Ready-to-Use Book Lists for Educators, Librarians, Parents, and Children.* Westport, CT: Libraries Unlimited, 2006. Copyright © 2006 by Libraries Unlimited.

Mathematics

Myller, Rolf. ***How Big Is a Foot?*** Bantam Doubleday Dell Books for Young Readers, 1991, c1990. 38pp.
An apprentice carpenter gets thrown into jail when the bed he builds for the Queen's birthday is too small. He soon solves the problem and is made a royal prince.

Pallotta, Jerry. ***The Hershey's Kisses Subtraction Book.*** Scholastic, c2002. 32pp. (NF)
Uses Hershey's kisses to teach subtraction.

Pinczes, Elinor J. ***One Hundred Hungry Ants.*** Houghton Mifflin, c1993. 32pp.
One hundred hungry ants head toward a picnic to get yummies for their tummies. They stop to change their line formation, showing different divisions of 100, causing them to lose both time and food in the end.

Pinczes, Elinor J. ***A Remainder of One.*** Houghton Mifflin, c1995. 32pp.
When the queen of the bugs demands that her army march in even lines, Private Joe divides the marchers into more and more lines so that he will not be left out of the parade.

Rylant, Cynthia. ***The Relatives Came.*** Atheneum Books for Young Readers, c2001. 32pp.
The relatives come to visit from Virginia and everyone has a wonderful time.

Schwartz, David M. ***How Much Is a Million?*** Lothrop, Lee & Shepard, c1985. 40pp. (NF)
Text and pictures try to make possible the conceptualization of a million, a billion, and a trillion.

Schwartz, David M. ***If You Hopped Like a Frog.*** Scholastic Press, c1999. 29pp. (NF)
Introduces the concept of ratio by comparing what humans would be able to do if they had bodies like various animals.

Schwartz, David M. ***If You Made a Million.*** HarperCollins, 1994, c1989. 40pp. (NF)
Describes the various forms money can take, including coins, paper money, and personal checks, and how it can be used to make purchases, pay off loans, or build interest in the bank.

Silverstein, Shel. ***A Giraffe and a Half.*** HarperCollins, c1992. 48pp.
Cumulative rhymed text explains what might happen if you had a giraffe that stretched another half, put on a hat in which lived a rat that looked cute in a suit, and so on.

Slate, Joseph. ***Miss Bindergarten Celebrates the 100th Day of Kindergarten.*** Dutton Children's Books, c1998. 40pp.
To celebrate 100 days in Miss Bindergarten's kindergarten class, all her students bring 100 of something to school, including a 100-year-old relative, 100 candy hearts, and 100 polka dots.

Sweeney, Joan. ***Me and The Measure of Things.*** Dell Dragonfly Books, 2002, c2001. 28pp. (NF)
Contains an introduction to the concept of measurement, in simple text with illustrations, and includes information on units of measure, such as how much, how many, how heavy, how tall, and how far.

Sweeney, Joan. ***Me Counting Time: From Seconds to Centuries.*** Dragonfly Books, 2001, c2000. 30pp. (NF)
Describes the relationships between second, minute, hour, day, week, month, year, decade, century, and millennium as measurements of time.

From Nancy J. Keane, *The Big Book of Children's Reading Lists: 100 Great, Ready-to-Use Book Lists for Educators, Librarians, Parents, and Children.* Westport, CT: Libraries Unlimited, 2006. Copyright © 2006 by Libraries Unlimited.

Mathematics

Tompert, Ann. ***Just a Little Bit.*** Houghton Mifflin, c1993. 32pp.
When Mouse and Elephant decide to go on the seesaw, Mouse needs a lot of help from other animals before they can go up and down.

Viorst, Judith. ***Alexander, Who Used to Be Rich Last Sunday.*** Atheneum, c1978. 32pp.
Although Alexander and his money are quickly parted, he comes to realize all the things that can be done with a dollar.

Wells, Rosemary. ***Max's Dragon Shirt.*** Puffin Books, 2000, c1991. 32pp.
On a shopping trip to the department store, Max's determination to get a dragon shirt leads him away from his distracted sister and into trouble.

Books for Children Ages 8–12

Anno, Masaichiro. ***Anno's Mysterious Multiplying Jar.*** Philomel, c1983. 45pp. (NF)
Simple text and pictures introduce the mathematical concept of factorials.

Cushman, Jean. ***Do You Wanna Bet?: Your Chance to Find Out About Probability.*** Clarion Books, c1991. 102pp. (NF)
Two boys find that the most ordinary events and activities such as card games, coin flips, sports scores and statistics, and even weather prediction are dependent on the subtle interplay of many factors of chance and probability.

DeFelice, Cynthia C. ***Under the Same Sky.*** Farrar, Straus & Giroux, c2003. 215pp.
While trying to earn money for a motor bike, fourteen-year-old Joe Pederson becomes involved with the Mexicans who work on his family's farm and develops a better relationship with his father.

Griffin, Adele. ***Hannah, Divided.*** Hyperion Books for Children, c2002. 264pp.
In 1934, a thirteen-year-old with a gift for numbers is offered the chance to leave her family's dairy farm to spend one term at an exclusive Philadelphia girls' school preparing for a scholarship exam.

Neuschwander, Cindy. ***Mummy Math: An Adventure in Math.*** H. Holt, c2005. 32pp. (NF)
Matt and Bibi accompany their scientist parents to Egypt to search for the mummy of an ancient pharaoh, and after becoming lost in the pyramid, must use their geometry skills to decipher the clues encoded in the hieroglyphics to locate the burial chamber and find their way out again.

Rodgers, Mary. ***A Billion for Boris.*** HarperTrophy, 2003, c1974. 216pp.
When they discover an old TV that plays tomorrow's programs, fourteen-year-old Annabel and her fifteen-year-old friend Boris try to use it to help humanity and earn money to refinish their apartment for Boris's eccentric mother.

Sachar, Louis. ***Sideways Arithmetic from Wayside School.*** Scholastic, c1989. 89pp. (NF)
Contains over fifty math puzzles and brainteasers.

Sachar, Louis. ***More Sideways Arithmetic from Wayside School.*** Scholastic, c1994. 94pp. (NF)
Try solving the more than fifty math brainteasers along with the kids from Mrs. Jewis's class.

Schwartz, David M. ***G Is for Googol: A Math Alphabet Book.*** Tricycle Press, c1998. 57pp. (NF)
Explains the meaning of mathematical terms that begin with the different letters of the alphabet, from abacus, binary, and cubit to zillion.

From Nancy J. Keane, *The Big Book of Children's Reading Lists: 100 Great, Ready-to-Use Book Lists for Educators, Librarians, Parents, and Children.* Westport, CT: Libraries Unlimited, 2006. Copyright © 2006 by Libraries Unlimited.

Black and White

Books for Children of All Ages

Bunting, Eve. ***Night of the Gargoyles.*** Clarion Books, c1994. 30pp.
In the middle of the night, the gargoyles that adorn the walls of a museum come to life and frighten the night watchman.

Henkes, Kevin. ***Kitten's First Full Moon.*** Greenwillow Books, c2004. 32pp.
When Kitten mistakes the full moon for a bowl of milk, she ends up tired, wet, and hungry trying to reach it.

Hoban, Tana. ***Over, Under & Through, and Other Spatial Concepts.*** Simon & Schuster Books for Young Readers, c1973. 32pp. (NF)
Photographs demonstrate the spatial concepts expressed in twelve words such as around, across, between, against, and behind.

Jonas, Ann. ***Round Trip.*** Greenwillow Books, c1983. 32pp.
Black-and-white illustrations and text record the sights on a day trip to the city and back home again to the country. The trip to the city is read from front to back and the return trip from back to front, upside down.

Macaulay, David. ***Black and White.*** Houghton Mifflin, c1990. 32pp.
Four brief "stories" about parents, trains, and cows, or is it really all one story? The author recommends careful inspection of words and pictures to both minimize and increase confusion.

Macaulay, David. ***Rome Antics.*** Houghton Mifflin, c1997. 79pp. (NF)
A pigeon carrying an important message takes the reader on a unique tour that includes both ancient and modern parts of the city of Rome.

MacLachlan, Patricia. ***What You Know First.*** Joanna Cotler Books, c1995. 32pp.
As a family prepares to move away from their farm, the daughter reflects on all the things she loves there so that when her baby brother is older she can tell him what it was like.

Van Allsburg, Chris. ***The Garden of Abdul Gasazi.*** Houghton Mifflin, c1979. 30pp.
When the dog he is caring for runs away from Alan into the forbidden garden of a retired dog-hating magician, a spell seems to be cast over the contrary dog.

Van Allsburg, Chris. ***The Widow's Broom.*** Houghton Mifflin, c1992. 32pp.
A witch's worn-out broom serves a widow well, until her neighbors decide the thing is wicked and dangerous.

Wright, Dare. ***The Lonely Doll.*** Houghton Mifflin Co. 1998, c1985. 55pp.
Edith, the doll, was lonely until two bears came to stay and play with her.

From Nancy J. Keane, *The Big Book of Children's Reading Lists: 100 Great, Ready-to-Use Book Lists for Educators, Librarians, Parents, and Children.* Westport, CT: Libraries Unlimited, 2006. Copyright © 2006 by Libraries Unlimited.

Artists' Biographies

Books for Children of All Ages

Burleigh, Robert. *Into the Woods: John James Audubon Lives His Dream.* Atheneum Books for Young Readers, c2003. 34pp. (NF)

Uses quotes from his journals to help explore Audubon's decision to follow his dream to paint every bird species in North America.

Davies, Jacqueline. *The Boy Who Drew Birds: A Story of John James Audubon.* Houghton Mifflin, c2004. 32pp. (NF)

John James Audubon, living in Pennsylvania far from his home and father in France, is obsessed with birds, and he comes up with the idea of banding the legs of his pewee bird friends to see if they will return in the spring to the nests they abandoned in the fall.

Frith, Margaret. *Frida Kahlo: The Artist Who Painted Herself.* Grosset & Dunlap, c2003. 32pp. (NF)

A biography of Mexican artist Frida Kahlo, written as a child's school report. Features photos of Kahlo and reproductions of her paintings.

Guarnieri, Paolo. *A Boy Named Giotto.* Farrar, Straus & Giroux, c1999. 26pp. (NF)

Eight-year-old Giotto the shepherd boy confesses his dream of becoming an artist to the painter Cimabue, who teaches him how to make marvelous pigments from minerals, flowers, and eggs and takes him on as his pupil.

Hart, Tony. *Leonardo da Vinci.* Barron's, 1994. 23pp. (NF)

Describes the childhood of noted fifteenth-century artist Leonardo da Vinci, discussing the development of his wide range of talents, including mathematics, music, art, and inventing.

Hart, Tony. *Michelangelo.* Barron's, c1994. 23pp. (NF)

Focuses on the childhood of the noted artist Michelangelo.

Lowery, Linda. *Georgia O'Keeffe.* Carolrhoda Books, c1996. 47pp. (NF)

Tells the story of how Georgia O'Keeffe overcame her frustration as an artist and found her own way of seeing and painting.

Lowery, Linda. *Pablo Picasso.* Carolrhoda Books, c1999. 48pp. (NF)

Tells the story of Pablo Picasso as he grows through his early days as an artist, his discovery of cubism, and his later years of sculpture and painting to become a famous artist.

Lucas, Eileen. *Vincent van Gogh.* Carolrhoda Books, c1997. 48pp. (NF)

Follows the life and artistic development of the painter who moved from Belgium and Holland to France, was influenced by Impressionism, and eventually created his own unique style.

Schaefer, A. R. *Grandma Moses.* Heinemann Library, c2003. 32pp. (NF)

Briefly examines the life and work of the twentieth-century American painter, describing and giving examples of her art.

From Nancy J. Keane, *The Big Book of Children's Reading Lists: 100 Great, Ready-to-Use Book Lists for Educators, Librarians, Parents, and Children.* Westport, CT: Libraries Unlimited, 2006. Copyright © 2006 by Libraries Unlimited.

Artists' Biographies

Slaymaker, Melissa Eskridge. ***Bottle Houses: The Creative World of Grandma Prisbrey.*** H. Holt, c2004. 32pp. (NF)
An introduction to the world of folk artist Grandma Prisbrey.

Stanley, Diane. ***Michelangelo.*** HarperCollins, c2000. 48pp. (NF)
A biography of the Renaissance sculptor, painter, architect, and poet, well known for his work on the Sistine Chapel in Rome's St. Peter's Cathedral.

Venezia, Mike. ***Andy Warhol.*** Children's Press, c1996. 32pp. (NF)
A simple biography of a man who helped develop pop art and made art fun for many people.

Wallner, Alexandra. ***Grandma Moses.*** Holiday House, c2004. 32pp. (NF)
A brief biography of Anna Mary Robertson, the artist who was known as Grandma Moses, describing the inspiration behind and development of her paintings.

Warhola, James. ***Uncle Andy's.*** Putnam, c2003. 32pp. (NF)
The author describes a trip to see his uncle, the soon-to-be-famous artist Andy Warhol, and the fun that he and his family had on the visit. (NF)

Winter, Jeanette. ***Beatrix: Various Episodes from the Life of Beatrix Potter.*** Farrar, Straus & Giroux, c2003. 62pp. (NF)
This simple biography of Beatrix Potter, best known for writing The tale of Peter Rabbit, includes excerpts from her published letters and journals and reveals why she drew and wrote about animals.

Winter, Jeanette. ***My Name Is Georgia: A Portrait.*** Silver Whistle/Harcourt Brace, c1998. 32pp. (NF)
Presents, in brief text and illustrations, the life of the painter who drew much of her inspiration from nature.

Winter, Jonah. ***Frida.*** Arthur A. Levine Books, 2002. 32pp. (NF)
Illustrations and simple text help chronicle the life of artist Magdalena Carmen Frida Kahlo, discussing how she learned to paint, how painting saved her life, and why her paintings are so unique.

Witteman, Barbara. ***Leonardo da Vinci.*** Bridgestone Books, c2004. 24pp. (NF)
Discusses the life, works, and lasting influence of Leonardo da Vinci.

Books for Children Ages 8–12

Bogart, Jo Ellen. ***Emily Carr: At the Edge of the World.*** Tundra Books, Tundra Books of Northern New York, c2003. 40pp. (NF)
Reproduces the paintings of Emily Carr and describes what the world was like in her lifetime.

From Nancy J. Keane, *The Big Book of Children's Reading Lists: 100 Great, Ready-to-Use Book Lists for Educators, Librarians, Parents, and Children.* Westport, CT: Libraries Unlimited, 2006. Copyright © 2006 by Libraries Unlimited.

Artists' Biographies

Butler, Jerry. ***A Drawing in the Sand: The Story of African American Art.*** Zino Press Children's Books, c1998. 63pp. (NF)

Describes Jerry Butler's development as an artist and his discovery of the long and beautiful tradition of African American art that preceded him.

Casey, Carolyn. ***Mary Cassatt: The Life of an Artist.*** Enslow, c2004. 48pp. (NF)

Discusses the life and the work of the Impressionist painter Mary Cassatt.

Greenberg, Jan. ***Romare Bearden: Collage of Memories.*** Harry N. Abrams, c2003. 52pp. (NF)

Recounts the life of the twentieth-century African-American collage artist whose bold and meaningful art was influenced by his Southern childhood, New York City, jazz, and Paris.

Igus, Toyomi. ***Going Back Home: An Artist Returns to the South.*** Children's Book Press, c1996. 32pp. (NF)

Narrative text describes the artist's paintings and their portrayal of the lives of her African American relatives in the rural American South.

Kucharczyk, Emily Rose. ***Georgia O'Keeffe: Desert Painter.*** Blackbirch Press, Thomson/Gale, c2002. 32pp. (NF)

Introduces the life of the painter whose fame came to rest in her large works from nature.

Langley, Andrew. ***Michelangelo.*** Raintree, c2003. 32pp. (NF)

Examines the life and accomplishments of sixteenth-century Italian sculptor and painter Michelangelo, with illustrations and photographs of his work.

Stanley, Diane. ***Leonardo da Vinci.*** Morrow Junior Books, c1996. 48pp. (NF)

A biography of the Italian Renaissance artist and inventor who, at about age thirty, began writing his famous notebooks, which contain the outpourings of his amazing mind.

Stanley, Diane. ***Michelangelo.*** HarperCollins, c2000. 48pp. (NF)

A biography of the Renaissance sculptor, painter, architect, and poet, well known for his work on the Sistine Chapel in Rome's St. Peter's Cathedral.

Woronoff, Kristen. ***Frida Kahlo: Mexican Painter.*** Blackbirch Press, Thomson/Gale, c2002. 32pp. (NF)

Examines the life of Mexican artist Frida Kahlo, discussing some of the many difficulties she endured throughout her life, including polio, a near-fatal bus accident, and her tempestuous marriage to fellow artist Diego Rivera.

From Nancy J. Keane, *The Big Book of Children's Reading Lists: 100 Great, Ready-to-Use Book Lists for Educators, Librarians, Parents, and Children.* Westport, CT: Libraries Unlimited, 2006. Copyright © 2006 by Libraries Unlimited.

Part 2

Character and Values

Managing Anger

Books for Children of All Ages

Agassi, Martine. ***Hands Are Not for Hitting.*** Free Spirit, c2000. 35pp. (NF)
Demonstrates that "hands are not for hitting" by suggesting many positive uses for them, such as saying hello, playing, creating, and helping.

Bang, Molly. ***When Sophie Gets Angry—: Really, Really Angry.*** Blue Sky Press, c1999. 36pp.
When Sophie gets angry, she goes outside and runs, cries, climbs her favorite tree—and then, calmed by the breeze, she is soon ready to go back home.

Barnes, Derrick D. ***Stop, Drop, and Chill.*** Scholastic, c2004. 32pp.
Rhyming words help a grade-schooler deal with his angry feelings in a more constructive way.

Brisson, Pat. ***The Summer My Father Was Ten.*** Boyds Mills Press, c1998. 32pp.
A father tells his daughter the story of how he damaged a neighbor's tomato garden when he was a boy and what he did to make amends.

Collins, Pat Lowery. ***Come Out, Come Out!*** Philomel Books, c2005. 32pp.
Hildy is so angry that she thinks she will hide from her family forever, but they manage to find her and make things right.

Ditta-Donahue, Gina. ***Josh's Smiley Faces: A Story About Anger.*** Magination Press, c2003. 31pp.
With the help of a smiley-face chart, Josh learns to express his anger appropriately.

Doudna, Kelly. ***I Feel Angry.*** Abdo, c1999. 24pp. (NF)
Describes some things that can make you angry and ways to deal with these feelings.

Frost, Helen. ***Feeling Angry.*** Pebble Books, 2000, c2001. 24pp. (NF)
Simple text and photographs describe and illustrate anger and ways to alleviate it.

Harris, Robie H. ***I'm So Mad!*** Little, Brown, c2005. 28pp.
A little girl and her mother enjoy shopping at the grocery store until the girl has a tantrum when her mother will not buy ice cream. Includes brief notes on handling a child's tantrums.

Johansen, Heidi Leigh. ***What I Look Like When I Am Angry.*** PowerStart Press, c2004. 24pp. (NF)
Describes what different parts of the face look like when a person is angry.

Johnston, Marianne. ***Dealing with Anger.*** PowerKids Press, c1996. 24pp. (NF)
A discussion of anger, including suggestions for ways to deal with it directly, channel it to something productive, and avoid its destructiveness.

Kroll, Steven. ***That Makes Me Mad!*** SeaStar Books, c2002. 32pp.
A little girl gets mad at a lot of things in her daily life but is comforted that her mother understands her anger.

Lachner, Dorothea. ***Andrew's Angry Words.*** North-South Books, 1997, c1995. 27pp.
When his sister trips and sends all his toys flying, Andrew lets loose a lot of nasty, angry words that start to spread from person to person, creating trouble wherever they go.

From Nancy J. Keane, *The Big Book of Children's Reading Lists: 100 Great, Ready-to-Use Book Lists for Educators, Librarians, Parents, and Children.* Westport, CT: Libraries Unlimited, 2006. Copyright © 2006 by Libraries Unlimited.

Managing Anger

Lachner, Dorothea. ***Danny, the Angry Lion.*** North-South Books, c2000. 28pp.
Danny turns into a prowling lion with a big appetite when he doesn't get the sausages and raspberry juice he wanted for lunch.

O'Neill, Alexis. ***The Recess Queen.*** Scholastic Press, c2002. 32pp.
Mean Jean is the biggest bully on the school playground, until a new girl arrives and challenges Jean's status as the Recess Queen.

Palatini, Margie. ***Goldie Is Mad.*** Hyperion Books for Children, c2001. 24pp.
A little girl is very upset when her baby brother drools on her doll, but during a time-out, she thinks of some of the things she likes about her brother.

Robberecht, Thierry. ***Angry Dragon.*** Clarion Books, 2004, c2003. 29pp.
A young boy is sometimes so angry that he becomes a dragon, turning red, spitting out angry words, and destroying everything in his path, but later he turns back into a boy and can feel his parents' love again.

Schami, Rafik. ***Fatima and the Dream Thief.*** North-South Books, c1996. 34pp.
Fatima accepts the challenge to work for the mean-tempered lord of the castle, who steals the dreams of anyone who becomes angry with him.

Spelman, Cornelia Maude. ***When I Feel Angry.*** Whitman, c2000. 24pp.
A little rabbit describes what makes her angry and the different ways she can control her anger.

Stadler, Alexander. ***Lila Bloom.*** Farrar, Straus & Giroux, 2004, c2003. 33pp.
Angry after a difficult day, Lila decides to quit ballet class, but reconsiders after she realizes that dancing makes her feel much better.

Vail, Rachel. ***Sometimes I'm Bombaloo.*** Scholastic, c2002. 32pp.
When Katie Honors feels angry and out of control, her mother helps her to be herself again.

Books for Children Ages 8–12

Althea. ***Feeling Angry.*** Gareth Stevens, c1998. 32pp. (NF)
Examines the nature, causes, and effects of anger and discusses how to deal with it.

Fox, Laura. ***I Am So Angry, I Could Scream: Helping Children Deal with Anger.*** Small Horizons, c2000. 46pp.
Penny's aunt, who is a school counselor, shows Penny how to control her anger by using an anger chart.

Guest, Jacqueline. ***A Goal in Sight.*** J. Lorimer (distributed in the United States by Orca Book Publishers), c2002. 113pp.
Having developed a reputation for being an enforcer both on and off the hockey rink, Aiden learns the value of controlling his anger when his bullying goes too far and he is placed on probation, assigned to do community service with a young blind boy.

Moser, Adolph. ***Don't Rant & Rave on Wednesdays!: The Children's Anger-Control Book.*** Landmark Editions, . c1994. 61pp. (NF)
Explains the causes of anger and offers methods to reduce anger children feel.

Poems About Anger. Benchmark Books, c2003. 32pp.
A collection of poetry and art by children describing their feelings about anger.

From Nancy J. Keane, *The Big Book of Children's Reading Lists: 100 Great, Ready-to-Use Book Lists for Educators, Librarians, Parents, and Children.* Westport, CT: Libraries Unlimited, 2006. Copyright © 2006 by Libraries Unlimited.

Compassion

Books for Children of All Ages

Fleming, Candace. ***Boxes for Katje.*** Farrar, Straus & Giroux, c2003. 34pp.
After a young Dutch girl writes to her new American friend in thanks for the care package sent after World War II, she begins to receive increasingly larger boxes.

Luttrell, William. ***Redheaded Robbie's Christmas Story.*** Sleeping Bear Press, c2003. 32pp.
Every time Robbie gets excited, his words come out all wrong, and when he is selected to write and tell a special Christmas story at the school assembly, he needs plenty of help from his friends.

McCourt, Lisa. ***Chicken Soup for Little Souls: A Dog of My Own.*** Health Communications, c1998. 32pp.
Ben rescues a dog who is afraid of everything and uses love and patience to win the dog's confidence and bring out his good qualities.

McCourt, Lisa. ***Chicken Soup for Little Souls: The Braids Girl.*** Health Communications, c1998. 32pp.
While helping Grandpa Mike do volunteer work at a shelter for less fortunate people, Izzy tries to figure out the best way to help a girl her own age who is staying there.

Myers, Christopher A. ***Wings.*** Scholastic Press, c2000. 40pp.
Ikarus Jackson, the new boy in school, is outcast because he has wings. But his resilient spirit inspires one girl to speak up for him, in this thought-provoking story about celebrating individuality.

Polacco, Patricia. ***Chicken Sunday.*** Philomel Books, c1992. 32pp.
To thank Miss Eula for her wonderful Sunday chicken dinners, three children sell decorated eggs to buy her a beautiful Easter hat.

Polacco, Patricia. ***Christmas Tapestry.*** Philomel Books, c2002. 48pp.
A tapestry that is being used to cover a hole in a church wall at Christmas brings together an elderly couple who were separated during World War II.

Polacco, Patricia. ***Thank You, Mr. Falker.*** Philomel Books, c1998. 40pp.
At first, Trisha loves school, but her difficulty learning to read makes her feel dumb, until, in the fifth grade, a new teacher helps her understand and overcome her problem.

Polacco, Patricia. ***Welcome Comfort.*** Philomel Books, c1999. 32pp.
Welcome Comfort, a lonely foster child, is assured by his friend the school custodian that there is a Santa Claus, but he does not discover the truth until one wondrous and surprising Christmas Eve.

Rylant, Cynthia. ***An Angel for Solomon Singer.*** Orchard Books, 1996, c1992. 30pp.
A lonely New York City resident finds companionship and good cheer at the Westway Cafe, where dreams come true.

From Nancy J. Keane, *The Big Book of Children's Reading Lists: 100 Great, Ready-to-Use Book Lists for Educators, Librarians, Parents, and Children.* Westport, CT: Libraries Unlimited, 2006. Copyright © 2006 by Libraries Unlimited.

Compassion

Tyler, Linda Wagner. ***The After-Christmas Tree.*** Viking Press, c1990. 32pp.
Family members take their Christmas tree into the back yard and decorate it with edible trimmings for the wild birds and animals.

Wojciechowski, Susan. ***The Christmas Miracle of Jonathan Toomey.*** Candlewick Press, 2002, c1995. 34pp.
The widow McDowell and her seven-year-old son Thomas ask the gruff Jonathan Toomey, the best wood-carver in the valley, to carve the figures for a Christmas crèche. Includes a reading on CD.

Books for Children Ages 8–12

Farrell, Donna. ***Cesar Chavez: With a Discussion of Compassion.*** Reading Challenge, c2004. 47pp. (NF)
Tells the life story of twentieth-century labor organizer Cesar Chavez, describing the recognition and benefits he brought to migrant farm workers in California and the rest of the United States.

Kerley, Barbara. ***Walt Whitman: Words for America.*** Scholastic Press, c2004. 42pp. (NF)
A biography of the American poet whose compassion led him to nurse soldiers during the Civil War, give voice to the nation's grief at Lincoln's assassination, and capture the true American spirit in verse.

Ludy, Mark. ***The Grump.*** Green Pastures. c2000. 32pp.
Grumpy Mr. Howlweister, a feared legend in the town of Dinkerwink, has his heart changed by the compassion and love of a little deaf girl.

Nichol, Barbara. ***Beethoven Lives Upstairs.*** Orchard Books, c1994. 48pp.
The letters that ten-year-old Christoph and his uncle exchange show how Christoph's feelings for Mr. Beethoven, the eccentric boarder who shares his house, change from anger and embarrassment to compassion and admiration.

Roberts, Ken. ***Past Tense.*** Douglas & McIntyre, c1994. 110pp.
Thirteen-year-old Max has always looked forward to Elspeth the clown's mysterious annual appearance on Halloween. One summer, when Elspeth suddenly appears to perform for a terminally ill friend, Max must confront questions of mortality, loyalty, and compassion.

Weston, Martha. ***Act I, Act II, Act Normal.*** Roaring Brook Press, c2003. 148pp.
Topher Blakely gets the lead in the eighth-grade play, but unfortunately the play is *Rumpelstiltskin,* the class bully picks on him relentlessly, and his beloved cat dies, all of which teaches him a lot about compassion, friendship, and life.

From Nancy J. Keane, *The Big Book of Children's Reading Lists: 100 Great, Ready-to-Use Book Lists for Educators, Librarians, Parents, and Children.* Westport, CT: Libraries Unlimited, 2006. Copyright © 2006 by Libraries Unlimited.

Dealing with Loss and Grief

Books for Children of All Ages

Aliki. ***The Two of Them.*** Mulberry Books, 1987, c1979. 30pp.
Describes the relationship of a grandfather and his granddaughter, from her birth to his death.

Buscaglia, Leo F. ***The Fall of Freddie the Leaf: A Story of Life for All Ages.*** Slack (distributed to the trade by H. Holt). 2002, c1982. 32pp.
As Freddie experiences the changing seasons along with his companion leaves, he learns about the delicate balance between life and death.

Clifton, Lucille. ***Everett Anderson's Goodbye.*** H. Holt, 1988, c1983. 26pp.
Everett Anderson has a difficult time coming to terms with his grief after his father dies.

De Paola, Tomie. ***Nana Upstairs & Nana Downstairs.*** Putnam, c1998. 32pp.
Four-year-old Tommy enjoys his relationship with both his grandmother and great-grandmother, but eventually he learns to face their inevitable deaths.

De Paola, Tomie. ***Now One Foot, Now the Other.*** Putnam, 2005, c1981. 48pp.
When his grandfather suffers a stroke, Bobby teaches him to walk, just as his grandfather had once taught him.

Durant, Alan. ***Always and Forever.*** Harcourt, 2004, c2003. 26pp.
A family of forest animals learns to cope with the death of a loved one.

Jukes, Mavis. ***Blackberries in the Dark.*** Dell Yearling, 2001, c1985. 58pp.
Nine-year-old Austin visits his grandmother the summer after his grandfather dies, and together they try to come to terms with their loss.

Maddern, Eric. ***Death in a Nut.*** Frances Lincoln Children's Books (distributed in the United States by Publishers Group West), c2005. 28pp.
Jack learns a valuable lesson about life when he tries to keep Old Man Death from taking his mother.

Mills, Joyce C. ***Gentle Willow: A Story for Children About Dying.*** Magination Press, c2004. 32pp.
Amanda the squirrel is upset that she is going to lose her friend Gentle Willow, but the tree wizards advise that both she and Gentle Willow should accept the change that comes with death.

Rylant, Cynthia. ***Cat Heaven.*** Blue Sky Press, c1997. 34pp.
God created Cat Heaven, with fields of sweet grass where cats can play, kitty-toys for them to enjoy, and angels to rub their noses and ears.

From Nancy J. Keane, *The Big Book of Children's Reading Lists: 100 Great, Ready-to-Use Book Lists for Educators, Librarians, Parents, and Children.* Westport, CT: Libraries Unlimited, 2006. Copyright © 2006 by Libraries Unlimited.

Dealing with Loss and Grief

Rylant, Cynthia. ***Dog Heaven.*** Blue Sky Press, c1995. 34pp.
God created Dog Heaven, a place where dogs can eat ice cream biscuits, sleep on fluffy clouds, and run through unending fields.

Schotter, Roni. ***In the Piney Woods.*** Farrar, Straus & Giroux, c2003. 32pp.
Grandpa and his granddaughter spend his last summer visiting and enjoying the pine woods near their house.

Spero, Moshe HaLevi. ***Saying Goodbye to Grandpa.*** Pitspopany, c1997. 63pp.
Teaches Jewish children about death through the story of a young boy whose grandfather, Zeydeh, dies.

Varley, Susan. ***Badger's Parting Gifts.*** Lothrop, Lee & Shepard, c1984. 25pp.
Badger's friends are sad when he dies, but they treasure the legacies he left them.

Viorst, Judith. ***The Tenth Good Thing About Barney.*** Atheneum Books for Young Readers, c1971. 25pp.
In an attempt to overcome his grief, a boy tries to think of the ten best things about his dead cat.

Wilhelm, Hans. ***I'll Always Love You.*** Crown, c1985. 31pp.
A child's sadness at the death of a beloved dog is tempered by the remembrance of saying to it every night, "I'll always love you."

Wood, Nancy C. ***Old Coyote.*** Candlewick Press, c2004. 26pp.
Realizing that he has come to the end of his days, Old Coyote recalls many of the good things about his life.

Books for Children Ages 8–12

Bredsdorff, Bodil. ***The Crow-Girl: The Children of Crow Cove.*** Farrar, Straus & Giroux, c2004. 155pp.
After the death of her grandmother, a young orphaned girl leaves her house by the cove and begins a journey, which leads her to people and experiences that exemplify the wisdom her grandmother had shared with her.

Carey, Janet Lee. ***Wenny Has Wings.*** Atheneum Books, c2002. 232pp.
Having had a near-death experience in the accident that killed his younger sister, eleven-year-old Will tries to cope with the situation by writing her letters.

Gilbert, Sheri L. ***The Legacy of Gloria Russell.*** Knopf (distributed by Random House), c2004. 218pp.
Twelve-year-old Billy James tries to come to terms with the sudden death of his best friend and learns about himself, his own family history, and life in his small hometown in the Ozark mountains.

From Nancy J. Keane, *The Big Book of Children's Reading Lists: 100 Great, Ready-to-Use Book Lists for Educators, Librarians, Parents, and Children.* Westport, CT: Libraries Unlimited, 2006. Copyright © 2006 by Libraries Unlimited.

Dealing with Loss and Grief

Grimes, Nikki. ***What Is Goodbye?*** Hyperion Books for Children, c2004. 64pp.
Alternating poems by a brother and sister convey their feelings about the death of their older brother and the impact it had on their family.

Hopkinson, Deborah. ***Bluebird Summer.*** Greenwillow Books, c2001. 32pp.
Gramps's farm isn't the same after Grandma's death, but slowly Mags and Cody work to recreate her spirit by bringing back some of the things she loved.

Kornblatt, Marc. ***Understanding Buddy.*** Margaret K. McElderry Books, c2001. 113pp.
When a new classmate stops speaking because of the sudden death of his mother, fifth-grader Sam tries to befriend him and risks destroying his relationship with his best friend Alex.

Rosen, Michael. ***Michael Rosen's Sad Book.*** Candlewick Press, 2005, c2004. 34pp.
A man tells about all the emotions that accompany his sadness over the death of his son, and how he tries to cope.

Stalfelt, Pernilla. ***The Death Book.*** Douglas & McIntyre (distributed in the United States by Publishers Group West), c2002. 27pp. (NF)
A discussion of death for children, explaining why people die, speculating on what happens after death, and exploring some of the feelings and activities that may occur after someone dies.

Wallace, Bill. ***No Dogs Allowed!*** Holiday House, c2004. 214pp.
Twelve-year-old Kristina, still struggling to come to terms with the death of her beloved horse, finds it difficult to accept the new dog she receives for her birthday.

Wiles, Debbie. ***Each Little Bird That Sings.*** Harcourt, c2005. 247pp.
Comfort Snowberger is well acquainted with death, because her family runs the funeral parlor in their small Southern town, but even so the ten-year-old is unprepared for the series of heart-wrenching events that begin on the first day of Easter vacation with the sudden death of her beloved great-uncle Edisto.

From Nancy J. Keane, *The Big Book of Children's Reading Lists: 100 Great, Ready-to-Use Book Lists for Educators, Librarians, Parents, and Children.* Westport, CT: Libraries Unlimited, 2006. Copyright © 2006 by Libraries Unlimited.

Friendship

Books for Children of All Ages

Grimes, Nikki. *Meet Danitra Brown.* Mulberry Books, 1997, c1994. 32pp.
A little girl introduces her best friend through a collection of thirteen poems.

Havill, Juanita. *Brianna, Jamaica, and the Dance of Spring.* Houghton Mifflin, c2002. 32pp.
When her sister Nikki gets sick, Brianna hopes to play her part as the butterfly queen in the Dance of Spring, but then another disaster strikes.

Hoban, Russell. a *Bargain for Frances.* HarperCollins, 1992, c1970. 62pp.
Frances foils Thelma's plot to trick her out of a new china set.

Hobbie, Holly. *Toot & Puddle.* Little, Brown, c1997. 32pp.
Toot and Puddle are best friends with very different interests, so when Toot spends the year traveling around the world, Puddle enjoys receiving his postcards.

Holabird, Katharine. *Angelina and Alice.* Pleasant Company Publications, c2001. 25pp.
Angelina and her best friend Alice discover the importance of teamwork when their acrobatics are the hit of the gymnastics show at the village fair.

Johnston, Tony. *Amber on the Mountain.* Puffin Books, 1998, c1994. 32pp.
Isolated on her mountain, Amber meets and befriends a girl from the city, who gives her the determination to learn to read and write.

Kellogg, Steven. *Best Friends.* Puffin Books, 1990, c1986. 32pp.
Kathy feels lonely and betrayed when her best friend goes away for the summer and has a wonderful time.

Parr, Todd. *The Best Friends Book.* Little, Brown, c2000. 26pp.
Illustrations and brief text describe how best friends treat each other.

Ryan, Pam Munoz. *Amelia and Eleanor Go for a Ride.* Scholastic, c1999. 44pp.
A fictionalized account of the night Amelia Earhart flew Eleanor Roosevelt over Washington, D.C. in an airplane.

Woodson, Jacqueline. *The Other Side.* Putnam, c2001. 32pp.
Two girls, one white and one African American, gradually get to know each other as they sit on the fence that divides their town.

Books for Children Ages 8–12

Bradby, Marie. *Some Friend.* Atheneum Books for Young Readers, c2004. 245pp.
Fifth-grader Pearl Jordan learns some difficult lessons about friendship when she befriends the odd but artistically talented Artemesia, then shuns her in favor of the popular Lenore.

Cox, Judy. *That Crazy Eddie: And the Science Project of Doom.* Holiday House, c2005. 88pp.
Best friends Matt and Eddie have a falling out that threatens to ruin their science fair project. Includes instructions for making a model of an erupting volcano.

From Nancy J. Keane, *The Big Book of Children's Reading Lists: 100 Great, Ready-to-Use Book Lists for Educators, Librarians, Parents, and Children.* Westport, CT: Libraries Unlimited, 2006. Copyright © 2006 by Libraries Unlimited.

Friendship

Dowell, Frances O'Roark. *The Secret Language of Girls.* Atheneum Books for Young Readers, c2004. 247pp.

Marylin and Kate have been friends since nursery school, but when Marylin becomes a middle school cheerleader and Kate begins to develop other interests, their relationship is put to the test.

Friedman, Laurie B. *Mallory on the Move.* Carolrhoda Books, c2004. 158pp.

After moving to a new town, eight-year-old Mallory keeps throwing stones in the "Wishing Pond," but things will not go back to the way they were before, and she remains torn between old and new best friends.

Marsden, Carolyn. *The Gold-Threaded Dress.* Candlewick Press, c2002. 73pp.

When Oy and her Thai American family move to a new neighborhood, her third-grade classmates tease and exclude her because she is different.

Matlin, Marlee. *Deaf Child Crossing.* Simon & Schuster Books for Young Readers, c2002. 200pp.

Despite the fact that Megan is deaf and Cindy can hear, the two girls become friends when Cindy moves into Megan's neighborhood, but when they go away to camp, their friendship is put to the test.

McKay, Hilary. *Permanent Rose.* Margaret K. McElderry Books, c2005. 234pp.

While trying to reconnect with her friend Tom, who has returned to the United States without leaving a forwarding address, eight-year-old Rose inadvertently discovers the identity of her adopted sister Saffy's father.

Myracle, Lauren. *Eleven.* Dutton Children's Books, c2004. 201pp.

The year between turning eleven and turning twelve brings many changes for Winnie and her friends.

Sateren, Shelley Swanson. *Cat on a Hottie's Tin Roof: A Novel.* Delacorte Press, c2003. 196pp.

Sixth-grader Cat tries to hide the fact that she is a good student to make friends with Cassidy, but when a third girl who likes the same music and fashions as Cassidy comes on the scene, Cat is afraid she will lose her new friend.

Schumacher, Julie. *Grass Angel.* Delacorte Press, c2004. 196pp.

Rather than go to a spiritual retreat in Oregon with her mother and brother, eleven-year-old Frances insists on staying in Ohio with her odd aunt, but she soon begins to worry that the retreat may really be a cult.

Shreve, Susan Richards. *Trout and Me.* Dell Yearling, 2004, c2002. 135pp.

Ben's troubles at school get progressively worse when he starts hanging around Trout, a new boy in his fifth-grade class, who is also labeled as learning disabled.

Stauffacher, Sue. *Donuthead.* Knopf (distributed by Random House), c2003. 144pp.

Franklin Delano Donuthead, a fifth-grader obsessed with hygiene and safety, finds an unlikely friend and protector in Sarah Kervick, the tough new student who lives in a dirty trailer, bonds with his mother, and is as "irregular" as Franklin is.

Van Draanen, Wendelin. *Swear to Howdy.* Knopf (distributed by Random House), c2003. 126pp.

Two thirteen-year-old boys share neighborhood adventures, complaints about their older sisters, family secrets, and even guilt, which binds them together in a special friendship.

Yee, Lisa. *Millicent Min, Girl Genius.* Arthur A. Levine Books, c2003. 248pp.

In a series of journal entries, eleven-year-old child prodigy Millicent Min records her struggles to learn to play volleyball, tutor her enemy, deal with her grandmother's departure, and make friends, over the course of a tumultuous summer.

From Nancy J. Keane, *The Big Book of Children's Reading Lists: 100 Great, Ready-to-Use Book Lists for Educators, Librarians, Parents, and Children.* Westport, CT: Libraries Unlimited, 2006. Copyright © 2006 by Libraries Unlimited.

Honesty

Books for Children of All Ages

Brown, Marc Tolon. ***Arthur and the True Francine.*** Little, Brown, c1996. 32pp.
Francine and Muffy are good friends, until Muffy lets Francine take the blame for cheating on a test.

Carlson, Nancy L. ***Harriet and the Garden.*** Carolrhoda Books, c2004. 32pp.
Harriet feels terrible after accidentally trampling a neighbor's garden and ruining her prize dahlia, until she confesses and sets things right.

De Groat, Diane. ***Liar, Liar, Pants on Fire.*** SeaStar Books, c2003. 32pp.
Gilbert is nervous about portraying George Washington in front of the class, and he feels even worse when he cannot find his main prop.

Demi. ***The Empty Pot.*** H. Holt, c1990. 32pp.
When Ping admits that he is the only child in China unable to grow a flower from the seeds distributed by the Emperor, he is rewarded for his honesty.

Eriksson, Eva. ***Molly Goes Shopping.*** R&S Books, c2003. 26pp.
Little Molly learns about the importance of honesty after lying to her grandmother instead of admitting she forgot which item to buy at the store.

Gutman, Anne. ***Lisa in the Jungle.*** Knopf (distributed by Random House), c2003. 26pp.
Although she spent the summer at the community swimming pool, Lisa tells her classmates that she visited the jungle, where her uncle raises panthers and leopards.

Schecter, Ellen. ***The Boy Who Cried "Wolf!"*** Gareth Stevens. c1997. 32pp.
Uses rebuses to retell the Aesop fable about a young boy whose false cries for help bring him to an unfortunate end.

Sharmat, Marjorie Weinman. ***A Big Fat Enormous Lie.*** Puffin Books, 1986, c1978. 32pp.
A child's simple lie grows to enormous proportions.

Stevens, Janet. ***Jackalope.*** Harcourt, c2003. 52pp.
A jackrabbit who wishes to be feared asks his fairy godrabbit for horns and becomes the first jackalope, but there's one condition: he must not tell lies.

Books for Children Ages 8–12

Bawden, Nina. ***Humbug.*** Clarion Books, c1992. 133pp.
When eight-year-old Cora is sent to stay next door with the seemingly pleasant woman called Aunt Sunday, she is tormented by Aunt Sunday's mean-spirited, deceitful daughter, but finds an ally in Aunt Sunday's elderly mother.

From Nancy J. Keane, *The Big Book of Children's Reading Lists: 100 Great, Ready-to-Use Book Lists for Educators, Librarians, Parents, and Children.* Westport, CT: Libraries Unlimited, 2006. Copyright © 2006 by Libraries Unlimited.

Honesty

Bowen, Fred. ***Winners Take All.*** Peachtree, c2000. 104pp.
When Kyle fakes a catch, his baseball team goes on to win the league championship, but Kyle doesn't feel good about winning by cheating. Includes a section on the sportsmanship of Christy Mathewson, a pitcher who played professional baseball in the early 1900s.

Greenburg, Dan. ***Tell a Lie and Your Butt Will Grow.*** Grosset & Dunlap, c2002. 58pp.
Zack's science fair partner, Andrew, has always boasted and told lies, but now each time Andrew fibs his butt gets bigger, and Zack must find a way to help before their science project is destroyed.

Greene, Stephanie. ***Owen Foote, Super Spy.*** Clarion Books, c2001. 90pp.
Owen and his friends decide that spying on the school principal at his own house will be a fun challenge.

Hershey, Mary. ***My Big Sister Is So Bossy She Says You Can't Read This Book.*** Wendy Lamb Books, c2005. 164pp.
Ten-year-old Effie, bursting with secrets since her best friend moved leaving her without a confidante, tries to deal with her problems on her own, certain there is no help to be found in her big sister, Maxey.

Hurwitz, Johanna. ***The Cold & Hot Winter.*** Morrow Junior Books, c1988. 132pp.
Fifth-grader Derek and his best friend Rory are delighted when their neighbor's niece Bolivia comes to town for another visit, until a lot of missing objects make Derek begin to doubt Rory's honesty. Sequel to *The Hot & Cold Summer.*

Kline, Suzy. ***Mary Marony and the Chocolate Surprise.*** Putnam, c1995. 85pp.
Mary decides it's all right to cheat to make sure she wins a special lunch with her favorite teacher, but the results of her dishonesty end up surprising the whole second-grade class.

Korman, Gordon. ***Liar, Liar, Pants on Fire.*** Scholastic, 1999, c1997. 86pp.
Zoe, an imaginative third-grader, thinks that she has to make things up to be interesting, until a good friend and an eagle convince her that she does not have to lie to be special.

Kramer, Barbara. ***Dave Thomas: Honesty Pays.*** Enslow, c2005. 48pp. (NF)
Examines the life of Dave Thomas, founder of the Wendy's hamburger restaurants, discussing his childhood, his success in the restaurant business, his devotion to the cause of adoption, and his policy of honesty.

Lewis, Barbara A. ***Being Your Best: Character Building for Kids 7–10.*** Free Spirit, c2000. 165pp. (NF)
Text, anecdotes, and activities introduce and discuss how to build important character traits, such as caring, citizenship, cooperation, courage, fairness, honesty, respect, and responsibility.

From Nancy J. Keane, *The Big Book of Children's Reading Lists: 100 Great, Ready-to-Use Book Lists for Educators, Librarians, Parents, and Children.* Westport, CT: Libraries Unlimited, 2006. Copyright © 2006 by Libraries Unlimited.

Importance of Reading

Books for Children of All Ages

Bradby, Marie. ***More Than Anything Else.*** Orchard Books, c1995. 32pp.
Nine-year-old Booker works with his father and brother at the saltworks but dreams of the day when he'll be able to read.

Conover, Chris. ***The Lion's Share.*** Farrar, Straus & Giroux, 2003, c2000. 32pp.
With the help of two animal fishermen, a young winged lion learns to read, to love books, and to fly properly.

Deedy, Carmen Agra. ***The Library Dragon.*** Peachtree, c1994. 32pp.
Miss Lotta Scales is a dragon who believes her job is to protect the school's library books from the children, but when she finally realizes that books are meant to be read, the dragon turns into Miss Lotty, librarian and storyteller.

Duvoisin, Roger. ***Petunia.*** Dragonfly Books, 2002, c1950. 32pp.
Petunia, the goose, learns that possessing knowledge involves more than just carrying a book around under her wing.

Ernst, Lisa Campbell. ***Stella Louella's Runaway Book.*** Simon & Schuster Books for Young Readers, c1998. 34pp.
As she tries to find the book that she must return to the library that day, Stella gathers a growing group of people who have all enjoyed reading the book.

Fox, Mem. ***A Bedtime Story.*** Mondo, c1996. 24pp.
Polly and her friend Bed Rabbit have lots of books, but they don't know how to read, so Polly's parents interrupt their own reading for a bedtime story.

Heide, Florence Parry. ***The Day of Ahmed's Secret.*** Mulberry Books, 1995, c1990. 32pp.
Ahmed rides his donkey cart throughout the city of Cairo, hurrying to finish his work, so he can return home and share his secret with his family.

Hest, Amy. ***Mr. George Baker.*** Candlewick Press, c2004. 25pp.
Harry sits on the porch with Mr. George Baker, an African American who is 100 years old but can still dance and play the drums. They are waiting for the school bus that will take them both to the class where they are learning to read.

Johnston, Tony. ***Amber on the Mountain.*** Puffin Books, 1998, c1994. 32pp.
Isolated on her mountain, Amber meets and befriends a girl from the city, who gives her the determination to learn to read and write.

From Nancy J. Keane, *The Big Book of Children's Reading Lists: 100 Great, Ready-to-Use Book Lists for Educators, Librarians, Parents, and Children.* Westport, CT: Libraries Unlimited, 2006. Copyright © 2006 by Libraries Unlimited.

Importance of Reading

McGill, Alice. ***Molly Bannaky.*** Houghton Mifflin, c1999. 32pp.
Relates how Benjamin Banneker's grandmother journeyed from England to Maryland in the late seventeenth century, worked as an indentured servant, began a farm of her own, and married a freed slave.

McPhail, David. ***Edward and the Pirates.*** Little, Brown, c1997. 32pp.
Once Edward has learned to read, books and his vivid imagination provide him with great adventures.

Mora, Pat. ***Tomas and the Library Lady.*** Knopf (distributed by Random House), c1997. 32pp.
While helping his family in their work as migrant laborers far from their home, Tomas finds an entire world to explore in the books at the local public library.

Numeroff, Laura Joffe. ***Beatrice Doesn't Want To.*** Candlewick Press, c2004. 32pp.
On the third afternoon of going to the library with her brother Henry, Beatrice finally finds something she enjoys doing.

Parr, Todd. ***Reading Makes You Feel Good.*** Little, Brown, c2005. 32pp. (NF)
Describes the characteristics and various advantages of reading.

Polacco, Patricia. ***Aunt Chip and the Great Triple Creek Dam Affair.*** Philomel Books, c1996. 40pp.
Aunt Chip saves the town of Triple Creek, where everyone has forgotten how to read because of the invasion of television.

Polacco, Patricia. ***Thank You, Mr. Falker.*** Philomel Books, c1998. 40pp.
At first Trisha loves school, but her difficulty learning to read makes her feel dumb, until, in the fifth grade, a new teacher helps her understand and overcome her problem.

Rylant, Cynthia. ***Poppleton.*** Scholastic, c1997. 48pp.
Poppleton the pig makes a friend, reads a library book about adventure, and helps a sick friend get better.

Smet, Marian De. ***Anna's Tight Squeeze.*** Tiger Tales, c2003. 28pp.
Anna makes a new friend and discovers reading is a good way to pass the time when she gets locked in the bathroom at the library.

Smothers, Ethel Footman. ***The Hard-Times Jar.*** Farrar, Straus & Giroux, c2003. 32pp.
Emma, the daughter of poor migrant workers, longs to own a real book, and when she turns eight and must attend school for the first time, she is amazed to discover a whole library in her classroom.

Wells, Rosemary. ***Bunny Cakes.*** Viking Press, 2002, c1997. 26pp.
Max makes an earthworm cake for Grandma's birthday and helps Ruby with her angel surprise cake. At the store, the grocer can't read the entire shopping list, until Max solves the problem by drawing a picture.

From Nancy J. Keane, *The Big Book of Children's Reading Lists: 100 Great, Ready-to-Use Book Lists for Educators, Librarians, Parents, and Children.* Westport, CT: Libraries Unlimited, 2006. Copyright © 2006 by Libraries Unlimited.

Manners

Books for Children of All Ages

Aliki. *Manners.* Greenwillow Books, c1990. 32pp. (NF)
Discusses manners and gives examples of good and bad manners.

Allen, Kathryn Madeline. *This Little Piggy's Book of Manners.* H. Holt, c2003. 32pp.
Some little pigs remember their manners, and others do not.

Bloom, Becky. *Leo and Lester.* Mondo, 2003, c2002. 32pp.
When Leo the raccoon and Lester the hippopotamus go to town, Leo has the challenging job of monitoring Lester's manners.

Bloom, Suzanne. *Piggy Monday: A Tale about Manners.* Whitman, 2001. 32pp.
The children in Mrs. Hubbub's class are so rude and thoughtless one day that they turn into pigs and need the help of the Pig Lady to help them remember their manners.

Cole, Babette. *Lady Lupin's Book of Etiquette.* Peachtree, c2002. 32pp.
Lady Lupin undertakes the education of her puppies in the art of manners.

Cosgrove, Stephen. *The Grumpling.* Price Stern Sloan, c2003. 32pp.
Buttermilk Bunny baked all night to prepare special cookies and crumpets, only to have the ill-mannered and uninvited Grumpling stuff them all into his mouth. Then Buttermilk devised a way to teach the rude bear some manners.

Curtis, Jamie Lee. *It's Hard to Be Five: Learning How to Work My Control Panel.* Joanna Cotler Books, c2004. 30pp.
A child finds that learning to have self-control is hard, but it can also be fun.

Cuyler, Margery. *Please Say Please!: Penguin's Guide to Manners.* Scholastic, c2004. 32pp.
Penguin teaches his animal friends how to behave when they are invited for dinner.

DeGezelle, Terri. *Manners in the Classroom.* Capstone Press, c2005. 24pp. (NF)
Describes good manners and shows how different character values can be used in the classroom.

DeGezelle, Terri. *Manners on the Playground.* Capstone Press, c2005. 24pp. (NF)
Explains to children the importance of kindness, respectfulness, patience, and other qualities on the playground and includes instructions for the English game Tig.

Edwards, Pamela Duncan. *Rude Mule.* Holt, c2002. 25pp.
A rude mule learns that he has more fun when he uses good manners.

From Nancy J. Keane, *The Big Book of Children's Reading Lists: 100 Great, Ready-to-Use Book Lists for Educators, Librarians, Parents, and Children.* Westport, CT: Libraries Unlimited, 2006. Copyright © 2006 by Libraries Unlimited.

Manners

Gibbs, Lynne. ***Don't Slurp Your Soup!*** McGraw-Hill Children's Publishing, 2003, c2002. 29pp. (NF)
Explains to youngsters the components of and reasons for good manners, covering table manners, introductions, letter writing, phone and e-mail etiquette, being a host, attending parties, good sportsmanship, and other related topics.

Holyoke, Nancy. ***Oops!: The Manners Guide for Girls.*** Pleasant Company Publications, c1997. 116pp. (NF)
An introduction to socially acceptable conduct in all sorts of situations.

Kopelke, Lisa. ***Excuse Me!*** Simon & Schuster Books for Young Readers, c2003. 32pp.
A frog who loves to burp learns the value of good manners.

Levin, Bridgette. ***Rules of the Wild: An Unruly Book of Manners.*** Chronicle Books, c2004. 30pp.
Rhyming text explores how proper behavior for young animals is different from what is expected of young children.

Roberts, Bethany. ***Monster Manners.*** Clarion Books, c1996. 32pp.
Three little monsters demonstrate good and bad manners, proving that even though they don't always show it, they can behave.

Tryon, Leslie. ***Patsy Says.*** Atheneum Books for Young Readers, c2001. 32pp.
Patsy Pig is determined to teach Ms. Klingensmith's first-grade class some manners before their parents come to the Open House.

Willems, Mo. ***Time To Say Please!*** Hyperion Books for Children, c2005.
Presents a children's book and board game on why it is important to say "please."

Ziefert, Harriet. ***Someday We'll Have Very Good Manners.*** Putnam, c2001. 28pp.
Characters discuss what they know about good manners and how they will have them some day, but for now they are "just kids."

Books for Children Ages 8–12

Cooney, Doug. ***I Know Who Likes You.*** Simon & Schuster Books for Young Readers, c2004. 217pp.
When Swimming Pool's mother insists she graduate from charm school or give up baseball, Ernie, who is the reluctant team manager, and Dusty, the catcher, pull together to help the team and their friend.

Holyoke, Nancy. ***Oops!: The Manners Guide for Girls.*** Pleasant Company Publications, c1997. 116pp. (NF)
An introduction to socially acceptable conduct in all sorts of situations.

Polisar, Barry Louis. ***Don't Do That!: A Child's Guide to Bad Manners, Ridiculous Rules, and Inadequate Etiquette.*** Rainbow Morning Music (distributed by Independent Publishers Group), c1994. 32pp. (NF)
A humorous introduction to good manners and behavior in relation to home and school activities.

From Nancy J. Keane, *The Big Book of Children's Reading Lists: 100 Great, Ready-to-Use Book Lists for Educators, Librarians, Parents, and Children.* Westport, CT: Libraries Unlimited, 2006. Copyright © 2006 by Libraries Unlimited.

Overcoming Perfectionism

Books for Children of All Ages

De Paola, Tomie. ***Meet the Barkers: Morgan and Moffat Go to School.*** Putnam, c2001. 32pp.
Bossy Moffie and her quiet twin brother Morgie both enjoy starting school, especially getting gold stars and making new friends.

Graves, Keith. ***Loretta: Ace Pinky Scout.*** Scholastic, c2002. 32pp.
Loretta, unrelenting perfectionist, is devastated when she fails to earn the Golden Marshmallow Badge, but her grandmother's picture gives her a new perspective on things.

Harris, Peter. ***Perfect Prudence.*** Gingham Dog Press, c2003. 28pp.
Prudence, just perfect at everything, is cast in every single role of the school play, and things are of course going perfectly until she discovers she has made one big mistake.

Manes, Stephen. ***Be a Perfect Person in Just Three Days!*** Clarion Books, c1982. 76pp.
Milo, tired of problems with his sister, parents, and classmates, finds a book in the library that promises to make him perfect in just three days.

Moss, Marissa. ***Regina's Big Mistake.*** Houghton Mifflin, c1990. 28pp.
When told to draw a jungle in art class, Regina experiences feelings of failure and creative insecurity, but manages to create a beautiful picture that's all her own.

Simon, Norma. ***Nobody's Perfect, Not Even My Mother.*** Whitman, c1981. 32pp.
A young child learns that nobody's perfect, yet people can be wonderful just the same.

Books for Children Ages 8–12

Becker, Bonny. ***My Brother, the Robot.*** Dutton Children's Books, c2001. 136pp.
When his father buys a SIMON Robot, advertised as "the perfect son," Chip decides that he can't compete with his new brother, but in the end, the whole family learns that perfection may not be so great after all.

Mills, Claudia. ***Perfectly Chelsea.*** Farrar, Straus & Giroux, c2004. 119pp.
Nine-year-old Chelsea's experiences, which include a fight with her best friend, making mistakes in the handbell concert, and saying goodbye to the only church minister she has ever known, help her to accept that things change and that people, including herself, are not perfect.

Smith, Anne Warren. ***Turkey Monster Thanksgiving.*** Whitman, c2003. 103pp.
When her perfectionist classmate and neighbor plans an elaborate Thanksgiving dinner, Katie begins to wonder if the relaxed day she, her father, and her messy little brother usually enjoy means they are not a "real" family.

Walters, Eric. ***Long Shot.*** Orca, c2001. 140pp.
Nick and Kia's new basketball coach is a strict disciplinarian with aggressive coaching techniques who expects near perfection and does not deal well with anything less.

From Nancy J. Keane, *The Big Book of Children's Reading Lists: 100 Great, Ready-to-Use Book Lists for Educators, Librarians, Parents, and Children.* Westport, CT: Libraries Unlimited, 2006. Copyright © 2006 by Libraries Unlimited.

Perseverance

Books for Children of All Ages

Bianco, Margery Williams. *The Velveteen Rabbit, Or, How Toys Become Real.* Doubleday, c1922. 44pp.
By the time the velveteen rabbit is dirty, worn out, and about to be burned, he has almost given up hope of ever finding the magic called Real.

Blume, Judy. *The One in the Middle Is the Green Kangaroo.* Atheneum Books for Young Readers, c1991. 32pp.
Freddy hates being the middle one in the family, until he gets a part in the school play.

Burton, Virginia Lee. *Katy and the Big Snow.* Houghton Mifflin, c1971. 36pp.
Katy is a crawler tractor who saves the city when it is snowed in by a blizzard.

Cosgrove, Stephen. *Dragolin.* Price Stern Sloan, c1995. 32pp.
Short, plump, and unable to breathe fire like the other dragons, Dragolin is in despair, until he learns the importance of believing in oneself.

Cosgrove, Stephen. *The Grumpling.* Price Stern Sloan, c2003. 32pp.
Buttermilk Bunny baked all night to prepare special cookies and crumpets, only to have the ill-mannered and uninvited Grumpling stuff them all into his mouth; then Buttermilk devised a way to teach the rude bear some manners.

Forest, Heather. *Stone Soup.* August House LittleFolk, c1998. 32pp.
Two hungry travelers use a stone as a soup starter and demonstrate the benefits of sharing. Includes a recipe for soup.

Kroll, Steven. *The Biggest Pumpkin Ever.* Holiday House, c1984. 32pp.
Two mice, each without the other's knowledge, help a pumpkin grow into "the biggest pumpkin ever"—but for different purposes.

Piper, Watty, pseud. *The Little Engine That Could.* Platt & Munk, c1990. 43pp.
When the other engines refuse, the Little Blue Engine tries to pull a stranded train full of toys and good food over the mountain.

Seuss, Dr. *The 500 Hats of Bartholomew Cubbins.* Random House, c1965. 47pp.
Each time Bartholomew Cubbins attempts to obey the king's order to take off his hat, he finds there is another one on his head.

Seuss, Dr. *The Lorax.* Random House, c1971. 64pp.
The Once-ler describes the results of the local pollution problem.

Seuss, Dr. *The Sneetches: And Other Stories.* Random House, c1989. 65pp.
A collection of four humorous fantasies, told in rhyme.

Silverstein, Shel. *The Giving Tree.* HarperCollins, c1964. 57pp.
A young boy grows to manhood and old age experiencing the love and generosity of a tree, which gives to him without thought of return.

From Nancy J. Keane, *The Big Book of Children's Reading Lists: 100 Great, Ready-to-Use Book Lists for Educators, Librarians, Parents, and Children.* Westport, CT: Libraries Unlimited, 2006. Copyright © 2006 by Libraries Unlimited.

Perseverance

Udry, Janice May. ***What Mary Jo Shared.*** Whitman, c1966. 32pp.
Mary Jo is faced with the problem of what to bring to "show and tell" at school.

Viorst, Judith. ***Alexander, Who Used to Be Rich Last Sunday.*** Atheneum, c1978. 32pp.
Although Alexander and his money are quickly parted, he comes to realize all the things that can be done with a dollar.

Ward, Lynd. ***The Biggest Bear.*** Houghton Mifflin, 1988, c1952. 84pp.
Johnny goes hunting for a bearskin to hang on his family's barn and returns with a small bundle of trouble.

Wells, Rosemary. ***Timothy Goes to School.*** Viking Press, c2000. 32pp.
Timothy learns about being accepted and making friends during the first week of his first year at school.

Books for Children Ages 8–12

Fritz, Jean. ***The Cabin Faced West.*** Putnam's, c1958. 124pp.
Ten-year-old Ann overcomes loneliness and learns to appreciate the importance of her role in settling the wilderness of western Pennsylvania.

Gilson, Jamie. ***Do Bananas Chew Gum?*** Beech Tree Books, c1997. 158pp.
Able to read and write at only a second-grade level, sixth-grader Sam Mott considers himself dumb, until he is prompted to cooperate with those who think something can be done about his problem.

Konigsburg, E. L. ***From the Mixed-Up Files of Mrs. Basil E. Frankweiler.*** Atheneum Books for Young Readers, c1967. 162pp.
Two suburban children run away from their Connecticut home and go to New York's Metropolitan Museum of Art, where their ingenuity enables them to live in luxury.

O'Brien, Robert C. ***Mrs. Frisby and the Rats of NIMH.*** Atheneum, c1971. 233pp.
With nowhere else to turn, a field mouse asks the clever escaped lab rats living under the rosebush to help save her son, who lies in the path of the farmer's tractor, too ill to be moved.

Sachs, Marilyn. ***Veronica Ganz.*** Puffin Books, 1995, c1968. 134pp.
Thirteen-year-old Veronica manages to bully everyone in her class, except for shrimpy Peter Wedemeyer, who keeps taunting and outsmarting her at every opportunity.

Sperry, Armstrong. ***Call It Courage.*** Macmillan, c1968. 95pp.
Based on a Polynesian legend, this is the story of a youth who overcomes his fear of the sea and proves his courage to himself and his tribe.

White, E. B. ***The Trumpet of the Swan.*** HarperCollins, 2000, c1970. 251pp.
A voiceless trumpeter swan named Louis, attempting to win the love of a beautiful swan named Serena, learns to play a trumpet stolen for him by his father. He finds himself far from his wilderness home when he sets out to become a trumpeter and pay his father back.

From Nancy J. Keane, *The Big Book of Children's Reading Lists: 100 Great, Ready-to-Use Book Lists for Educators, Librarians, Parents, and Children.* Westport, CT: Libraries Unlimited, 2006. Copyright © 2006 by Libraries Unlimited.

Responsibility

Books for Children of All Ages

Brisson, Pat. ***The Summer My Father Was Ten.*** Boyds Mills Press, c1998. 32pp.
A father tells his daughter the story of how he damaged a neighbor's tomato garden when he was a boy and what he did to make amends.

Brown, Marc Tolon. ***Arthur's New Puppy.*** Little, Brown, c1993. 30pp.
Arthur's new puppy causes problems when it tears the living room apart, wets on everything, and refuses to wear a leash; later, Buster wonders if he has made an archaeological discovery when he finds a very interesting bone.

Hassett, John. ***Cat up a Tree.*** Houghton Mifflin, c1998. 28pp.
With rapidly increasing numbers of cats stuck in her tree, Nana Quimby asks for help from the firehouse, the police, the pet shop, the zoo, the library, and even city hall, but no one will help rescue the cats.

Henkes, Kevin. ***Lilly's Purple Plastic Purse.*** Greenwillow Books, c1996. 32pp.
Lilly loves everything about school, especially her teacher, but when he asks her to wait a while before showing the class her new purse, she does something for which she is very sorry later.

James, Simon. ***Sally and the Limpet.*** Candlewick Press, c2002. 26pp.
While exploring on the beach, Sally gets a limpet stuck to her finger, and no one can help her get it off.

Joyce, William. ***Bently & Egg.*** Laura Geringer Book, c1992. 32pp.
A shy, singing frog is left in charge of a very special egg that changes his life.

Levitin, Sonia. ***Taking Charge.*** Orchard Books, c1999. 32pp.
When her mother has to leave home suddenly, Amanda learns how demanding it is to run a household and care for a baby.

Lewin, Betsy. ***What's the Matter, Habibi?*** Clarion Books, c1997. 29pp.
One day, instead of following Ahmed around in a circle giving children rides, Habibi the camel runs through the bazaar, with Ahmed following him and trying to figure out what is wrong.

McKissack, Pat. ***The Honest-to-Goodness Truth.*** Atheneum Books for Young Readers, c2000. 32pp.
After promising never to lie, Libby learns that it's not always necessary to blurt out the whole truth, either.

From Nancy J. Keane, *The Big Book of Children's Reading Lists: 100 Great, Ready-to-Use Book Lists for Educators, Librarians, Parents, and Children.* Westport, CT: Libraries Unlimited, 2006. Copyright © 2006 by Libraries Unlimited.

Responsibility

Books for Children Ages 8–12

Graeber, Charlotte Towner. ***Fudge.*** Pocket Books, 1988, c1987. 123pp.
Chad's parents agree to let him take the puppy, Fudge, on a trial basis, if he takes care of her.

McDonald, Megan. ***Judy Moody Declares Independence.*** Candlewick Press, c2005. 144pp.
After learning about the American Revolution on a family trip to Boston, Judy Moody makes her own Declaration of Independence and tries to prove that she is responsible enough to have more freedoms, such as a larger allowance and her own bathroom.

Nix, Garth. ***Grim Tuesday.*** Scholastic, 2005, c2004. 321pp.
Seventh-grader Arthur Penhaligon returns to the parallel universe known as the House to fight his latest enemy, Grim Tuesday, whose greed threatens to destroy both the House and the Earth.

Peters, Stephanie True. ***All Keyed Up.*** Little, Brown, c2002. 50pp.
When his soccer teammate and new friend Stookie asks him to take care of his gerbils while he is on vacation, Jerry is happy to agree, but then disaster strikes.

Sachar, Louis. ***Marvin Redpost: Alone in His Teacher's House.*** Random House, c1994. 83pp.
Marvin is pleased when his teacher asks him to take care of her dog while she's away, but he soon finds that there's more pressure involved than he likes.

Wesley, Valerie Wilson. ***How to Lose Your Class Pet.*** Jump at the Sun/Hyperion Books for Children, c2003. 88pp.
When third-grader Willimena loses the class pet, her teacher helps her to understand that responsibility means doing one's best, and that animals can't always be controlled.

From Nancy J. Keane, *The Big Book of Children's Reading Lists: 100 Great, Ready-to-Use Book Lists for Educators, Librarians, Parents, and Children.* Westport, CT: Libraries Unlimited, 2006. Copyright © 2006 by Libraries Unlimited.

Self-Esteem

Books for Children of All Ages

Beaumont, Karen. ***I Like Myself!*** Harcourt, c2004. 32pp.
In rhyming text, a child expresses her self-esteem and exults in her unique identity.

Blume, Judy. ***The One in the Middle Is the Green Kangaroo.*** Atheneum Books for Young Readers, c1991. 32pp.
Freddy hates being the middle one in the family, until he gets a part in the school play.

Carlson, Nancy L. ***I Like Me!*** Viking Kestrel, c1988. 32pp.
By admiring her finer points and showing that she can take care of herself and have fun even when there's no one else around, a charming pig proves the best friend you can have is yourself.

De Paola, Tomie. ***Oliver Button Is a Sissy.*** Harcourt Brace, c1979. 48pp.
His classmates' taunts don't stop Oliver Button from doing what he likes best.

Henkes, Kevin. ***Chrysanthemum.*** Greenwillow Books, c1991. 32pp.
Chrysanthemum loves her name, until she starts going to school and the other children make fun of it.

Henkes, Kevin. ***Lilly's Purple Plastic Purse.*** Greenwillow Books, c1996. 32pp.
Lilly loves everything about school, especially her teacher, but when he asks her to wait a while before showing the class her new purse, she does something for which she is very sorry later.

Kraus, Robert. ***Leo the Late Bloomer.*** Windmill (distributed by HarperCollins), c1971. 32pp.
Leo, a young tiger, finally blooms under the anxious eyes of his parents.

Books for Children Ages 8–12

Birdseye, Tom. ***Just Call Me Stupid.*** Holiday House, c1993. 181pp.
Terrified of failing and believing that he is stupid, a fifth grader who has never learned to read begins to believe in himself, with the help of an outgoing new girl next door.

Codell, Esme Raji. ***Sahara Special.*** Hyperion Books for Children, c2003. 175pp.
Struggling with school and her feelings since her father left, Sahara gets a fresh start with a new and unique teacher who supports her writing talents and the individuality of each of her classmates.

Danziger, Paula. ***I, Amber Brown.*** Putnam, c1999. 140pp.
Because her divorced parents share joint custody of her, nine-year-old Amber suffers from lack of self-esteem and feels that she is a piece of jointly owned property.

Graves, Keith. ***Down in the Dumps with the 3 Nasty Gnarlies: (Featuring Snooty Judy Butterfly).*** Scholastic, c2003. 33pp.
In an effort to improve their cleanliness and appearance, three nasty gnarlies follow a butterfly's advice.

Korman, Gordon. ***Liar, Liar, Pants on Fire.*** Scholastic, 1999, c1997. 86pp.
Zoe, an imaginative third-grader, thinks that she has to make things up to be interesting, until a good friend and an eagle convince her that she does not have to lie to be special.

Seidler, Tor. ***Brothers Below Zero.*** Laura Geringer Books, c2002. 137pp.
Having lived for years in the shadow of his younger, more talented brother, middle schooler Tim takes painting lessons from his beloved Great Aunt Winifred and discovers that he is a gifted artist.

From Nancy J. Keane, *The Big Book of Children's Reading Lists: 100 Great, Ready-to-Use Book Lists for Educators, Librarians, Parents, and Children.* Westport, CT: Libraries Unlimited, 2006. Copyright © 2006 by Libraries Unlimited.

Part 3

Genres and Themes

Animal ABC

Books for Children of All Ages

Cassie, Brian. ***The Butterfly Alphabet Book.*** Charlesbridge, c1995. 32pp. (NF)
Introduces butterflies from A to Z, describing their distinctive features while highlighting each letter of the alphabet.

Dodson, Peter. ***An Alphabet of Dinosaurs.*** Scholastic, c1995. 72pp. (NF)
Illustrations and text present information on the physical appearance and eating habits of twenty-six dinosaurs.

The Dog: From Arf! Arf! to Zzzzzz. HarperCollins, c2004. 32pp. (NF)
Presents twenty-six amusing color photos of a wide variety of dog breeds, accompanied by simple dog-related words or phrases, one for each letter of the alphabet.

Edwards, Wallace. ***Alphabeasts.*** Kids Can Press, c2002. 32pp.
Introduces the letters of the alphabet through short verses about the animal inhabitants of a remarkable old house.

Fleming, Denise. ***Alphabet Under Construction.*** H. Holt, c2002. 32pp.
A mouse works his way through the alphabet as he folds the "F," measures the "M," and rolls the "R."

Gag, Wanda. The ***ABC Bunny.*** University of Minnesota Press, 2004, c1933. 38pp. (NF)
A children's alphabet rhyming book that follows Bunny from Bunnyland to Elsewhere and describes what he eats and the friends he meets.

Grossman, Bill. ***My Little Sister Hugged An Ape.*** Knopf (distributed by Random House), c2004. 44pp.
Little sister is on a hugging spree, out to hug a different animal for every letter of the alphabet.

Hoena, B. A. ***Dog's ABC: An Alphabet Book.*** Capstone Press, c2005. 32pp. (NF)
Introduces dogs through photographs and brief texts that use one word relating to dog for each letter of the alphabet.

Knox, Barbara. ***Animal Babies ABC: An Alphabet of Animal Offspring.*** Capstone Press, c2003. 32pp. (NF)
Introduces baby animals through photographs and text that describe one animal for each letter of the alphabet.

Most, Bernard. ***ABC T-Rex.*** Harcourt, c2000. 34pp.
A young T-rex loves his ABCs so much that he eats them up, experiencing for each letter a word that begins with that letter.

Pallotta, Jerry. ***The Beetle Alphabet Book.*** Charlesbridge, c2004. 32pp. (NF)
Uses letters of the alphabet to introduce various kinds of beetles.

Smith, Marie. ***Z Is for Zookeeper: A Zoo Alphabet.*** Sleeping Bear Press, Thomson/Gale, c2005. 40pp. (NF)
A children's A to Z alphabet picture book that describes the various animals and other things found in a zoo.

Thornhill, Jan. ***The Wildlife ABC & 123: A Nature Alphabet & Counting Book.*** Maple Tree Press (distributed by Publishers Group West), c2004. 64pp. (NF)
An alphabet book and a counting book featuring illustrations of animals.

From Nancy J. Keane, *The Big Book of Children's Reading Lists: 100 Great, Ready-to-Use Book Lists for Educators, Librarians, Parents, and Children.* Westport, CT: Libraries Unlimited, 2006. Copyright © 2006 by Libraries Unlimited.

Food ABC

Books for Children of All Ages

Azarian, Mary. ***A Gardener's Alphabet.*** Houghton Mifflin, c2000. 32pp. (NF)
An alphabet book featuring words associated with gardening, including bulbs, compost, digging, insects, and weeds.

Banks, Kate. ***Alphabet Soup.*** Knopf (distirbuted by Random House), 1994, c1988. 25pp.
A boy's ability to spell words with his alphabet soup comes in handy during the magical journey he takes in his mind with a friendly bear.

Dahl, Michael. ***Chewy Chuckles: Deliciously Funny Jokes About Food.*** Picture Window Books, c2003. 24pp.
An easy-to-read collection of riddles about strawberries, alphabet soup, and other foods.

Doering, Amanda. ***Food ABC: An Alphabet Book.*** Capstone Press, c2005. 32pp. (NF)
Introduces food through photographs and brief text that uses one word relating to food for each letter of the alphabet.

Dragonwagon, Crescent. ***Alligator Arrived with Apples: A Potluck Alphabet Feast.*** Aladdin Paperbacks, 1992, c1987. 40pp.
From Alligator's apples to Zebra's zucchini, a multitude of alphabetical animals and foods celebrate Thanksgiving with a grand feast.

Ehlert, Lois. ***Eating the Alphabet: Fruits and Vegetables from A to Z.*** Harcourt Brace, c1989. 34pp. (NF)
An alphabetical tour of the world of fruits and vegetables, from apricot and artichoke to yam and zucchini.

Gustafson, Scott. ***Alphabet Soup: A Feast of Letters.*** Greenwich Workshop, c1994. 44pp.
A host of animals from A to Z come to Otter's housewarming party, bringing a wide variety of foods for his alphabetical soup.

Kalman, Maira. ***What Pete Ate from A-Z: Where We Explore the English Alphabet (In Its Entirety) in Which a Certain Dog Devours a Myriad of Items Which He Should Not.*** Putnam, c2001. 40pp.
In this alphabet book, a child relates some of the unusual things eaten by Pete the dog, including an accordion, a lucky quarter, and Uncle Norman's underpants.

Pallotta, Jerry. ***The Spice Alphabet Book: Herbs, Spices, and Other Natural Flavors.*** Charlesbridge. c1994. 32pp. (NF)
An alphabet book of herbs and spices, from Anise to Zatar.

From Nancy J. Keane, *The Big Book of Children's Reading Lists: 100 Great, Ready-to-Use Book Lists for Educators, Librarians, Parents, and Children.* Westport, CT: Libraries Unlimited, 2006. Copyright © 2006 by Libraries Unlimited.

Food ABC

Richard, David. ***My Whole Food A B C's.*** Vital Health Publishing. c1997. 28pp. (NF)
A collection of rhymes about whole foods—one for each letter of the alphabet.

Schuette, Sarah L. ***An Alphabet Salad: Fruits and Vegetables from A to Z.*** Capstone Press, c2003. 32pp. (NF)
Introduces fruits and vegetables through photographs and brief text that describe one item for each letter of the alphabet.

Sloat, Teri. ***Patty's Pumpkin Patch.*** Putnam, c1999. 30pp.
Rhyming text and illustrations featuring the letters from A to Z follow Patty as she plants pumpkins and watches them grow.

Watson, Clyde. ***Applebet: An ABC.*** Farrar, Straus & Giroux, 1987, c1982. 32pp.
Short verses introduce scenes from a fair in which letters of the alphabet figure prominently.

Whitehouse, Patricia. ***Food ABC.*** Heinemann Library, c2002. 24pp.
An alphabet book presenting information on the various colors and qualities of different kinds of food.

From Nancy J. Keane, *The Big Book of Children's Reading Lists: 100 Great, Ready-to-Use Book Lists for Educators, Librarians, Parents, and Children.* Westport, CT: Libraries Unlimited, 2006. Copyright © 2006 by Libraries Unlimited.

Nature ABC

Books for Children of All Ages

Azarian, Mary. ***A Gardener's Alphabet.*** Houghton Mifflin, c2000. 32pp. (NF)
An alphabet book featuring words associated with gardening, including bulbs, compost, digging, insects, and weeds.

Diebel, Lynne Smith. ***ABCs Naturally: A Child's Guide to the Alphabet Through Nature.*** Trail Books, c2003.32pp. (NF)
A collection of photographs in which elements of nature are used to form the letters of the alphabet.

Doering, Amanda. ***A Rain Forest ABC: An Alphabet Book.*** Capstone Press, c2005. 32pp. (NF)
An alphabet book that helps preschool children learn their letters while also learning about the plants and animals that live in rain forests.

Grassby, Donna. ***A Seaside Alphabet.*** Tundra Books of Northern New York, c2000. 32pp. (NF)
Teaches young readers the alphabet by means of simple text and pictures of the coasts of Maine, Nova Scotia, and Prince Edward Island.

Hoena, B. A. ***A Desert ABC: An Alphabet Book.*** Capstone Press, c2005. 32pp. (NF)
Contains an alphabet book that helps preschool children learn their letters while also learning about plants and animals that live in deserts.

Hoena, B. A. ***Farms ABC: An Alphabet Book.*** Capstone Press, c2005. 32pp. (NF)
Photographs and brief text describe a word used on a farm for each letter of the alphabet.

Hoena, B. A. ***Weather ABC: An Alphabet Book.*** Capstone, c2005. 32pp. (NF)
Introduces weather through photographs and brief text that uses one word relating to weather for each letter of the alphabet.

Knox, Barbara. ***ABC Under the Sea: An Ocean Life Alphabet Book.*** Capstone Press, c2003. 32pp. (NF)
Introduces ocean creatures through photographs and brief text that describe one animal for each letter of the alphabet.

Kratter, Paul. ***The Living Rain Forest: An Animal Alphabet.*** Charlesbridge, c2004. 57pp. (NF)
Introduces twenty-six rain forest animals from A to Z, providing the name, favorite foods, and unique characteristics of each.

From Nancy J. Keane, *The Big Book of Children's Reading Lists: 100 Great, Ready-to-Use Book Lists for Educators, Librarians, Parents, and Children.* Westport, CT: Libraries Unlimited, 2006. Copyright © 2006 by Libraries Unlimited.

Nature ABC

Maurer, Tracy. ***A to Z of Autumn.*** Rourke Press. c2003. 32pp. (NF)
Illustrations and simple text present a variety of things seen in the fall.

Maurer, Tracy. ***A to Z of Spring.*** Rourke Press. c2003. 32pp. (NF)
Presents an alphabet of spring activities.

Maurer, Tracy. ***A to Z of Summer.*** Rourke Press, c2003. 32pp. (NF)
Illustrations and simple text present an alphabet of things to see and do in the summer.

Maurer, Tracy. ***A to Z of Winter.*** Rourke Press, c2003. 32pp. (NF)
Illustrations and simple text present an alphabet of things to see and do in the winter.

McGehee, Claudia. ***A Tallgrass Prairie Alphabet.*** University of Iowa Press, c2004. 32pp. (NF)
Contains twenty-six scratchboard illustrations of plants and animals that once lived in the tallgrass prairies of America's heartland, each of which corresponds to a letter of the alphabet.

Miller, Jane. ***Farm Alphabet Book.*** Scholastic, c2000. 32pp. (NF)
Photographs of farm animals and objects, accompanied by simple descriptions, illustrate the letters of the alphabet.

Rose, Deborah Lee. ***Into the A, B, Sea: An Ocean Alphabet.*** Scholastic, c2000. 40pp. (NF)
Features twenty-six animals found in the ocean and includes endnotes giving additional details about each of these sea creatures.

Whitehouse, Patricia. ***Plant ABC.*** Heinemann Library, c2002. 24pp. (NF)
Introduces the letters of the alphabet while providing information about various plants. Includes photographs.

Whitehouse, Patricia. ***Seasons A B C.*** Heinemann Library, c2003. 24pp. (NF)
An alphabet book that features items associated with particular seasons, such as fall, when apples are picked, and summer, when it is hot and people eat ice cream.

Wisnewski, Andrea. ***A Cottage Garden Alphabet.*** D. Godine, c2002. 62pp. (NF)
Pictures and text associate some aspect of cottage gardening with each letter of the alphabet.

From Nancy J. Keane, *The Big Book of Children's Reading Lists: 100 Great, Ready-to-Use Book Lists for Educators, Librarians, Parents, and Children.* Westport, CT: Libraries Unlimited, 2006. Copyright © 2006 by Libraries Unlimited.

Silly ABC

Books for Children of All Ages

Dodd, Emma. ***Dog's ABC: A Silly Story About the Alphabet.*** Dutton Children,s Books, 2002, c2000. 32pp.

Dog finds an alphabet's worth of adventure as he patrols his neighborhood.

The Dog: From Arf! Arf! to Zzzzzz. HarperCollins, c2004. 32pp.

Presents twenty-six amusing color photos of a wide variety of dog breeds, accompanied by simple dog-related words or phrases, one for each letter of the alphabet.

Edwards, Wallace. ***Alphabeasts.*** Kids Can Press, c2002. 32pp.

Introduces the letters of the alphabet through short verses about the animal inhabitants of a remarkable old house.

Gerstein, Mordicai. ***The Absolutely Awful Alphabet.*** Harcourt Brace, c1999. 32pp.

An alliterative alphabet book presenting mean and monstrous letters, from A (an awfully arrogant amphibian) to Z (a zig-zagging zoological zany).

Hepworth, Catherine. ***Antics!: An Alphabetical Anthology.*** Putnam, c1992. 32pp.

Alphabet entries from A to Z all have an "ant" somewhere in the word, such as E for Enchanter, P for Pantaloons, S for Santa Claus, and Y for Your Ant Yetta.

Lester, Mike. ***A Is for Salad.*** Putnam & Grosset, c2000. 32pp.

Each letter of the alphabet is presented in an unusual way, such as: "A is for salad," showing an alligator eating a bowl of greens.

Macdonald, Ross. ***Achoo! Bang! Crash!: The Noisy Alphabet.*** Roaring Brook Press, c2003. 32pp.

Words about sound and noise illustrate the letters of the alphabet.

Seuss, Dr. ***Dr. Seuss's ABC.*** Beginner Books, c1991. 63pp.

An alphabet book filled with funny creatures.

Van Allsburg, Chris. ***The Alphabet Theatre Proudly Presents the Z Was Zapped: A Play in Twenty-Six Acts.*** Houghton Mifflin, c1987. 56pp.

Depicts how A was in an avalanche, B was badly bitten, C was cut to ribbons, and the other letters of the alphabet suffered similar mishaps.

From Nancy J. Keane, *The Big Book of Children's Reading Lists: 100 Great, Ready-to-Use Book Lists for Educators, Librarians, Parents, and Children.* Westport, CT: Libraries Unlimited, 2006. Copyright © 2006 by Libraries Unlimited.

U.S. ABC

Books for Children of All Ages

Bannatyne-Cugnet, Jo. ***A Prairie Alphabet.*** Tundra, c1992. 32pp. (NF)
Text and illustrations of the prairie in an alphabet book for children and an art book for adults.

Bellefontaine, Kim. ***ABC of America.*** Kids Can Press, c2004. 32pp. (NF)
An illustrated alphabet book in which American places, symbols, and traditions are used to describe each letter.

Bowen, Betsy. ***Antler, Bear, Canoe: A Northwoods Alphabet Year.*** Houghton, Mifflin, c1991. 32pp. (NF)
Introduces the letters of the alphabet in woodcut illustrations and brief text depicting the changing seasons in the northern woods.

Butler, Dori Hillestad. ***ABCs of Wisconsin.*** Trails Books, c2000. 32pp. (NF)
Showcases the joys of everyday life in Wisconsin while teaching the letters of the alphabet.

Cheney, Lynne V. ***America: A Patriotic Primer.*** Simon & Schuster Books for Young Readers, c2002. 40pp. (NF)
Each letter of the alphabet is represented by important people, ideas, and events in the history of the United States.

Chial, Debra. ***M Is for Minnesota.*** Voyageur Press, c1994. 32pp. (NF)
Each letter of the alphabet serves to highlight special features, places, and people of Minnesota. Includes a list of interesting facts about the state.

Cummings, Priscilla. ***Chesapeake ABC.*** Tidewater Publishers, c2000. 24pp. (NF)
An illustrated alphabet story in which each letter provides information about a different feature of the Chesapeake Bay area.

Dartez, Cecilia Casrill. ***L Is for Louisiana.*** Pelican. c2002. 32pp. (NF)
An alphabet book featuring words and photographs from Louisiana, such as alligators, bayous, and steamboats.

Golembe, Carla. ***M Is for Maryland: An Alphabet Picture Book About Maryland.*** VSP Books, c2000. 30pp. (NF)
An illustrated alphabet book that celebrates the many attractions of the State of Maryland.

From Nancy J. Keane, *The Big Book of Children's Reading Lists: 100 Great, Ready-to-Use Book Lists for Educators, Librarians, Parents, and Children.* Westport, CT: Libraries Unlimited, 2006. Copyright © 2006 by Libraries Unlimited.

U.S. ABC

Golembe, Carla. ***Washington, DC ABC's: An Alphabet Picture Book About Our Nation's Capital.*** VSP Books, c2001. 32pp. (NF)

Presents the letters of the alphabet accompanied by color artwork and descriptions of places and things that shape the capital city of the United States, such as "A" for "Archives" and "S" for "Smithsonian."

Grimes, Nikki. ***C Is for City.*** Wordsong/Boyds Mills Press, 2002. 40pp. (NF)

Rhyming verses describe different aspects of life in a city, featuring each letter of the alphabet. Includes a complete list of all objects and actions featured in the illustrations that begin with the particular letter of the alphabet.

Helman, Andrea. ***C Is for Coyote: A Southwest Alphabet Book.*** Rising Moon, c2002. 32pp. (NF)

Photographs and simple text provide an alphabetical profile of the animals, plants, and places of the Southwest.

Hoena, B. A. ***A Desert ABC: An Alphabet Book.*** Capstone Press, c2005. 32pp. (NF)

An alphabet book that helps preschool children learn their letters while also learning about plants and animals that live in deserts.

Kreeger, Charlene. ***Alaska ABC Book.*** Paws IV Publishing. c1978. 32pp. (NF)

An alphabet book describing life in Alaska, from caribou and Eskimos to the northern lights and zero temperatures.

McGehee, Claudia. ***A Tallgrass Prairie Alphabet.*** University of Iowa Press, c2004. 32pp. (NF)

Contains twenty-six scratchboard illustrations of plants and animals that once lived in the tallgrass prairies of America's heartland, each of which corresponds to a letter of the alphabet.

Medley, Steven P. ***Antelope, Bison, Cougar: A National Park Wildlife Alphabet Book.*** Yosemite Association, c2001. 62pp. (NF)

An alphabet book designed to teach children about the different kinds of wild mammals, birds, and other creatures that live in various sites throughout the U.S. national park system.

Melmed, Laura Krauss. ***Capital!: Washington, D.C. from A to Z.*** HarperCollins, c2003. 42pp. (NF)

Rhyming text and illustrations present the sights of Washington, D.C. from A to Z.

From Nancy J. Keane, *The Big Book of Children's Reading Lists: 100 Great, Ready-to-Use Book Lists for Educators, Librarians, Parents, and Children.* Westport, CT: Libraries Unlimited, 2006. Copyright © 2006 by Libraries Unlimited.

U.S. ABC

Pack, Linda Hager. ***A Is for Appalachia: The Alphabet Book of Appalachian Heritage.*** Harmony House, 2003, c2002. 44pp. (NF)

Text and illustrations associate each letter of the alphabet with an aspect of the heritage of the Appalachian Region; for example, "B" is for baskets, and "C" is for coal.

Parker, Laurie. ***Louisiana Alphabet.*** Quail Ridge Press, c2001. 32pp. (NF)

Illustrations and the letters of the alphabet describe various aspects of Louisiana's history, people, animals, and culture.

Parker, Laurie. ***Mississippi Alphabet.*** Quail Ridge Press, c1998. 32pp. (NF)

An alphabet book about things in or relating to Mississippi, from azaleas and armadillos to Yazoo and the great Jackson zoo.

Reynolds, Jeff E. ***United States of America.*** Children's Press, c2004. 40pp. (NF)

An A to Z alphabet book on the history and culture of the United States; includes information on important and historic cities and landmarks; traditional Native American, Amish, and colonial dress; exports; and important people in American history.

Rice, James. ***Texas Alphabet.*** Pelican. c1988. 40pp. (NF)

Introduces words and names, from A to Z, significant to Texas history, beginning with Austin and concluding with Lorenzo De Zavala.

Schroeder, Holly. ***The United States ABCs: A Book About the People and Places of the United States of America.*** Picture Window Books, c2004. 32pp. (NF)

An alphabetical exploration of the people, geography, animals, plants, history, and culture of the United States.

Wagner, Jay. ***H Is for Hawkeye.*** Trails Books, c2003. 32pp. (NF)

Colorful illustrations and the alphabet teach young readers about Iowa.

Weaver, Dorothy Hines. ***California A to Z.*** Rising Moon, c1999. 29pp. (NF)

Presents fascinating facts about California, representing each letter of the alphabet, from amusement parks to zebra perch zipping by Zuma Beach.

Wolfe, Art. ***O Is for Orca: A Pacific Northwest Alphabet Book.*** Sasquatch Books, c1995. 32pp. (NF)

Simple text and illustrations introduce the characteristics of various animals, people and areas found in the Pacific Northwest.

From Nancy J. Keane, *The Big Book of Children's Reading Lists: 100 Great, Ready-to-Use Book Lists for Educators, Librarians, Parents, and Children.* Westport, CT: Libraries Unlimited, 2006. Copyright © 2006 by Libraries Unlimited.

Regional/World ABC

Books for Children of All Ages

Berge, Ann. ***Russia ABCs: A Book About the People and Places of Russia.*** Picture Window Books, c2004. 32pp. (NF)

An alphabetical exploration of the people, geography, animals, plants, history, and culture of Russia.

Chester, Jonathan. ***A Is for Antarctica.*** Tricycle Press, c1995. 32pp. (NF)

A photographic dictionary of words about Antarctica.

Chin-Lee, Cynthia. ***A Is for Asia.*** Orchard Books, c1997. 32pp. (NF)

An alphabetical introduction to the diverse peoples, lands, and cultures of the world's largest continent.

Fontes, Justine. ***Brazil.*** Children's Press, c2003. 40pp. (NF)

Explores the history, geography, economy, people, culture, and other aspects of Brazil, featuring a topic for each letter of the alphabet.

Fontes, Justine. ***China.*** Children's Press, c2003. 40pp. (NF)

Explores the history, geography, economy, people, culture, and other aspects of China, featuring a topic for each letter of the alphabet.

Fontes, Justine. ***India.*** Children's Press, c2003. 40pp. (NF)

Explores the history, geography, economy, people, culture, and other aspects of India, featuring a topic for each letter of the alphabet.

Fontes, Justine. ***Israel.*** Children's Press, c2003. 40pp. (NF)

Explores the history, geography, economy, people, culture, and other aspects of Israel, featuring a topic for each letter of the alphabet.

Fontes, Justine. ***Italy.*** Children's Press, c2003. 40pp. (NF)

Explores the history, geography, economy, people, culture, and other aspects of Italy, featuring a topic for each letter of the alphabet.

Fontes, Justine. ***Kenya.*** Children's Press, c2003. 40pp. (NF)

Explores the history, geography, economy, people, culture, and other aspects of Kenya, featuring a topic for each letter of the alphabet.

Fontes, Justine. ***Mexico.*** Children's Press, c2003. 40pp. (NF)

Contains twenty-six entries—one for each letter of the alphabet—that provide information about different aspects of Mexico, from animals to zapatos, or shoes.

Fontes, Justine. ***Russia.*** Children's Press, c2003. 40pp. (NF)

Explores the history, geography, economy, people, culture, and other aspects of Russia, featuring a topic for each letter of the alphabet.

From Nancy J. Keane, *The Big Book of Children's Reading Lists: 100 Great, Ready-to-Use Book Lists for Educators, Librarians, Parents, and Children.* Westport, CT: Libraries Unlimited, 2006. Copyright © 2006 by Libraries Unlimited.

Regional/World ABC

Haugen, Brenda. ***Canada ABCs: A Book About the People and Places of Canada.*** Picture Window Books, c2004. 32pp. (NF)

An alphabetical exploration of the people, geography, animals, plants, history, and culture of Canada.

Heiman, Sarah. ***Australia ABCs: A Book About the People and Places of Australia.*** Picture Window Books, c2003. 31pp. (NF)

An alphabetical exploration of the people, geography, animals, plants, history, and culture of Australia.

Heiman, Sarah. ***Egypt ABCs: A Book About the People and Places of Egypt.*** Picture Window Books, c2003. 31pp. (NF)

An alphabetical exploration of the people, geography, animals, plants, history, and culture of Egypt.

Heiman, Sarah. ***Germany ABCs: A Book About the People and Places of Germany.*** Picture Window Books, c2003. 28pp. (NF)

An alphabetical exploration of the people, geography, animals, plants, history, and culture of Germany.

Hieman, Sara. ***Japan ABCs: A Book About the People and Places of Japan.*** Picture Window Books, c2003. 31pp. (NF)

An alphabetical exploration of the people, geography, animals, plants, history, and culture of Japan.

Heiman, Sara. ***Kenya ABCs: A Book About the People and Places of Kenya.*** Picture Window Books, c2003. 31pp. (NF)

An alphabetical exploration of the people, geography, animals, plants, history, and culture of Kenya.

Heiman, Sarah. ***Mexico ABCs: A Book About the People and Places of Mexico.*** Picture Window Books, c2003. 31pp. (NF)

An alphabetical explanation of the people, geography, animals, plants, history, and culture of Mexico. Includes directions for making crepe paper flowers and "Fun phrases in Spanish."

Onyefulu, Ifeoma. ***A Is for Africa.*** Puffin, 1997, c1993. 32pp. (NF)

The author, a member of the Igbo tribe in Nigeria, presents text and her own photographs of twenty-six things, from A to Z, representative of all African peoples.

Schroeder, Holly. ***China ABCs: A Book About the People and Places of China.*** Picture Window Books, c2004. 32pp. (NF)

An alphabetical exploration of the people, geography, animals, plants, history, and culture of China.

Schroeder, Holly. ***Israel ABCs: A Book About the People and Places of Israel.*** Picture Window Books, c2004. 32pp. (NF)

Each letter of the alphabet is represented by illustrations and information related to Israel.

Schroeder, Holly. ***New Zealand ABCs: A Book About the People and Places of New Zealand.*** Picture Window Books, c2004. 32pp. (NF)

An alphabetical exploration of the people, geography, animals, plants, history, and culture of New Zealand.

From Nancy J. Keane, *The Big Book of Children's Reading Lists: 100 Great, Ready-to-Use Book Lists for Educators, Librarians, Parents, and Children.* Westport, CT: Libraries Unlimited, 2006. Copyright © 2006 by Libraries Unlimited.

Cumulative Stories

Books for Children of All Ages

Bell, Babs. ***The Bridge Is Up!*** HarperCollins, c2004. 32pp.
In this cumulative story, a traffic jam is created when everyone has to wait for the bridge to come down.

Brisson, Pat. ***Benny's Pennies.*** Dell Dragonfly Books, c2002, c1993. 32pp.
Benny sets off in the morning with five shiny new pennies to spend and eventually buys something for his mother, brother, sister, dog, and cat.

Burningham, John. ***Mr. Gumpy's Outing.*** H. Holt, 1990, c1970. 32pp.
Mr. Gumpy accepts more and more riders on his boat, until the inevitable occurs.

Carle, Eric. ***Today Is Monday.*** Philomel Books, c1993. 25pp.
Each day of the week brings a new food, until on Sunday all the world's children can come and eat it up.

Cole, Henry. ***Jack's Garden.*** Greenwillow Books, c1995. 25pp.
Cumulative text and illustrations depict what happens in Jack's garden after he plants his seeds.

Crummel, Susan Stevens. ***All in One Hour.*** Marshall Cavendish, c2003. 40pp.
In this cumulative rhyming story, a cat runs after a mouse in the middle of the night, giving rise to a more complicated chase.

Fearnley, Jan. ***A Perfect Day for It.*** Harcourt, c2002. 33pp.
Bear announces that it's "a perfect day for it" and his friends follow him up the mountain, each imagining what special treat they might share there, but all come to agree that Bear's "it" is just right.

Garriel, Barbara S. ***I Know a Shy Fellow Who Swallowed a Cello.*** Boyds Mills Press, c2004. 32pp.
An adaptation of the folk rhyme "There was an old woman who swallowed a fly," featuring musical instruments.

Harley, Bill. ***Sitting Down to Eat.*** August House LittleFolk, c1996. 32pp.
In this cumulative story, a young boy agrees to share his snack with an ever-growing menagerie of animals, each insisting that there is room for one more.

Jackson, Alison. ***I Know an Old Lady Who Swallowed a Pie.*** Dutton Children's Books, c1997. 32pp.
A cumulative rhyme in which an old lady who comes for Thanksgiving swallows her pie before dinner is served, and continues to eat until she has gobbled down the entire feast, pot and all.

From Nancy J. Keane, *The Big Book of Children's Reading Lists: 100 Great, Ready-to-Use Book Lists for Educators, Librarians, Parents, and Children.* Westport, CT: Libraries Unlimited, 2006. Copyright © 2006 by Libraries Unlimited.

Cumulative Stories

Kimmel, Eric A. ***The Old Woman and Her Pig.*** Holiday House, c1992. 32pp.
When her newly bought pig won't go over the stile, an old woman tries to enlist the aid of some reluctant helpers so that she can get home that night.

Lewis, Kevin. ***The Lot At the End of My Block.*** Hyperion Books for Children, c2001. 32pp.
A cumulative story about the construction of a building, beginning with an empty lot at the end of the block and ending with a new house and neighbors.

Lobel, Arnold. ***The Rose in My Garden.*** Mulberry Books, 1993, c1984. 40pp.
Various flowers grow near the hollyhocks that give shade to the bee that sleeps on the only rose in a garden.

Oxenbury, Helen. ***It's My Birthday.*** Candlewick Press, 1996, c1993. 32pp.
The birthday child's animal friends bring ingredients and help him make a birthday cake.

Polacco, Patricia. ***In Enzo's Splendid Gardens.*** Philomel Books, c1997. 32pp.
A cumulative rhyme that describes the uproarious chain of events that ensue when a waiter trips over a book dropped by a boy watching a bee.

Taback, Simms. ***This Is the House That Jack Built.*** Puffin Books, 2004, c2002. 27pp.
Jack sets out to build a house like no other and fill it with wild and wacky objects.

Waber, Bernard. ***Bearsie Bear and the Surprise Sleepover Party.*** Houghton Mifflin, c1997. 40pp.
In a cumulative story, one animal after another asks to come in out of the winter cold to sleep in Bearsie Bear's big bed.

Waddell, Martin. ***The Pig in the Pond.*** Candlewick Press, 1996, c1992. 32pp.
An overheated pig who doesn't swim throws himself into a pond, throwing the farmyard into an uproar.

West, Colin. ***"Have You Seen the Crocodile?"*** Candlewick Press, 1999, c1986. 24pp.
A group of animal friends look for the cunning crocodile, little realizing that he is right under their noses.

Westcott, Nadine Bernard. ***I Know an Old Lady Who Swallowed a Fly.*** Little, Brown, c2004. 28pp.
A cumulative folk song in which the solution proves worse than the predicament when an old lady swallows a fly.

From Nancy J. Keane, *The Big Book of Children's Reading Lists: 100 Great, Ready-to-Use Book Lists for Educators, Librarians, Parents, and Children.* Westport, CT: Libraries Unlimited, 2006. Copyright © 2006 by Libraries Unlimited.

Memoirs

Books for Children of All Ages

Carling, Amelia Lau. ***Mama & Papa Have a Store.*** Dial Books for Young Readers, c1998. 32pp.
A little girl describes what a day is like in her parents' Chinese store in Guatemala City.

Cooney, Barbara. ***Miss Rumphius.*** Viking Press, c1982. 32pp.
After making her girlhood dreams of world travel and living by the sea come true, a retired librarian follows her grandfather's advice to do something to make the world more beautiful, and then passes that wisdom on to her grandniece.

Curtis, Jamie Lee. ***When I Was Little: A Four-Year-Old's Memoir of Her Youth.*** HarperCollins, c1993. 32pp.
A four-year-old describes how she has changed since she was a baby.

De Paola, Tomie. ***26 Fairmount Avenue.*** Putnam, c1999. 56pp.
Children's author-illustrator Tomie De Paola describes his experiences at home and in school when he was a boy.

De Paola, Tomie. ***The Art Lesson.*** Putnam, c1989. 32pp.
Having learned to be creative in drawing pictures at home, young Tommy is dismayed when he goes to school and finds the art lesson there much more regimented.

De Paola, Tomie. ***The Baby Sister.*** Putnam, c1996. 32pp.
When he learns that his mother is going to have a baby, Tommy is very excited and hopes that the baby will be a sister.

Houston, Gloria. ***The Year of the Perfect Christmas Tree: An Appalachian Story.*** Dial Books for Young Readers, c1988. 32pp.
Ruthie and her mother wonder how they will fulfill their obligation of getting the perfect Christmas tree to the town for the holiday celebration, since Papa has left the Appalachian area to go to war.

Hurst, Carol Otis. ***Rocks in His Head.*** Greenwillow Books, c2001. 32pp.
A young man has a lifelong love of rock collecting that eventually leads him to work at a science museum.

Lied, Kate. ***Potato: A Tale from the Great Depression.*** National Geographic Society, 2002, c1997. 32pp.
During the "Great Depression," a family seeking work finds employment for two weeks digging potatoes in Idaho.

Lyon, George Ella. ***Come a Tide.*** Orchard Books, 1993, c1990. 32pp.
A girl provides a lighthearted account of the spring floods at her rural home.

From Nancy J. Keane, *The Big Book of Children's Reading Lists: 100 Great, Ready-to-Use Book Lists for Educators, Librarians, Parents, and Children.* Westport, CT: Libraries Unlimited, 2006. Copyright © 2006 by Libraries Unlimited.

Memoirs

MacLachlan, Patricia. ***All the Places to Love.*** HarperCollins, c1994. 32pp.
A young boy describes the favorite places that he shares with his family on his grandparents' farm and in the nearby countryside.

McLerran, Alice. ***Roxaboxen.*** Lothrop, Lee & Shepard, c1991. 32pp.
A hill covered with rocks and wooden boxes becomes an imaginary town for Marian, her sisters, and their friends.

Polacco, Patricia. ***Thank You, Mr. Falker.*** Philomel Books, c1998. 40pp.
At first Trisha loves school, but her difficulty learning to read makes her feel dumb, until, in the fifth grade, a new teacher helps her understand and overcome her problem.

Pomerantz, Charlotte. ***The Chalk Doll.*** HarperCollins, c1989. 30pp.
Rosy's mother remembers the pleasures of her childhood in Jamaica and the very special dolls she used to play with.

Ringgold, Faith. ***Tar Beach.*** Crown, c1991. 32pp.
A young girl dreams of flying above her Harlem home, claiming all she sees for herself and her family. Based on the author's quilt painting of the same name.

Rylant, Cynthia. ***The Relatives Came.*** Atheneum Books for Young Readers, c2001. 32pp.
The relatives come to visit from Virginia, and everyone has a wonderful time.

Rylant, Cynthia. ***When I Was Young in the Mountains.*** Dutton Children's Books, c1982. 32pp.
Reminiscences of the pleasures of life in the mountains as a child.

Say, Allen. ***El Chino.*** Houghton Mifflin, c1990. 32pp.
A biography of Bill Wong, a Chinese American who became a famous bullfighter in Spain.

Say, Allen. ***Grandfather's Journey.*** Houghton Mifflin, c1993. 32pp.
A Japanese American man recounts his grandfather's journey to America, which he later also undertakes, and the feelings of being torn by a love for two different countries.

Wells, Rosemary. ***Streets of Gold.*** Dial Books for Young Readers, c1999. 39pp.
Based on a memoir written in the early twentieth century; tells the story of a young girl and her life in Russia, her travels to America, and her subsequent life in the United States.

Books for Children Ages 8–12

Alcott, Louisa May. ***The Girlhood Diary of Louisa May Alcott, 1843–1846: Writings of a Young Author*.** Blue Earth Books, c2001. 32pp. (NF)
Excerpts from the girlhood diary of Louisa May Alcott, describing her family life, lessons, and experiences on a communal farm in the 1840s. Includes sidebars, activities, and a timeline related to this era.

From Nancy J. Keane, *The Big Book of Children's Reading Lists: 100 Great, Ready-to-Use Book Lists for Educators, Librarians, Parents, and Children.* Westport, CT: Libraries Unlimited, 2006. Copyright © 2006 by Libraries Unlimited.

Memoirs

Ashby, Ruth. ***Rocket Man: The Mercury Adventure of John Glenn.*** Peachtree, c2004. 105pp. (NF)
Presents the story of John Glenn's flight into space, taken from Glenn's own memoirs and dialogue from the transcripts of the actual Friendship 7 flight.

Berry, Carrie. ***A Confederate Girl: The Diary of Carrie Berry, 1864.*** Blue Earth Books, c2000. 32pp. (NF)
Excerpts from the diary of Carrie Berry, describing her family's life in the Confederate South in 1864. Supplemented by sidebars, activities, and a timeline of the era.

Bircher, William. ***A Civil War Drummer Boy: The Diary of William Bircher, 1861–1865.*** Blue Earth Books, c2000. 32pp. (NF)
Excerpts from the diary of William Bircher, a fifteen-year-old Minnesotan who was a drummer during the Civil War. Supplemented by sidebars, activities, and a timeline of the era.

Bolden, Tonya. ***Maritcha: A Nineteenth-Century American Girl.*** Harry N. Abrams, c2005. 47pp. (NF)
The memoirs of Maritcha Remond Lyons, who was born in New York in the nineteenth-century, describing how she and her family escaped to Rhode Island during the 1863 draft riots and how she overcame prejudice to become the first African American person to graduate from Providence High School.

Murphy, Jim. ***A Young Patriot: The American Revolution As Experienced by One Boy.*** Clarion Books, c1996. 101pp. (NF)
The memoirs of Joseph Plumb Martin, a fifteen-year-old boy who enlisted in the revolutionary army in 1776, fighting under Washington, wintering at Valley Forge, and staying in the fight until the end of the war in 1783.

Pavlova, Anna. ***I Dreamed I Was a Ballerina: A Girlhood Story.*** Metropolitan Museum of Art/Atheneum Books for Young Readers, c2001. 32pp. (NF)
A children's story, drawn from the memoirs of famous dancer Anna Pavlova, in which she shares her love of ballet and describes what it was like to see Tchaikovsky's *Sleeping Beauty* performed onstage.

Roosevelt, Theodore. ***The Boyhood Diary of Theodore Roosevelt, 1869–1870: Early Travels of the 26th U.S. President.*** Blue Earth Books, c2001. 32pp. (NF)
The diary of Theodore Roosevelt records his travels through Europe with his family in 1869 and 1870. Includes sidebars, activities, and a timeline related to this era.

Wister, Sarah. ***A Colonial Quaker Girl: The Diary of Sally Wister, 1777–1778.*** Blue Earth Books, c2000. 32pp. (NF)
The diary of the sixteen-year-old daughter of a prominent Quaker family who moved with her family from British-occupied Philadelphia to the safety of the countryside during the Revolutionary War. Includes sidebars, activities, and a timeline related to this era.

From Nancy J. Keane, *The Big Book of Children's Reading Lists: 100 Great, Ready-to-Use Book Lists for Educators, Librarians, Parents, and Children.* Westport, CT: Libraries Unlimited, 2006. Copyright © 2006 by Libraries Unlimited.

Mother Goose Stories

Books for Children of All Ages

Animal Crackers: A Delectable Collection of Pictures, Poems, Songs, and Lullabies for the Very Young. Little, Brown, c1996. 64pp.
An illustrated collection of Mother Goose rhymes, lullabies, and contemporary verses that celebrate special times in a child's first years.

The Arnold Lobel Book of Mother Goose. Knopf, 1997, c1986. 176pp.
An illustrated collection of Mother Goose nursery rhymes, including well-known ones such as "Bah, Bah, Black Sheep" and "Little Boy Blue" and less familiar ones such as "Doctor Foster Went to Gloucester" and "When Clouds Appear Like Rocks and Towers."

Dan Yaccarino's Mother Goose. Golden Books, c2004. 41pp.
A collection of well-known Mother Goose rhymes illustrated by the renowned illustrator of children's books, Dan Yaccarino.

Edwards, Pamela Duncan. *The Neat Line: Scribbling Through Mother Goose.* Katherine Tegen Books, c2005. 32pp.
A young scribble matures into a neat line, then wriggles into a book of nursery rhymes, where he transforms himself into different objects to assist the characters he meets there.

Here Comes Mother Goose. Candlewick Press, c1999. 107pp.
Presents more than sixty traditional nursery rhymes, including "Old Mother Hubbard," "I'm a Little Teapot," and "One, Two, Buckle My Shoe," accompanied by illustrations of various animals.

Hoberman, Mary Ann. *You Read to Me, I'll Read to You: Very Short Mother Goose Tales to Read Together.* Little, Brown, c2005. 32pp.
A collection of short retellings of familiar Mother Goose fairy tales, each told in two voices designed especially for young children and adults to read together.

Michael Foreman's Mother Goose. Harcourt Brace Jovanovich, c1991. 152pp.
A classic Mother Goose collection that features intriguing visual links from one scene to the next.

Moses, Will. *Mother Goose.* Philomel Books, c2003. 61pp.
Folk art paintings accompany this compilation of over sixty of the best-loved Mother Goose rhymes.

Mother Goose: A Sampler. Douglas & McIntyre (distributed in the United States by Publishers Group West), c1996. 63pp.
An illustrated collection of traditional nursery rhymes.

Mother Goose Remembers. Barefoot Books, c2000. 56pp.
An illustrated collection of forty-six Mother Goose nursery rhymes, including "Three Little Kittens," "I See the Moon," "Polly Put the Kettle On," and "Hey Diddle Diddle."

The Neighborhood Mother Goose. Greenwillow Books/Amistad, c2004. 63pp.
A collection of nursery rhymes, both familiar and lesser known, illustrated with photographs in a city setting.

From Nancy J. Keane, *The Big Book of Children's Reading Lists: 100 Great, Ready-to-Use Book Lists for Educators, Librarians, Parents, and Children.* Westport, CT: Libraries Unlimited, 2006. Copyright © 2006 by Libraries Unlimited.

Mother Goose Stories

Polacco, Patricia. ***Babushka's Mother Goose.*** Philomel Books, c1995. 64pp.
A collection of traditional rhymes, rewritten to feature Russian characters and scenes.

Sylvia Long's Mother Goose. Chronicle Books, c1999. 109pp.
An illustrated collection of familiar nursery rhymes.

Tomie dePaola's Mother Goose. Putnam, c1985. 127pp.
An illustrated collection of 204 Mother Goose nursery rhymes, including well-known ones such as "Little Boy Blue" and less familiar ones such as "Charlie Warlie and His Cow."

Books for Children Ages 8–12

The Charles Addams Mother Goose. Simon & Schuster Books for Young Readers, c2002. 64pp.
Traditional Mother Goose rhymes illustrated by the cartoonist who created *The Addams Family.*

Engelbreit, Mary. ***Mary Engelbreit's Mother Goose.*** HarperCollins, c2004. 119pp.
An illustrated collection of nearly a hundred nursery rhymes, including "Twinkle, Twinkle, Little Star" and other familiar poems, as well as "Mary Had a Pretty Bird" and other less familiar ones.

Gosling, Gabby. ***The Top Secret Files of Mother Goose!*** Gareth Stevens. c2004. 31pp.
When "Mother" Goose tracks down the thief who stole the queen's tarts, she runs into several nursery rhyme characters.

Greenberg, David. ***Whatever Happened to Humpty Dumpty?: And Other Surprising Sequels to Mother Goose Rhymes.*** Little, Brown, c1999. 32pp.
Humorous verses are added to traditional Mother Goose rhymes.

Still, James. ***An Appalachian Mother Goose.*** University Press of Kentucky, c1998. 55pp.
A compilation of Mother Goose rhymes as collected from the Appalachian region oral tradition.

From Nancy J. Keane, *The Big Book of Children's Reading Lists: 100 Great, Ready-to-Use Book Lists for Educators, Librarians, Parents, and Children.* Westport, CT: Libraries Unlimited, 2006. Copyright © 2006 by Libraries Unlimited.

Multicultural

Compiled by Charity Huechteman, Children's Association, Brentwood Library, Springfield, MO (charityh@mail.sgcl.org).

Books for Children of All Ages

Adoff, Arnold. *Black Is Brown Is Tan.* Amistad, c2002. 32pp.
Describes in verse a family with a brown-skinned mother, white-skinned father, two children, and their various relatives.

Anholt, Catherine. *What I Like.* Candlewick Press, c1998. 30pp.
A variety of children describe their likes and dislikes in rhymed text and illustrations.

Bunting, Eve. *A Picnic in October.* Harcourt Brace, c1999. 28pp.
A boy finally comes to understand why his grandmother insists that the family come to Ellis Island each year to celebrate Lady Liberty's birthday.

Cheng, Andrea. *Grandfather Counts.* Lee & Low Books, c2000. 32pp.
When her maternal grandfather comes from China, Helen, who is biracial, develops a special bond with him despite their age and language differences.

Davol, Marguerite W. *Black, White, Just Right.* Whitman, c1993. 32pp.
A girl explains how her parents are different in color, tastes in art and food, and pet preferences, and how she herself is different too—but just right.

Hamanaka, Sheila. *Grandparents Song.* HarperCollins, c2003. 32pp.
A rhyming celebration of ancestry and of the diversity that flourishes in this country.

hooks, bell. *Skin Again.* Jump at the Sun/Hyperion Books for Children, c2004. 32pp.
Children note that skin color is not as important as what is inside for determining who a person really is.

Hubbell, Patricia. *Black All Around!* Lee & Low Books, c2003. 32pp.
An African American girl contemplates the many wonderful black things around her, from the inside of a pocket, where surprises hide, to the cozy night where there is no light.

Igus, Toyomi. *Two Mrs. Gibsons.* Children's Book Press (distributed to the book trade by Publishers Group West), c1996. 32pp.
The biracial daughter of an African American father and a Japanese mother fondly recalls growing up with her mother and her father's mother, two very different but equally loving women.

Jones, Rebecca C. *Matthew and Tilly.* Puffin Books, 1995, c1991. 32pp.
Like all good friends, Matthew and Tilly have an occasional tiff, but their friendship prevails despite their differences.

Kates, Bobbi Jane. *We're Different, We're the Same.* Random House, 1992. 32pp.
Illustrations and simple rhyming text show that while the body parts of various human and Muppet characters may look different, they have similar uses.

From Nancy J. Keane, *The Big Book of Children's Reading Lists: 100 Great, Ready-to-Use Book Lists for Educators, Librarians, Parents, and Children.* Westport, CT: Libraries Unlimited, 2006. Copyright © 2006 by Libraries Unlimited.

Multicultural

Katz, Karen. ***The Colors of Us.*** H. Holt, c1999. 26pp.
Seven-year-old Lena and her mother observe the variations in the color of their friends' skin, viewed in terms of foods and things found in nature.

Lorbiecki, Marybeth. ***Sister Anne's Hands.*** Dial Books for Young Readers, c1998. 34pp.
Seven-year-old Anna has her first encounter with racism in the 1960s when an African American nun comes to teach at her parochial school.

Mandelbaum, Pili. ***You Be Me, I'll Be You.*** Kane/Miller, 1993, c1989. 34pp.
A brown-skinned daughter and her white father experiment to see what it would be like to have the other's skin color.

Ormerod, Jan. ***Who's Whose?*** Lothrop, Lee & Shepard, c1998. 32pp.
Three very busy families engage in such activities as school, soccer, piano playing, and cooking.

Starr, Meg. ***Alicia's Happy Day.*** Star Bright Books, c2002. 28pp.
Alicia receives greetings from her Hispanic neighborhood as she walks to her birthday party.

Walsh, Melanie. ***My Nose, Your Nose.*** Houghton Mifflin, c2002. 34pp.
Agnes and Kit compare various parts of their bodies to see how they are similar and different.

Yolen, Jane. ***Miz Berlin Walks.*** Puffin Books, 2000, c1997. 32pp.
Mary Louise gradually gets to know and love her elderly neighbor lady, who tells wonderful stories as she walks around the block of her Virginia home.

Books for Children Ages 8–12

Hamilton, Virginia. ***Plain City.*** Scholastic, c1993. 194pp.
Twelve-year-old Buhlaire, a "mixed" child who feels out of place in her community, struggles to unearth her past and her family history as she gradually discovers more and more about her long-missing father.

Meyer, Carolyn. ***Jubilee Journey.*** Harcourt Brace, c1997. 271pp.
Emily Rose has always felt comfortable growing up in Connecticut with her African American mother and her French American father, but when they spend some time with her great-grandmother in Texas, Emily Rose learns about her black heritage and uncovers some new and exciting parts of her own identity.

Taylor, Mildred D. ***The Land.*** P. Fogelman, c2001. 375pp.
Paul-Edward, the son of a part-Indian, part-African slave mother and a white plantation owner father, finds himself caught between the two worlds of his parents as he pursues his dream of owning land in the aftermath of the Civil War.

Wilson, Barbara. ***A Clear Spring.*** Feminist Press at the City University of New York, c2002. 173pp.
While visiting relatives in Seattle, twelve-year-old Willa explores the ethnic diversity of her family and investigates the pollution of a salmon stream.

Wyeth, Sharon Dennis. ***The World of Daughter McGuire.*** Bantam Doubleday Dell Books for Young Readers, c1994. 167pp.
Eleven-year-old Daughter, called a "zebra" by a boy at school because one of her parents is black and the other is white, wonders exactly who and what she is.

From Nancy J. Keane, *The Big Book of Children's Reading Lists: 100 Great, Ready-to-Use Book Lists for Educators, Librarians, Parents, and Children.* Westport, CT: Libraries Unlimited, 2006. Copyright © 2006 by Libraries Unlimited.

Mysteries

Books for Children of All Ages

Adler, David A. ***Young Cam Jansen and the Double Beach Mystery.*** Viking Press, c2002. 30pp.
Cam uses her photographic memory and her brain to solve two mysteries at the beach, involving a missing mother and a missing set of papers.

Adler, David A. ***Young Cam Jansen and the Library Mystery.*** Viking Press, c2001. 30pp.
Cam uses her photographic memory to find a shopping list that her dad lost at the library.

Adler, David A. ***Young Cam Jansen and the Zoo Note Mystery.*** Viking Press, c2003. 30pp.
Cam helps her friend Eric when he misplaces his permission slip to go on the school field trip.

Bonsall, Crosby Newell. ***The Case of the Hungry Stranger.*** HarperCollins, c1992. 64pp.
Soon after Wizard decided to become a private eye, he had to solve the mystery of Mrs. Meech's missing blueberry pie.

Carlson, Nancy L. ***Louanne Pig in the Mysterious Valentine.*** Carolrhoda Books, c2004. 32pp.
Louanne Pig tries to discover the identity of her secret admirer after receiving an anonymous valentine.

Christelow, Eileen. ***The Robbery at the Diamond Dog Diner.*** Clarion Books, c1986. 32pp.
When she hears there are jewel thieves in town, Lola Dog doesn't wear her usual diamonds to the Diamond Dog Diner, but she doesn't take into account Glenda Feathers's loud talk about where Lola should hide her jewels.

Clement, Rod. ***Grandpa's Teeth.*** HarperCollins, 1998, c1997. 28pp.
Soon after Grandpa's teeth disappear from a glass of water near his bed, Inspector Rate has the whole town under investigation.

Cushman, Doug. ***Aunt Eater Loves a Mystery.*** Harper & Row, c1987. 64 p.
Aunt Eater loves mystery stories so much that she sees mysterious adventures wherever she looks.

Hurd, Thacher. ***Mystery on the Docks.*** HarperCollins, c1983. 32pp.
Ralph, a short order cook, rescues a kidnapped opera singer from Big Al and his gang of nasty rats.

Kellogg, Steven. ***The Missing Mitten Mystery.*** Dial Books for Young Readers, c2000. 33pp.
Annie searches the neighborhood for her red mitten, the fifth she's lost this winter.

Kellogg, Steven. ***The Mystery of the Stolen Blue Paint.*** Dial Books for Young Readers, 1986, c1982. 32pp.
Suspicious that one of her younger friends is the culprit, a little girl named Belinda investigates the disappearance of her can of blue paint.

From Nancy J. Keane, *The Big Book of Children's Reading Lists: 100 Great, Ready-to-Use Book Lists for Educators, Librarians, Parents, and Children.* Westport, CT: Libraries Unlimited, 2006. Copyright © 2006 by Libraries Unlimited.

Mysteries

Macaulay, David. ***Black and White.*** Houghton Mifflin, c1990. 32pp.
Four brief "stories" about parents, trains, and cows, or is it really all one story? The author recommends careful inspection of words and pictures to both minimize and enhance confusion.

Palatini, Margie. ***The Web Files.*** Hyperion Books for Children, c2001. 32pp.
Ducktective Web and his partner try to quack the case of the pilfered peck of perfectly picked pickled peppers.

Quackenbush, Robert M. ***Danger in Tibet: A Miss Mallard Mystery.*** Pippin Press, c1989. 32pp.
The world-famous ducktective investigates the disappearance of her nephew, Inspector Willard Widgeon, during a secret mission in the Himalayas, and uncovers a dastardly plot that could destroy Mt. Everest.

Rylant, Cynthia. ***The High-Rise Private Eyes: The Case of the Baffled Bear.*** Greenwillow Books, c2004. 48pp.
Bunny and Jack, animal detectives, take a break from playing cards to look for Bernard Bear's missing messenger whistle.

Sharmat, Marjorie Weinman. ***Nate the Great.*** Dell Yearling, 2004, c1972. 60pp.
Nate the Great solves the mystery of the missing picture.

Van Allsburg, Chris. ***The Mysteries of Harris Burdick.*** Houghton Mifflin, c1984. 31pp.
A series of loosely related drawings, each accompanied by a title and a caption, which the reader may use to make up his or her own story.

Van Allsburg, Chris. ***The Stranger.*** Houghton Mifflin, c1986. 32pp.
The enigmatic origins of the stranger Farmer Bailey hits with his truck and brings home to recuperate seem to have a mysterious relation to the changing season.

Van Allsburg, Chris. ***The Wretched Stone.*** Houghton Mifflin, c1991. 31pp.
A strange, glowing stone picked up on a sea voyage captivates a ship's crew and has a terrible transforming effect on them.

Yolen, Jane. ***Piggins.*** Harcourt, c1987. 32pp.
During a dinner party, the lights go out and Mrs. Reynard's beautiful diamond necklace is stolen, but Piggins the butler quickly discovers the real thief.

Books for Children Ages 8–12

Adler, David A. ***Cam Jansen and the Chocolate Fudge Mystery.*** Viking Press, c1993. 58pp.
When Cam Jansen and her friend Eric uncover a mystery while selling fudge door-to-door to raise money for the local library, Cam uses her photographic memory to foil a crime. See also other titles in the series.

From Nancy J. Keane, *The Big Book of Children's Reading Lists: 100 Great, Ready-to-Use Book Lists for Educators, Librarians, Parents, and Children.* Westport, CT: Libraries Unlimited, 2006. Copyright © 2006 by Libraries Unlimited.

Mysteries

Cushman, Doug. ***The Mystery of King Karfu.*** HarperCollins, c1996. 32pp.
The great detective Seymour Sleuth and his assistant Muggs journey to Egypt in search of a missing stone chicken, an important clue to the location of the lost treasure of King Karfu.

Hale, Bruce. ***The Mystery of Mr. Nice: From the Tattered Casebook of Chet Gecko, Private Eye.*** Harcourt, . c2000. 96pp.
When the principal of his school begins acting nice to him, Chet Gecko realizes that he is an imposter and so sets out to find the real one. See also other titles in the series.

Levy, Elizabeth. ***The Mystery of the Missing Dog.*** Scholastic, c1995. 48pp.
The invisible boy Chip intends to enter his invisible dog Max in the dog show, but when Max comes up missing, Chip and his Invisible Inc. friends suspect foul play. See also other titles in the series.

Preller, James. ***The Case of Hermie the Missing Hamster.*** Scholastic, c1998. 76pp.
Jigsaw Jones, private eye, and his partner Mila, investigate the disappearance of their friend Wingnut's hamster. See also other titles in the series.

Roy, Ron. ***The Absent Author.*** Random House, c1997. 86pp.
Dink Duncan and his two friends investigate the apparent kidnapping of famous mystery author Wallis Wallace. See also other titles in the series.

Sobol, Donald J. ***Encyclopedia Brown, Boy Detective.*** Dell Yearling, 2002, c1963. 111pp.
Encyclopedia Brown, a ten-year-old detective, uses his intelligence to help solve ten puzzling crimes. See also other titles in the series.

Torrey, Michele. ***The Case of the Gasping Garbage.*** Dutton Children's Books, c2001. 71pp.
Fourth-graders Drake Doyle and Nell Fossey combine their detective and scientific investigative skills to solve a variety of cases, involving a noisy garbage can, endangered frogs, a stuck truck, and a mysterious love letter. Includes a section of scientific experiments and activities.

Torrey, Michele. ***The Case of the Mossy Lake Monster and Other Super-Scientific Cases.*** Dutton Children's Books, c2002. 83pp.
Fourth-graders Drake Doyle and Nell Fossey combine their detective and scientific investigative skills to solve a variety of cases, involving a hungry cat, endangered penguins, a fish-stealing monster, and a dirty election. Includes a section of scientific experiments and activities.

Warner, Gertrude Chandler. ***The Boxcar Children.*** Whitman, c1977. 154pp.
Four orphans, two boys and two girls, set up housekeeping in an old boxcar. See also other titles in the series.

From Nancy J. Keane, *The Big Book of Children's Reading Lists: 100 Great, Ready-to-Use Book Lists for Educators, Librarians, Parents, and Children.* Westport, CT: Libraries Unlimited, 2006. Copyright © 2006 by Libraries Unlimited.

Pop-Up Books

Books for Children of All Ages

De Paola, Tomie. ***The First Christmas.*** Putnam, c1984. 13pp. (NF)
Simple text and pop-up illustrations retell the story of the birth of Jesus, from the Annunciation to the visit of the shepherds and the three kings.

Faulkner, Keith. ***The Wide-Mouthed Frog: A Pop-Up Book***. Dial Books for Young Readers, c1996. 14pp.
A wide-mouthed frog is interested in what other animals eat—until he meets a creature that eats only wide-mouthed frogs!

Moore, Clement Clarke. ***The Night Before Christmas: A Pop-Up.*** Little Simon, c2002. 12pp.
Presents the familiar poem "The Night Before Christmas," with intricate pop-ups that portray scenes from the text.

Murphy, Chuck. ***Chuck Murphy's Black Cat, White Cat: A Pop-Up Book of Opposites.*** Little Simon, c1998. 8pp. (NF)
A pop-up book for children that uses pictures of cats to demonstrate opposites.

Old Macdonald Had a Farm. Orchard Books, c1999. 12pp.
Pop-ups of animals illustrate the song "Old MacDonald Had a Farm."

Priceman, Marjorie. ***Little Red Riding Hood.*** Little Simon, c2001. 16pp.
A pop-up adaptation of the classic children's story "Little Red Riding Hood" in which the young girl employs some clever thinking to find out what the wolf has done with her grandmother.

Sabuda, Robert. ***The 12 Days of Christmas: A Pop-Up Celebration.*** Little Simon, c1996. 12pp.
A sophisticated pop-up book that uses white paper cutouts by paper engineer Robert Sabuda to illustrate the traditional holiday song.

Sabuda, Robert. ***Alice's Adventures in Wonderland: A Pop-Up Adaptation of Lewis Carroll's Original Tale.*** Little Simon, c2003. 12pp.
A detailed, pop-up adaptation of *Alice's Adventures in Wonderland,* the story of a little girl who falls down a rabbit hole and discovers a world of nonsensical and amusing characters.

Sabuda, Robert. ***Cookie Count: A Tasty Pop-Up.*** Little Simon, c1997. 22pp.
A pop-up book of ten tasty types of cookies, ready to be devoured by a crew of tiny mice.

Sabuda, Robert. ***The Movable Mother Goose.*** Little Simon, c1999. 12pp.
A collection of Mother Goose nursery rhymes in the form of a pop-up book.

From Nancy J. Keane, *The Big Book of Children's Reading Lists: 100 Great, Ready-to-Use Book Lists for Educators, Librarians, Parents, and Children.* Westport, CT: Libraries Unlimited, 2006. Copyright © 2006 by Libraries Unlimited.

Pop-Up Books

Seibold, J. Otto. ***J. Otto Seibold's Alice in Pop-Up Wonderland: With Original Text from the Lewis Carroll Classic.*** Orchard Books, c2003. 14pp.
A visual retelling of *Alice in Wonderland,* featuring pop-up illustrations by J. Otto Seibold.

Terreson, Jeffrey. ***Animal Homes.*** National Geographic Society, c1992. 10pp. (NF)
Text and pop-up illustrations depict how animals build homes for protection and to raise their young.

Williams, Nancy. ***A Kwanzaa Celebration Pop-Up Book.*** Little Simon, c1995. 14pp. (NF)
A description of the seven-day African American harvest festival, explaining the activities of each day and their special significance.

The Wonderful Wizard of Oz: A Commemorative Pop-Up. Little Simon, c2000. 14pp.
After a cyclone transports her to the land of Oz, Dorothy must seek out the great Wizard so she can return to Kansas.

Zelinsky, Paul O. ***Knick-Knack Paddywhack!: A Moving Parts Book.*** Dutton Children's Books, c2002. 32pp. (NF)
A moving-parts book based on the familiar counting song, with tiny old men that appear to act out the refrain.

Books for Children Ages 8–12

Abrahams, Peter. ***The Girl Who Loved Tom Gordon.*** Little Simon, 2004, c1999. 14pp.
Presents a pop-up book about nine-year-old Trisha McFarland, lost in the woods after she wanders off to escape the bickering between her mom and her brother. She boosts her courage by imagining that her hero, Boston Red Sox relief pitcher Tom Gordon, is with her helping her deal with an unknown enemy.

Carter, David. ***The Nutcracker: A Pop-Up Adaptation of E.T.A. Hoffmann's Original Tale.*** Little Simon, c2000. 18pp.
Adapts the original version of the Christmas tale "The Nutcracker," in which a young girl's love for a nutcracker shaped like a soldier brings him to life, and illustrates the story with elaborate pop-ups that resemble lavish theater sets.

Forward, Toby. ***Shakespeare's Globe: An Interactive Pop-up Theatre.*** Candlewick Press, c2005. 14pp. (NF)
Presents a pop-up model of the Globe Theater as it appeared in the time of William Shakespeare, features a tour of the theater hosted by actor Richard Burbage of the King's Men troupe, and includes two scripts with scenes from twelve Shakespeare plays, as well as punch-out figures that can be moved around the theater for performances.

From Nancy J. Keane, *The Big Book of Children's Reading Lists: 100 Great, Ready-to-Use Book Lists for Educators, Librarians, Parents, and Children.* Westport, CT. Libraries Unlimited, 2006. Copyright © 2006 by Libraries Unlimited.

Pop-Up Books

Hawcock, David. ***The Amazing Pull-Out Pop-Up Body in a Book.*** DK Publishing, c1997.9pp. (NF)
Provides information about the organs, muscles, bones, and other parts of the human body. Includes fold-out spreads, flaps, and a paper sculpture of a skeleton that unfolds to a height of five feet.

Moore, Clement Clarke. ***The Night Before Christmas: A Pop-Up.*** Little Simon, c2002. 12pp.
Presents the familiar poem "The Night Before Christmas," with intricate pop-ups that portray scenes from the text.

Petty, Kate. ***The Amazing Pop-Up Geography Book.*** Dutton Children's Books, c2000. 14pp. (NF)
Designed to teach children about the physical structure of the earth.

Prokofiev, Sergey. ***Peter and the Wolf: A Mechanical Book.*** Viking Press, c1986. 10pp.
A pop-up version of the orchestral fairy tale in which a boy ignores his grandfather's warnings and proceeds to capture a wolf.

Putnam, James. ***The Ancient Egypt Pop-Up Book.*** Universe Publishing (distributed by St. Martin's Press), c2003. 14pp. (NF)
Contains pop-ups that showcase a selection of ancient Egypt's cultural wonders; includes photographs, text, and other interactive elements that provide information about Egyptian history.

Sabuda, Robert. ***America the Beautiful: A Pop-Up Book.*** Little Simon, c2004. 16pp. (NF)
Pop-up figures of such famous American landmarks as the Golden Gate Bridge and theU.S. Capitol are used to interpret Katherine Lee Bates's famous poem.

Sabuda, Robert. ***Dinosaurs—Encyclopedia Prehistorica.*** Candlewick Press, c2005. 12pp. (NF)
Contains a collection of facts and information on dinosaurs, including over thirty-five pop-ups of these prehistoric animals, as well as descriptions of more than fifty different species.

Seibold, J. Otto. ***J. Otto Seibold's Alice in Pop-Up Wonderland: with Original Text from the Lewis Carroll Classic.*** Orchard Books, c2003. 14pp.
A visual retelling of *Alice in Wonderland,* featuring pop-up illustrations by J. Otto Seibold.

Trivizas, Eugenios. ***The Three Little Wolves and the Big Bad Pig: A Pop-Up Storybook with a Twist in the Tale!*** Egmont, c2003. 16pp.
Three little wolves go out into the world, where they are terrorized by a big, bad pig until they realize they have been taking the wrong approach to dealing with their tormentor. Includes pop-ups and pull tabs.

The Wonderful Wizard of Oz: A Commemorative Pop-Up. Little Simon, c2000. 14pp.
After a cyclone transports her to the land of Oz, Dorothy must seek out the great Wizard so she can return to Kansas.

From Nancy J. Keane, *The Big Book of Children's Reading Lists: 100 Great, Ready-to-Use Book Lists for Educators, Librarians, Parents, and Children.* Westport, CT: Libraries Unlimited, 2006. Copyright © 2006 by Libraries Unlimited.

Repetition of Phrase

Books for Children of All Ages

Alborough, Jez. ***Watch Out! Big Bro's Coming!*** Candlewick Press, 1998, c1997. 26pp.
Terror spreads through the jungle as animals hear the news that rough, tough Big Bro is coming.

Brown, Margaret Wise. ***Goodnight Moon.*** Harper, c1947. 31pp.
As a little bunny says goodnight to each of the objects in the great green room, the illustrations grow progressively darker.

Butler, John. ***Ten in the Den.*** Peachtree, c2005. 32pp.
One by one, nine forest creatures fall out of bed when Little Mouse says "Roll over!"

Carle, Eric. ***Do You Want to Be My Friend?*** HarperCollins, c1976. 32pp.
A mouse searches everywhere for a friend.

Carle, Eric. ***Have You Seen My Cat?*** Simon & Schuster Books for Young Readers, c1987. 28pp.
A young boy encounters all sorts of cats while searching for the one he lost.

Fearnley, Jan. ***A Perfect Day for It.*** Harcourt, c2002. 33pp.
Bear announces that it's "a perfect day for it," and his friends follow him up the mountain, each imagining what special treat they might share there, but all come to agree that Bear's "it" is just right.

Fleming, Candace. ***Muncha! Muncha! Muncha!*** Atheneum Books for Young Readers, c2002. 32pp.
After planting the garden he has dreamed of for years, Mr. McGreely tries to find a way to keep some persistent bunnies from eating all his vegetables.

Guarino, Deborah. ***Is Your Mama a Llama?*** Scholastic, 2004, c1989. 32pp.
A young llama asks his friends if their mamas are llamas and finds out, in rhyme, that their mothers are other types of animals.

Hamsa, Bobbie. ***Dirty Larry.*** Children's Press, c2002. 23pp.
No matter what he does, Larry always gets dirty—except in the shower.

Hoberman, Mary Ann. ***A House Is a House for Me.*** Viking Press, c1978. 48pp.
Lists in rhyme the dwellings of various animals and things.

Kraus, Robert. ***Where Are You Going, Little Mouse?*** Greenwillow Books, c1986. 34pp.
A little mouse runs away from home to find a "nicer" family, but when darkness comes, he misses them and realizes how much he loves them.

Kraus, Robert. ***Come Out and Play, Little Mouse.*** Mulberry Books, 1995, c1987. 32pp.
Little mouse is busy helping his family five days of the week, but he gets to play with them on weekends.

From Nancy J. Keane, *The Big Book of Children's Reading Lists: 100 Great, Ready-to-Use Book Lists for Educators, Librarians, Parents, and Children.* Westport, CT. Libraries Unlimited, 2006. Copyright © 2006 by Libraries Unlimited.

Repetition of Phrase

Martin, Bill. ***Brown Bear, Brown Bear, What Do You See?*** H. Holt, c1992. 26pp.
Children see a variety of animals, each one a different color, and a teacher looking at them.

Most, Bernard. ***If the Dinosaurs Came Back.*** Harcourt, c1978. 32pp.
A young boy who wishes for the return of dinosaurs imagines how useful they would be.

Rathmann, Peggy. ***Good Night, Gorilla.*** Putnam, c1994. 36pp.
An unobservant zookeeper is followed home by all the animals he thinks he has left behind in the zoo.

Serfozo, Mary. ***Who Said Red?*** Aladdin Paperbacks, 1992, c1988. 32pp.
A little girl and her brother introduce red, green, blue, yellow, and other colors as they wander about their farm.

Shannon, George. ***Dance Away.*** Mulberry Books, 1991, c1982. 32pp.
A children's story for young readers about how Rabbit's dancing saves his friends from becoming Fox's supper.

Tafuri, Nancy. ***Have You Seen My Duckling?*** Greenwillow Books, c1984. 25pp.
A mother duck leads her brood around the pond as she searches for one missing duckling.

Van Laan, Nancy. ***Possum Come A-Knockin'***. Dragonfly Books, 1992, c1990. 28pp.
A cumulative tale in verse about a mysterious stranger that interrupts a family's daily routine.

West, Colin. ***"Have You Seen the Crocodile?"*** Candlewick Press, 1999, c1986. 24pp.
A group of animal friends look for the cunning crocodile, little realizing that he is right under their noses.

Wood, Audrey. ***Silly Sally.*** Harcourt Brace Jovanovich, c1992. 32pp.
A rhyming story of Silly Sally, who makes many friends as she travels to town—backward and upside down.

Wood, Jakki. ***Moo Moo, Brown Cow.*** Red Wagon Books, 1996, c1991. 20pp.
Teaches readers about numbers and colors as a kitten visits a barnyard, asking mother animals about their babies.

Zamorano, Ana. ***Let's Eat!*** Scholastic, c1999. 32pp.
Each day Antonio's Mama tries to get everyone to sit down together to eat, but someone is always busy elsewhere, until the family celebrates a new arrival.

From Nancy J. Keane, *The Big Book of Children's Reading Lists: 100 Great, Ready-to-Use Book Lists for Educators, Librarians, Parents, and Children.* Westport, CT: Libraries Unlimited, 2006. Copyright © 2006 by Libraries Unlimited.

Wordless

Books for Children of All Ages

Aruego, Jose. ***Look What I Can Do.*** Aladdin Paperbacks, 1988, c1971. 32pp.
Two carabaos discover that being a copycat can lead to trouble.

Baker, Jeannie. ***Home.*** Greenwillow Books, c2004. 32pp.
A wordless picture book that observes the changes in a neighborhood from before a girl is born until she is an adult, as it first decays and then is renewed by the efforts of the residents.

Baker, Jeannie. ***Window.*** Greenwillow Books, c1991. 32pp.
Chronicles the events and changes in a young boy's life and in his environment, from babyhood to grownup, through wordless scenes observed from the window of his room.

Banyai, Istvan. ***Re-zoom.*** Puffin Books, 1998, c1995. 64pp.
This wordless picture book presents a series of scenes, each one from farther away, showing, for example, a boat that becomes the image on a magazine, which is held in a hand, which belongs to a boy, and so on.

Banyai, Istvan. ***Zoom.*** Viking Press, c1995. 64pp.
This wordless picture book presents a series of scenes, each one from farther away, showing, for example, a girl playing with toys who is actually a picture on a magazine cover, which is part of a sign on a bus, and so on.

Blake, Quentin. ***Clown.*** H. Holt, 1998, c1995. 32pp.
After being discarded, Clown makes his way through town having a series of adventures as he tries to find a home for himself and his other toy friends.

Briggs, Raymond. ***The Snowman.*** Random House, c1978. 32pp.
A wordless book using over 175 picture frames to relate the adventure shared by a little boy and the snowman he built in the yard.

Carle, Eric. ***Do You Want to Be My Friend?*** HarperCollins, c1976. 32pp.
A mouse searches everywhere for a friend.

Catalanotto, Peter. ***Dylan's Day Out.*** Orchard Books, 1993, c1989. 32pp.
In a story where almost everything is black and white, Dylan, a Dalmatian, escapes from his home and becomes involved in a soccer game between penguins and skunks.

Collington, Peter. ***A Small Miracle.*** Knopf, c1997. 16pp.
The figures in a nativity scene come to life to help an old woman in need at Christmas.

Day, Alexandra. ***Carl Goes Shopping.*** Farrar, Straus & Giroux, c1989. 32pp.
While his mistress shops, Carl, a large dog, and the baby in his care explore the department store quite thoroughly and have a wonderful time.

Day, Alexandra. ***Carl Goes to Daycare.*** Farrar, Straus & Giroux, c1993. 32pp.
Carl the rottweiler takes charge when things take an unexpected turn at the day care center he is visiting.

From Nancy J. Keane, *The Big Book of Children's Reading Lists: 100 Great, Ready-to-Use Book Lists for Educators, Librarians, Parents, and Children.* Westport, CT: Libraries Unlimited, 2006. Copyright © 2006 by Libraries Unlimited.

Wordless

Day, Alexandra. *Carl's Birthday.* Farrar, Straus & Giroux, c1995. 32pp.
Carl, a rottweiler, and Madeline fool her mother once again as they inspect his presents and cake for his surprise birthday party, all while she thinks they are taking a nap.

Day, Alexandra. *Good Dog, Carl.* Aladdin Paperbacks, 1997, c1985. 36pp.
Lively and unusual things happen when Carl the dog is left in charge of the baby.

De Paola, Tomie. *The Hunter and the Animals: A Wordless Picture Book.* Holiday House, c1981. 32pp.
When a discouraged hunter falls asleep, the forest animals play a trick on him.

De Paola, Tomie. *Pancakes for Breakfast.* Harcourt Brace, c1978. 32pp.
A little old lady's attempts to have pancakes for breakfast are hindered by a scarcity of supplies and the participation of her pets.

Felix, Monique. *The Boat.* Creative Education, c1993. 28pp.
A mouse trapped inside a book makes a boat out of paper and goes sailing.

Felix, Monique. *The Colors.* Creative Education, c1991. 30pp.
A mouse trapped in a book discovers what colors are.

Felix, Monique. *The House.* Creative Education, c1991. 30pp.
A little mouse trapped in a book makes a house.

Felix, Monique. *The Wind.* Stewart, Tabori & Chang, Creative Education, c1991. 30pp.
A little mouse trapped in a book discovers the wind.

Hoban, Tana. *Shadows and Reflections.* Greenwillow Books, c1990. 32pp.
Photographs without text feature shadows and reflections of various objects, animals, and people.

Hutchins, Pat. *Changes, Changes.* Aladdin Paperbacks, 1987, c1971. 32pp.
Two wooden dolls rearrange wooden building blocks to form various objects.

Kalan, Robert. *Blue Sea.* Mulberry Books, 1992, c1979. 24pp.
Several fishes of varying size introduce space relationships and size differences.

Liu, Jae Soo. *Yellow Umbrella.* Kane/Miller, c2002. 32pp.
Combines a wordless picture book, in which an increasing number of colorful umbrellas appear in the falling rain, with a CD of background music designed to enrich the images.

Mayer, Mercer. *A Boy, a Dog, a Frog and a Friend.* Dial Books for Young Readers, c1971. 32pp.
A boy, a dog, and a frog catch a turtle while fishing down by the pond. Soon the three friends become four.

Mayer, Mercer. *Frog Goes to Dinner.* Dial Books for Young Readers, c1974. 32pp.
When a boy goes with his parents to a fancy restaurant, Frog cannot resist the temptation to stow away in an empty pocket.

Mayer, Mercer. *One Frog Too Many.* Dial Books for Young Readers, 2003?, c1975. 32pp.
A boy's pet frog thinks that the new little frog the boy gets for his birthday is one frog too many.

From Nancy J. Keane, *The Big Book of Children's Reading Lists: 100 Great, Ready-to-Use Book Lists for Educators, Librarians, Parents, and Children.* Westport, CT: Libraries Unlimited, 2006. Copyright © 2006 by Libraries Unlimited.

Wordless

McCully, Emily Arnold. ***Four Hungry Kittens.*** Dial Books for Young Readers, c2001. 32pp.
In this wordless story, four kittens share adventures while their mother is away hunting food.

Ormerod, Jan. ***Moonlight.*** Frances Lincoln Children's Books (distributed in the United States by Publishers Group West), 2004, c1982. 26pp.
As her parents attempt to help a child fall asleep at bedtime, they themselves become more and more sleepy.

Ormerod, Jan. ***Sunshine.*** Frances Lincoln Children's Books (distributed in the United States by Publishers Group West), 2004, c1981. 26pp.
Awakened by the sun, a little girl proceeds to wake her parents and sees that they all leave the house on time.

Rohmann, Eric. ***Time Flies.*** Crown, c1994. 32pp.
A wordless tale in which a bird flying around the dinosaur exhibit in a natural history museum has an unsettling experience when the dinosaurs seem to come alive and view it as a potential meal.

Sneed, Brad. ***Picture a Letter.*** Phyllis Fogelman Books, c2002. 32pp.
A wordless alphabet book in which the illustrations show people, objects, and animals that form the shapes of the individual letters.

Spier, Peter. ***Noah's Ark.*** Doubleday, c1977. 46pp.
Retells in pictures how a pair of every manner of creature climbed on board Noah's ark and thereby survived the Flood.

Turkle, Brinton. ***Deep in the Forest.*** Puffin Books, 1987, c1976. 32pp.
A curious bear explores a cabin in the forest, with disastrous results.

Vincent, Gabrielle. ***A Day, a Dog.*** Front Street, c2000. 64pp.
Pictures tell the story of a dog's day, from the moment he is abandoned on the highway until he finds a friend in a young boy.

Weitzman, Jacqueline Preiss. ***You Can't Take a Balloon into the Museum of Fine Arts.*** Dial Books for Young Readers, c2002. 35pp.
While a brother and sister, along with their grandparents, visit the Museum of Fine Arts, the balloon they were not allowed to bring into the museum floats around Boston, causing a series of mishaps at various tourist sites.

Wiesner, David. ***Free Fall.*** Lothrop, Lee & Shepard Books, c1988. 32pp.
A young boy dreams of daring adventures in the company of imaginary creatures inspired by the things surrounding his bed.

Wiesner, David. ***Sector 7.*** Clarion Books, c1999. 50pp.
While on a school trip to the Empire State Building, a boy is taken by a friendly cloud to visit Sector 7, where he discovers how clouds are shaped and channeled throughout the country.

Wilson, April. ***April Wilson's Magpie Magic: A Tale of Colorful Mischief.*** Dial Books for Young Readers, c1999. 36pp.
This wordless picture book depicts a young artist who draws a picture of a magpie that then comes to life and interacts with a series of colorful drawings.

From Nancy J. Keane, *The Big Book of Children's Reading Lists: 100 Great, Ready-to-Use Book Lists for Educators, Librarians, Parents, and Children.* Westport, CT: Libraries Unlimited, 2006. Copyright © 2006 by Libraries Unlimited.

Angels

Books for Children of All Ages

Anglund, Joan Walsh. ***Little Angels' Alphabet of Love.*** Simon & Schuster Books for Young Readers, c1997. 32pp.
Little angels illustrate the meaning of love using each letter of the alphabet.

Libby, Larry. ***Angels, Angels Everywhere.*** Zonderkidz, c2003. 34pp.
Illustrations and text teach children about angels and their presence in everyday life.

Magnier, Thierry. ***Isabelle and the Angel.*** Chronicle Books, c2000. 35pp.
Isabelle, a pretty pig with artistic aspirations, visits the museum and is shown all the paintings and statues by the little Angel, an experience that changes her life.

Otto, Gina. ***Cassandra's Angel.*** Illumination Arts Publishing, c2001. 36pp.
When she listens to the people around her, Cassandra feels that she cannot do anything right, but then a meeting with her Angel gives her a new perspective on herself and others.

Rylant, Cynthia. ***Cat Heaven.*** Blue Sky Press, c1997. 34pp.
God created Cat Heaven, with fields of sweet grass where cats can play, kitty-toys for them to enjoy, and angels to rub their noses and ears.

Spinelli, Eileen. ***City Angel.*** Dial Books for Young Readers, c2005. 36pp.
An angel spends her day watching over and taking care of the animals and people who are visiting or live in a busy city.

Stone, Phoebe. ***What Night Do the Angels Wander?*** Little, Brown, c1998. 32pp.
Rhyming text describes the one night of the year when the angels come together to celebrate with the children and animals of the earth.

Books for Children Ages 8–12

Absolutely Angels: Poems for Children and Other Believers. Wordsong/Boyds Mills Press, c1998. 32pp.
The glory and mystery of angels is the theme of this collection of poems.

Avi. ***The Christmas Rat.*** Atheneum Books for Young Readers, c2000. 135pp.
Alone in his apartment during Christmas vacation, eleven-year-old Eric finds himself caught in a battle between a strange exterminator and the rat he wants to kill.

Bauer, Jutta. ***Grandpa's Angel.*** Candlewick Press, c2005. 48pp.
An elderly man shares his life story with his grandson, complete with long, dangerous walks to school, war, love and marriage, and a very special protector.

Dalton, Annie. ***Calling the Shots.*** Avon, 2003, c2002. 154pp.
Mel has her hands full when her first mission as a guardian angel sends her back to Earth to watch over an aspiring Hollywood starlet in the 1920s.

Hendry, Diana. ***Harvey Angell Beats Time.*** Aladdin Paperbacks, 2002, c2000. 150pp.
Henry calls upon his friend, the mysterious and magical Harvey Angell, for help when a storm deposits an extraordinary baby in the garden—one with antennae instead of eyebrows, and ears that look like buttercups.

From Nancy J. Keane, *The Big Book of Children's Reading Lists: 100 Great, Ready-to-Use Book Lists for Educators, Librarians, Parents, and Children.* Westport, CT: Libraries Unlimited, 2006. Copyright © 2006 by Libraries Unlimited.

Cowboys

Books for Children of All Ages

Brett, Jan. ***Armadillo Rodeo.*** Putnam, c1995. 32pp.
Looking for adventure, Bo the armadillo follows a girl in red cowboy boots to the rodeo, where he rides a bronco, eats chili peppers, and tries the two-step.

Frank, John. ***The Toughest Cowboy, Or, How the Wild West Was Tamed.*** Simon & Schuster Books for Young Readers, c2004. 40pp.
A group of grizzly cowboys are transformed when Foofy, a French poodle, comes to live with them on the range.

Ketteman, Helen. ***Bubba the Cowboy Prince: A Fractured Texas Tale.*** Scholastic, 1997. 32pp.
Loosely based on "Cinderella," this story is set in Texas, the fairy godmother is a cow, and the hero, named Bubba, is the stepson of a wicked rancher.

Kimmel, Eric A. ***Four Dollars and Fifty Cents.*** Holiday House, c1990. 32pp.
To avoid paying the Widow Macrae the $4.50 he owes her, deadbeat cowboy Shorty Long plays dead and almost gets buried alive.

Lenski, Lois. ***Cowboy Small.*** Random House, 2001, c1949. 50pp.
Cowboy Small takes good care of his horse, rides the range, helps in the roundup, and rides a bucking bronco.

Lester, Julius. ***Black Cowboy, Wild Horses. A True Story.*** Dial Books, c1998. 40pp.
An African American cowboy is so in tune with wild mustangs that they accept him into the herd, thus enabling him to take them to the corral single-handedly.

Lowell, Susan. ***Cindy Ellen: A Wild Western Cinderella.*** HarperCollins, c2000. 40pp.
Cindy Ellen loses one of her diamond spurs at the square dance in this wild Western retelling of the classic "Cinderella."

Miller, Heather. ***Cowboy.*** Heinemann Library, c2003. 24pp.
Describes a day in a cowboy's life, covering what cowboys do, what they wear, what tools they use, how to become a cowboy, and other related topics; includes color photos, a cowboy quiz, and a picture glossary.

Murdoch, David Hamilton. ***Cowboy.*** Dorling Kindersley, c2000. 63pp.
Text and photographs trace the history and lore of cowboys around the globe.

Nolen, Jerdine. ***Thunder Rose.*** Harcourt, c2003. 32pp.
Unusual from the day she is born, Thunder Rose performs all sorts of amazing feats, including building metal structures, taming a stampeding herd of steers, capturing a gang of rustlers, and turning aside a tornado.

Pinkney, Andrea Davis. ***Bill Pickett: Rodeo-Ridin' Cowboy.*** Harcourt Brace, c1996. 32pp. (NF)
Describes the life and accomplishments of the son of a former slave, whose unusual bulldogging style made him a rodeo star.

From Nancy J. Keane, *The Big Book of Children's Reading Lists: 100 Great, Ready-to-Use Book Lists for Educators, Librarians, Parents, and Children.* Westport, CT. Libraries Unlimited, 2006. Copyright © 2006 by Libraries Unlimited.

Cowboys

Savage, Candace Sherk. ***Born to Be a Cowgirl: A Spirited Ride Through the Old West.*** Tricycle Press, c2001. 64pp. (NF)
Examines the lives of young women, most raised in the Wild West beginning in the mid-nineteenth century, who adopted the cowboy lifestyle; includes photographs and first-person quotations.

Smith, Janice Lee. ***Jess and the Stinky Cowboys.*** Dial Books for Young Readers, c2004. 48pp.
When a band of stinky cowboys comes to town while the sheriff is away and refuses to bathe, young Deputy Jess and her aunt, Deputy Gussy, must find a way to enforce the No-Stink Law.

Stanley, Diane. ***Saving Sweetness.*** Putnam, c1996. 32pp.
The sheriff of a dusty Western town rescues Sweetness, an unusually resourceful orphan, from nasty old Mrs. Sump and her terrible orphanage.

Timberlake, Amy. ***The Dirty Cowboy.*** Farrar, Straus & Giroux, c2003. 32pp.
Telling his faithful dog to make sure nobody touches his clothes but him, a cowboy jumps into a New Mexico river for a bath, not realizing just how much the scrubbing will change his scent.

Willis, Jeanne. ***I Want to Be a Cowgirl.*** H. Holt, c2002. 25pp.
Speaking in rhyme, a little girl tells her father that she would rather have the active outdoor life of a cowgirl than that of a girl who stays inside quietly reading, talking, or cleaning.

Books for Children Ages 8–12

Bial, Raymond. ***Cow Towns.*** Children's Press, c2004. 48pp. (NF)
Examines life in the cow towns that developed in the nineteenth century, primarily in Kansas, to provide goods and services to cattlemen looking to sell their herds.

Freedman, Russell. ***In the Days of the Vaqueros: America's First True Cowboys.*** Clarion Books, c2001. 70pp. (NF)
Describes the work, equipment, and culture of the vaqueros, the Spanish cowherders who shaped the Mexican plains 500 years ago, and traces their evolution over the centuries into "cowboys" and "buckaroos."

Scieszka, Jon. ***The Good, the Bad, and the Goofy.*** Viking Press, c1992. 70pp.
The Time Warp Trio find themselves in the Wild West of yesteryear, rubbing elbows with cowboys and Indians.

Sundling, Charles W. ***Cowboys of the Frontier.*** Abdo, c2000. 32pp. (NF)
A brief introduction to the day-to-day life of cowboys in the American West.

Worcester, Donald Emmet. ***Cowboy with a Camera: Erwin E. Smith, Cowboy Photographer.*** Amon Carter Museum, c1998. 48pp. (NF)
A historical account of cowboy life on the open range in the early twentieth century, featuring photographs by cowboy artist Erwin E. Smith.

From Nancy J. Keane, *The Big Book of Children's Reading Lists: 100 Great, Ready-to-Use Book Lists for Educators, Librarians, Parents, and Children.* Westport, CT: Libraries Unlimited, 2006. Copyright © 2006 by Libraries Unlimited.

Days of the Week

Books for Children of All Ages

Carle, Eric. ***Today Is Monday.*** Philomel Books, c1993. 25pp. (NF)
Each day of the week brings a new food, until on Sunday all the world's children can come and eat it up.

Fernandes, Eugenie. ***Big Week for Little Mouse.*** Kids Can Press, c2004. 24pp.
An introduction to the days of the week, in rhyming prose and illustrations that describe the various activities Little Mouse must do to get ready for the birthday party on Sunday.

Johnson, Dinah. ***Sunday Week.*** H. Holt, c1999. 32pp.
Describes the activities that a community of people engage in all week long as they wait for Sunday, the best day of all.

Katz, Karen. ***Twelve Hats for Lena: A Book of Months.*** Margaret K. McElderry Books, c2002. 32pp.
Lena Katz creates hats appropriate for each month of the year.

Koller, Jackie French. ***Seven Spunky Monkeys.*** Harcourt, c2005. 32pp.
One by one, seven monkeys who go out to have a good time wind up falling in love over the course of a week.

Kraus, Robert. ***Come Out and Play, Little Mouse.*** Mulberry Books, 1995, c1987. 32pp.
Little mouse is busy helping his family five days of the week, but he gets to play with them on weekends.

Llewellyn, Claire. ***My First Book of Time.*** Dorling Kindersley (distributed by Houghton Mifflin), c1992. 30pp. (NF)
Explains how to tell time and discusses such aspects of time as day and night, days of the week, and months of the year. Includes a fold-out clock face for practice.

Murphy, Patricia J. ***A Day.*** Capstone Press, c2005. 24pp. (NF)
Introduces the concept of the day, in simple text with illustrations; includes information on how many days are in a week, month, and year; explains the different times of day: morning, afternoon, and night.

Murphy, Patricia J. ***A Week.*** Capstone Press, c2005. 24pp. (NF)
Introduces the concept of the calendar week, in simple text with illustrations, and includes information how many days are in week, how many weeks are in year, and what happens during each of the different days, Monday through Friday. Includes a glossary.

Scheunemann, Pam. ***Days.*** Abdo, c2001. 24pp. (NF)
Simple text and color photos introduce children to the days of the week and the capital letters with which they are spelled.

Ward, Cindy. ***Cookie's Week.*** Penguin Putnam Books for Young Readers, 1997, c1988. 32pp.
Cookie the cat gets into a different kind of mischief every day of the week.

Wells, Rosemary. ***How Many? How Much?*** Puffin Books, c2001. 24pp. (NF)
Timothy and his kindergarten classmates learn about counting, measuring, money, and other math concepts. Includes activities on directionality, spatial relations, and the days of the week.

From Nancy J. Keane, *The Big Book of Children's Reading Lists: 100 Great, Ready-to-Use Book Lists for Educators, Librarians, Parents, and Children.* Westport, CT: Libraries Unlimited, 2006. Copyright © 2006 by Libraries Unlimited

Dragons

Books for Children of All Ages

Coville, Bruce. ***The Dragon of Doom.*** Simon & Schuster Books for Young Readers, c2003. 69pp.
Life in the village of Pigbone is boring until an aspiring magician and his talking toad come to town and ask Edward to help them slay the Dragon of Doom.

Davol, Marguerite W. ***The Paper Dragon.*** Atheneum Books for Young Readers, c1997. 32pp.
A humble artist agrees to confront the terrifying dragon that threatens to destroy his village.

De Paola, Tomie. ***The Knight and the Dragon.*** Putnam & Grosset, 1998, c1980. 32pp.
A knight who has never fought a dragon and an equally inexperienced dragon prepare to meet each other in battle.

Deedy, Carmen Agra. ***The Library Dragon.*** Peachtree, c1994. 32pp.
Miss Lotta Scales is a dragon who believes her job is to protect the school's library books from the children, but when she finally realizes that books are meant to be read, the dragon turns into Miss Lotty, librarian and storyteller.

Gibbons, Gail. ***Behold—the Dragons!*** Morrow Junior Books, c1999. 32pp.
Explains how myths about dragons developed, different types of dragons, what draconologists do, and how different cultures portray dragons.

Gray, Luli. ***Falcon's Egg.*** Houghton Mifflin, c1995. 133pp.
Taking care of her younger brother and a loving but flighty mother has made Falcon very responsible for an eleven-year-old, but she needs the help of her great-great aunt, a friendly neighbor, and an ornithologist when she finds an unusual egg in Central Park.

Munsch, Robert N. ***The Paper Bag Princess.*** Annick Press, c1980. 27pp.
Princess, Elizabeth, robbed of her beautiful clothes and her fiancé by a fierce dragon, dons a paper bag and marches off to rescue her prince, only to realize he is not worthy of her efforts.

San Souci, Robert D. ***The Reluctant Dragon.*** Orchard Books, c2004. 39pp.
A retelling of Kenneth Grahame's classic story in which Jack, aware that the fire-breathing dragon living near his home is really a gentle, poetic soul, must find a way to convince St. George the dragonslayer, as well as the villagers, that there is nothing to fear.

Thayer, Jane. ***The Popcorn Dragon.*** Morrow Junior Books, c1989. 32pp.
Though his hot breath is the envy of all the other animals, a young dragon learns that showing off does not make friends.

Thomas, Shelley Moore. ***Get Well, Good Knight.*** Dutton Children's Books, c2002. 44pp.
A good knight does his best to help his three ill dragon friends with a wizard's soups, but when these fail miserably, the knight realizes he needs a more dependable source of aid.

Ward, Helen. ***The Dragon Machine.*** Dutton Children's Books, c2003. 32pp.
George, ignored and overlooked, begins seeing dragons everywhere and soon comes to a decision that he alone must lead them back to their wilderness home.

Wilson, Gina. ***Ignis.*** Candlewick Press, c2001. 40pp.
Though he is admired by others, a young dragon does not feel complete because he cannot breathe fire.

From Nancy J. Keane, *The Big Book of Children's Reading Lists: 100 Great, Ready-to-Use Book Lists for Educators, Librarians, Parents, and Children.* Westport, CT: Libraries Unlimited, 2006. Copyright © 2006 by Libraries Unlimited.

Dragons

Books for Children Ages 8–12

Coville, Bruce. ***Jeremy Thatcher, Dragon Hatcher.*** Harcourt, 2002, c1991. 151pp.
Small for his age but artistically talented, twelve-year-old Jeremy Thatcher unknowingly buys a dragon's egg.

Cowell, Cressida. ***How to Train Your Dragon.*** Little, Brown, 2004, c2003. 214pp.
Chronicles the adventures and misadventures of Hiccup Horrendous Haddock the Third as he tries to pass the important initiation test of his Viking clan, the Tribe of the Hairy Hooligans, by catching and training a dragon.

Downer, Ann. ***Hatching Magic.*** Atheneum Books for Young Readers, c2003. 242pp.
When a thirteenth-century wizard confronts twenty-first-century Boston while seeking his pet dragon, he is followed by a rival wizard and a very unhappy demon, but eleven-year-old Theodora Oglethorpe may hold the secret to setting everything right.

Dr. Ernest Drake's Dragonology: The Complete Book of Dragons. Candlewick Press, c2003. 30pp.
An introduction to dragonology that includes spells to catch dragons, a chronology of their natural history, tips for catching a dragon, descriptions of legendary dragons, and numerous illustrations of dragons and dragon slayers.

Fire and Wings: Dragon Tales from East and West. Cricket Books, c2002. 146pp.
A collection of stories about all kinds of dragons, by such authors as Jane Yolen, Patricia MacLaughlin, Eric Kimmel, Vida Chu, and E. Nesbit.

Funke, Cornelia Caroline. ***Dragon Rider.*** Scholastic, c2004. 523pp.
After learning that humans are headed toward his hidden home, Firedrake, a silver dragon, is joined by a brownie and an orphan boy in a quest to find the legendary valley known as the Rim of Heaven, encountering friendly and unfriendly creatures along the way, and struggling to evade the relentless pursuit of an old enemy.

Grahame, Kenneth. ***The Reluctant Dragon.*** Candlewick Press, c2004. 54pp.
In this illustrated, abridged version of the original, the boy who finds the dragon in the cave knows it is a kindly, harmless one, but how can he convince the frightened villagers and, especially St. George the dragon killer, that there is no cause for concern?

Nesbit, E. ***The Book of Beasts.*** Candlewick Press, c2001. 53pp.
As young King Lionel turns the pages of his magical book, a hungry red dragon and other creatures in the illustrations come to life.

Rupp, Rebecca. ***The Dragon of Lonely Island.*** Candlewick Press, c1998. 160pp.
Three children spend the summer with their mother on a secluded island, where they discover a three-headed dragon living in a cave and learn what it means to be a Dragon Friend.

Yolen, Jane. ***The Dragon's Boy.*** HarperTrophy, 2001, c1990. 120pp.
Young Arthur meets a dragon and comes to accept him as a friend and mentor.

Zhang, Song Nan. ***A Time of Golden Dragons.*** Tundra Books, Tundra Books of Northern New York, c2000. 24pp.
Traces the history of dragon symbols and legends in the Chinese culture.

From Nancy J. Keane, *The Big Book of Children's Reading Lists: 100 Great, Ready-to-Use Book Lists for Educators, Librarians, Parents, and Children.* Westport, CT: Libraries Unlimited, 2006. Copyright © 2006 by Libraries Unlimited.

Chinese New Year

Books for Children of All Ages

Brown, Tricia. ***Chinese New Year.*** H. Holt, 1997, c1987. 48pp. (NF)
Text and photographs depict the celebration of Chinese New Year by Chinese Americans living in San Francisco's Chinatown.

Compestine, Ying Chang. ***The Runaway Rice Cake.*** Simon & Schuster Books for Young Readers, c2001. 34pp.
After chasing the special rice cake, Nian Gao, that their mother has made to celebrate the Chinese New Year, three poor brothers share it with an elderly woman and their generosity is richly rewarded.

Flanagan, Alice K. ***Chinese New Year.*** Compass Point Books, c2004. 32pp. (NF)
Explores the origins of Chinese New Year, a holiday that marks the end of winter and the beginning of spring, and describes the preparations, foods, customs, and symbols associated with the celebration.

Jango-Cohen, Judith. ***Chinese New Year.*** Carolrhoda Books, c2005. 48pp. (NF)
Describes how the Chinese New Year is celebrated with costumes, food, visiting, gifts, and other rituals.

Books for Children Ages 8–12

Demi. ***Happy New Year!: Kung-hsi fa-ts'ai!*** Crown, c1997. 34pp. (NF)
Examines the customs, traditions, foods, and lore associated with the celebration of Chinese New Year.

Hoyt-Goldsmith, Diane. ***Celebrating Chinese New Year.*** Holiday House, c1998. 32pp. (NF)
Depicts a San Francisco boy and his family preparing for and enjoying the celebration of the Chinese New Year, their most important holiday.

MacMillan, Dianne M. ***Chinese New Year.*** Enslow, c1994. 48pp. (NF)
Explains the history of Chinese New Year and tells how it is celebrated.

Yep, Laurence. ***When the Circus Came to Town.*** HarperCollins, c2002. 113pp.
An Asian cook and a Chinese New Year celebration help a ten-year-old girl at a Montana stage coach station regain her confidence after smallpox scars her face.

From Nancy J. Keane, *The Big Book of Children's Reading Lists: 100 Great, Ready-to-Use Book Lists for Educators, Librarians, Parents, and Children.* Westport, CT: Libraries Unlimited, 2006. Copyright © 2006 by Libraries Unlimited.

Easter

Books for Children of All Ages

Auch, Mary Jane. ***The Easter Egg Farm.*** Holiday House, c1992. 32pp.
Pauline the hen lays unusual eggs, but Mrs. Pennywort, her owner, thinks they're beautiful, and she and Pauline work together to open an Easter egg farm.

Dunn, Judy. ***The Little Rabbit.*** Random House, c1980. 32pp.
Sarah's Easter gift rabbit becomes her constant companion and eventually gives birth to seven little bunnies.

Friedrich, Priscilla. ***The Easter Bunny That Overslept.*** HarperCollins, c2002. 32pp.
Having slept past Easter, the Easter Bunny tries to distribute his eggs on Mother's Day, the Fourth of July, and Halloween, but no one is interested, until finally Santa Claus is able to get him back on track.

Gibbons, Gail. ***Easter.*** Holiday House, c1989. 32pp. (NF)
Examines the background, significance, symbols, and traditions of Easter.

Houselander, Caryll. ***Petook: An Easter Story.*** Holiday House, c1988. 30pp.
Petook the rooster witnesses the crucifixion of Christ and rejoices in the birth of new chicks three days later on Easter morning.

Kimmel, Eric A. ***The Birds' Gift: A Ukrainian Easter Story.*** Holiday House, c1999. 32pp.
Villagers take in a flock of golden birds nearly frozen by an early snow and are rewarded with beautifully decorated eggs the next spring.

Modesitt, Jeanne. ***Little Bunny's Easter Surprise.*** Aladdin Paperbacks, 2002, c1999. 28pp.
Little Bunny surprises her mother, father, and baby brother with Easter baskets for all of them.

Polacco, Patricia. ***Chicken Sunday.*** Philomel Books, c1992. 32pp.
To thank Miss Eula for her wonderful Sunday chicken dinners, three children sell decorated eggs to buy her a beautiful Easter hat.

Polacco, Patricia. ***Rechenka's Eggs.*** Philomel Books, c1988. 32pp.
Having broken the painted eggs intended for the Easter Festival in Moscva, an injured goose rescued by Babushka lays thirteen marvelously colored eggs to replace them, leaving behind one final miracle in egg form before returning to her own kind.

From Nancy J. Keane, *The Big Book of Children's Reading Lists: 100 Great, Ready-to-Use Book Lists for Educators, Librarians, Parents, and Children.* Westport, CT: Libraries Unlimited, 2006. Copyright © 2006 by Libraries Unlimited.

Easter

Zolotow, Charlotte. ***The Bunny Who Found Easter.*** Houghton Mifflin, 1998, c1959. 32pp.
A lonely rabbit searches for others of his kind from summer through winter, until spring arrives and he finds one special bunny.

Books for Children Ages 8–12

Barth, Edna. ***Lilies, Rabbits, and Painted Eggs: The Story of the Easter Symbols.*** Clarion, c1998. 63pp. (NF)
Traces the history of Easter symbols from their Christian and pagan origins to such present-day additions as rabbits and new clothes.

Chambers, Catherine. ***Easter.*** Raintree Steck-Vaughn, c1998. 31pp. (NF)
Introduces the holiday of Easter and explains how it is celebrated all over the world.

Fisher, Aileen Lucia. ***The Story of Easter.*** HarperCollins, c1997. 32pp. (NF)
Presents the background and significance of the Christian celebration of Easter.

Sanders, Nancy I. ***Easter.*** Children's Press, c2003. 47pp. (NF)
An introduction to the history, customs, meaning, and celebration of Easter.

From Nancy J. Keane, *The Big Book of Children's Reading Lists: 100 Great, Ready-to-Use Book Lists for Educators, Librarians, Parents, and Children.* Westport, CT: Libraries Unlimited, 2006. Copyright © 2006 by Libraries Unlimited.

Independence Day

Books for Children of All Ages

Chall, Marsha Wilson. ***Happy Birthday, America!*** HarperCollins, c2000. 32pp.
Joined by an army of aunts, uncles, and cousins, eight-year-old Kay and her family celebrate the Fourth of July.

Kimmelman, Leslie. ***Happy 4th of July, Jenny Sweeney!*** Whitman, c2003. 32pp.
Town residents prepare to celebrate the Fourth of July with food, a parade, and fireworks.

Lilly, Melinda. ***The Declaration of Independence.*** Rourke Press, c2003. 24pp. (NF)
A simple introduction to Independence Day and the writing of the Declaration of Independence.

Roberts, Bethany. ***Fourth of July Mice!*** Clarion Books, c2004. 31pp.
Four energetic mice enjoy a parade and other festivities on Independence Day.

Whitehead, Kathy. ***Looking for Uncle Louie on the Fourth of July.*** Boyds Mills Press, c2005. 32pp.
Joe and his parents go to the Fourth of July parade, and after looking for his Uncle Louie all day, Joe gets a big surprise when the decorated, low rider cars drive past.

Wong, Janet S. ***Apple Pie 4th of July.*** Harcourt, c2002. 32pp.
A Chinese American child fears that the food her parents are preparing to sell on the Fourth of July will not be eaten.

Books for Children Ages 8–12

Giblin, James. ***Fireworks, Picnics, and Flags.*** Clarion Books, c1983. 90pp. (NF)
Traces the social history behind the celebration of Independence Day and explains the background of such national symbols as the flag, the bald eagle, the Liberty Bell, and Uncle Sam.

Hess, Debra. ***The Fourth of July.*** Benchmark Books, c2004. 40pp. (NF)
Describes the history and symbolism of the Fourth of July holiday in the United States.

Hill, Elizabeth Starr. ***Wildfire!*** Farrar, Straus & Giroux, c2004. 66pp.
Living with his great-grandmother in rural Florida, ten-year-old Ben looks forward to the Fourth of July celebrations, but the day becomes complicated by the presence of a new neighbor boy, a stray puppy, and local wildfires.

Maguire, Gregory. ***One Final Firecracker.*** Clarion Books, c2005. 225pp.
A giant spider and several other odd creatures from the earlier books in the Hamlet Chronicles return as the small Vermont town celebrates a grammar school graduation, Miss Earth's wedding, and the Fourth of July.

From Nancy J. Keane, *The Big Book of Children's Reading Lists: 100 Great, Ready-to-Use Book Lists for Educators, Librarians, Parents, and Children.* Westport, CT: Libraries Unlimited, 2006. Copyright © 2006 by Libraries Unlimited.

Halloween

Books for Children of All Ages

Bailey, Mary Bryant. ***Jeoffry's Halloween.*** Farrar, Straus & Giroux, c2003. 32pp.
After roaming through fields, woods, and streets on Halloween night, Jeoffry the cat is glad to finally return home.

Bond, Felicia. ***The Halloween Play.*** Laura Geringer Books, 1999, c1983. 24pp.
Roger plays a small but important part in the school's Halloween play.

Brown, Margaret Wise. ***The Fierce Yellow Pumpkin.*** HarperCollins, c2003. 32pp.
A little pumpkin dreams of the day when he will be a big, fierce, yellow pumpkin who frightens away the field mice as the scarecrow does.

Costello, David. ***Here They Come.*** Farrar, Straus & Giroux, c2004. 32pp.
When a group of frightening creatures holds a Halloween party in the woods, some costumed children give them a scare.

Crimi, Carolyn. ***Boris and Bella.*** Harcourt, c2004. 32pp.
Bella Legrossi and Boris Kleanitoff, the messiest and cleanest monsters in Booville, respectively, do nothing but argue until the night of Harry Beastie's Halloween party.

Dillon, Jana. ***Jeb Scarecrow's Pumpkin Patch.*** Houghton Mifflin, c1992. 32pp.
Jeb Scarecrow comes up with a wonderful plan to scare the crows away from his pumpkin patch.

Gibbons, Gail. ***Halloween Is—.*** Holiday House, c2002. 32pp. (NF)
Looks at some of the many traditions associated with the celebration of Halloween, including pumpkin carving, trick-or-treating, and wearing costumes.

Hall, Zoe. ***It's Pumpkin Time!*** Blue Sky Press, 1999, c1994. 32pp.
A sister and brother plant and tend their own pumpkin patch so they will have jack-o'-lanterns for Halloween.

Krosoczka, Jarrett. ***Annie Was Warned.*** Knopf (distributed by Random House), c2003. 28pp.
Disregarding warnings about the creepy mansion outside of town, on Halloween night Annie bravely goes to investigate and gets a big surprise.

London, Jonathan. ***Froggy's Halloween.*** Viking Press, 1999. 32pp.
Froggy tries to find just the right costume for Halloween, and although his trick-or-treating does not go as he had planned, he enjoys himself anyway.

Parish, Herman. ***Happy Haunting, Amelia Bedelia.*** Greenwillow Books, c2004. 64pp.
Amelia Bedelia tries to help Mr. and Mrs. Rogers with their Halloween party.

Reeves, Howard W. ***There Was an Old Witch.*** Hyperion Books for Children, 2000, c1998. 24pp.
In this cumulative verse, an old witch collects a bat, a scratching scritching cat, a howling yowling creature, and other creepy crawly things to adorn her Halloween hat.

Rylant, Cynthia. ***Moonlight: The Halloween Cat.*** HarperCollins, c2003. 26pp.
Moonlight the cat loves everything about Halloween, from pumpkins to children to candy.

From Nancy J. Keane, *The Big Book of Children's Reading Lists: 100 Great, Ready-to-Use Book Lists for Educators, Librarians, Parents, and Children.* Westport, CT: Libraries Unlimited, 2006. Copyright © 2006 by Libraries Unlimited.

Halloween

Shaw, Nancy. ***Sheep Trick or Treat.*** Houghton Mifflin, c1997. 32pp.
When sheep dress up to go trick-or-treating at a nearby farm, their costumes scare away some wolves lurking in the woods.

Silverman, Erica. ***The Halloween House.*** Farrar, Straus & Giroux, 1999, c1997. 32pp.
The Halloween house, occupied by a variety of creatures, including werewolves, witches, bats, and skeletons, turns out to be an unfortunate choice as a hideout for a couple of escaped convicts.

Tegen, Katherine Brown. ***Dracula and Frankenstein Are Friends.*** HarperCollins, c2003. 30pp.
Dracula and Frankenstein are friends until they both decide to have a Halloween party, and Dracula misplaces Frankenstein's invitations.

Thompson, Lauren. ***Mouse's First Halloween.*** Simon & Schuster Books for Young Readers, c2000. 32pp.
On Halloween a mouse finds scary objects everywhere he goes.

Tunnell, Michael O. ***Halloween Pie.*** Boyds Mills Press, 2004, c1999. 24pp.
Old Witch smiles a crooked smile and makes a Halloween pie for vampire and ghoul and ghost and banshee to enjoy.

Van Rynbach, Iris. ***Five Little Pumpkins.*** Boyds Mills Press (distributed by St. Martin's Press), c1995. 24pp.
The traditional finger rhyme, illustrated with lively watercolors.

Waldron, Jan L. ***John Pig's Halloween.*** Puffin Books, 2001, c1998. 30pp.
Too scared to go trick-or-treating, John Pig stays home on Halloween and has an unplanned party with some unexpected, monstrous guests.

Books for Children Ages 8–12

Greene, Carol. ***The Story of Halloween.*** HarperCollins, c2004. 35pp. (NF)
Explores the history of Halloween from the holiday's Celtic origins over 2,000 years ago to present-day celebrations, and provides spooky riddles and ideas for pumpkin art.

Kline, Suzy. ***Horrible Harry at Halloween.*** Viking Press, c2000. 53pp.
The students in Miss Mackle's third-grade class enjoy a day of Halloween surprises, including Harry's unusual costume.

Robinson, Barbara. ***The Best Halloween Ever.*** Joanna Cotler Books, c2004. 117pp.
The six horrible Herdman children create mayhem during Halloween.

Seuling, Barbara. ***Robert and the Back-to-School Special.*** Cricket Books, c2002. 104pp.
The new school year gets off to a not-so-good start when Robert gets a bad haircut, but things improve when his father helps him plan a party for Halloween.

Vande Velde, Vivian. ***Witch's Wishes.*** Holiday House, c2003. 91pp.
On Halloween, six-year-old Sarah helps out a witch, who repays her kindness by making her magic wand real for the night, resulting in a series of wishes coming true that the witch then has to fix.

From Nancy J. Keane, *The Big Book of Children's Reading Lists: 100 Great, Ready-to-Use Book Lists for Educators, Librarians, Parents, and Children.* Westport, CT: Libraries Unlimited, 2006. Copyright © 2006 by Libraries Unlimited.

Thanksgiving

Books for Children of All Ages

Anderson, Laurie Halse. *Thank You, Sarah: The Woman Who Saved Thanksgiving.* Simon & Schuster Books for Young Readers, c2002. 40pp.
Relates how Sarah Hale, a magazine editor and author, persuaded President Lincoln to transform Thanksgiving Day into a national holiday.

Atwell, Debby. *The Thanksgiving Door.* Houghton Mifflin, c2003. 32pp.
After burning their Thanksgiving dinner, Ann and Ed head for the local cafe, where they are welcomed by an immigrant family to an unusual celebration that gives everyone cause to be thankful.

Balian, Lorna. *Sometimes It's Turkey, Sometimes It's Feathers.* Star Bright Books, c2004. 33pp.
When she finds a turkey egg, Mrs. Gumm decides to hatch it and have a turkey for Thanksgiving dinner.

Boelts, Maribeth. *The Firefighters' Thanksgiving.* Putnam, c2004. 32pp.
Calls to fires, an injured friend, and cooking disasters threaten to keep a group of firefighters from enjoying Thanksgiving dinner.

Bruchac, Joseph. *Squanto's Journey: The Story of the First Thanksgiving.* Harcourt, c2000. 32pp.
Squanto recounts how in 1614 he was captured by the British, sold into slavery in Spain, and ultimately returned to the New World to become a guide and friend for the colonists.

Bunting, Eve. *A Turkey for Thanksgiving.* Clarion Books, c1991. 31pp.
Mr. and Mrs. Moose try to invite a turkey to their Thanksgiving feast.

Capucilli, Alyssa Satin. *Happy Thanksgiving, Biscuit!* HarperFestival, c1999. 18pp.
Biscuit is fed by a little girl on Thanksgiving Day.

De Paola, Tomie. *My First Thanksgiving.* Putnam, c1992. 12pp.
Introduces in simple text some of the family activities associated with the celebration of Thanksgiving.

Devlin, Wende. *Cranberry Thanksgiving.* Aladdin Paperbacks, c1990. 38pp.
Grandmother almost loses her secret recipe for cranberry bread to one of the guests she and Maggie invite for Thanksgiving dinner. Includes the secret recipe.

Goode, Diane. *Thanksgiving Is Here!* HarperCollins, c2003. 32pp.
A family gathers to celebrate Thanksgiving at Grandma's house.

From Nancy J. Keane, *The Big Book of Children's Reading Lists: 100 Great, Ready-to-Use Book Lists for Educators, Librarians, Parents, and Children.* Westport, CT: Libraries Unlimited, 2006. Copyright © 2006 by Libraries Unlimited.

Thanksgiving

Herman, Charlotte. ***The Memory Cupboard: A Thanksgiving Story.*** Whitman, c2003. 32pp.
When Katie breaks a gravy boat at Thanksgiving dinner, her grandmother shows her that love is more important than objects.

Hoban, Lillian. ***Silly Tilly's Thanksgiving Dinner.*** HarperTrophy, 1991, c1990. 63pp.
Forgetful Silly Tilly Mole nearly succeeds in ruining her Thanksgiving dinner, but her animal friends come to the rescue with tasty treats.

Kamma, Anne. ***If You Were At—the First Thanksgiving.*** Scholastic, c2001. 64pp. (NF)
Presents color-illustrated answers to nearly fifty questions about the first Thanksgiving, from "Why did the Pilgrims come to America?" to "Who had to clean the dishes?"

Levine, Abby. ***This Is the Turkey.*** Whitman, c2000. 24pp.
Describes in rhyme the activities of a young boy and his extended family as they share a special Thanksgiving.

Milgrim, David. ***Thank You, Thanksgiving.*** Clarion Books, c2003. 32pp.
While on a Thanksgiving Day errand for her mother, a girl says thank you to all the things around her.

Nikola-Lisa, W. ***Setting the Turkeys Free.*** Jump at the Sun/Hyperion Books for Children, c2004. 32pp.
A little boy makes several paper turkeys that come to life and now have to be protected from Foxy the Fox, who is on the prowl for something good to eat.

Rael, Elsa. ***Rivka's First Thanksgiving.*** Margaret K. McElderry, c2001. 32pp.
Having heard about Thanksgiving in school, nine-year-old Rivka tries to convince her immigrant family and her rabbi that it is a holiday for all Americans, Jews and non-Jews alike.

Rockwell, Anne F. ***Thanksgiving Day.*** HarperCollins, c1999. 33pp.
Mrs. Madoff's preschool class learns about Thanksgiving and puts on a play about the origins of the holiday.

Spinelli, Eileen. ***The Perfect Thanksgiving.*** H. Holt, c2003. 32pp.
Two families—one that is perfect and one that is far from it—celebrate Thanksgiving in their own loving ways.

Spinelli, Eileen. ***Thanksgiving at the Tappletons'.*** HarperCollins, 2003, c1982. 32pp.
When calamity stalks every step of the preparations for the Tappletons' Thanksgiving dinner, they realize that there is more to Thanksgiving than turkey and trimmings.

From Nancy J. Keane, *The Big Book of Children's Reading Lists: 100 Great, Ready-to-Use Book Lists for Educators, Librarians, Parents, and Children.* Westport, CT: Libraries Unlimited, 2006. Copyright © 2006 by Libraries Unlimited.

Thanksgiving

Stanley Diane. *Thanksgiving on Plymouth Plantation.* Joanna Cotler Books, c2004. 42pp.
Twins Liz and Lenny, along with their time-traveling grandmother, visit Plymouth Plantation to see how the Pilgrims lived and to celebrate a big feast with the Pilgrims and Native Americans.

Books for Children Ages 8–12

Cohen, Barbara. *Molly's Pilgrim.* Lothrop, Lee & Shepard Books, c1998. 32pp.
Told to make a Pilgrim doll for the Thanksgiving display at school, Molly is embarrassed when her mother tries to help her out by creating a doll dressed as she herself was dressed before leaving Russia to seek religious freedom.

De Groat, Diane. *Annie Pitts, Burger Kid.* SeaStar Books, c2000. 107pp.
Third-grader Annie Pitts loves hamburgers and is determined to become the Burger Barn's next poster child.

Grace, Catherine O'Neill. *1621: A New Look at Thanksgiving.* National Geographic Society, c2001. 47pp. (NF)
Chronicles the events of the first Thanksgiving and discusses how the holiday has changed over time.

Greenwood, Barbara. *A Pioneer Thanksgiving: A Story of Harvest Celebrations in 1841.* Kids Can Press, c1999. 48pp.
Tells the story of what Thanksgiving was like for the Robertsons, a pioneer family living on a backwoods farm in 1841.

Lowry, Lois. *Gooney Bird and the Room Mother.* Houghton Mifflin, c2005. 76pp.
Gooney Bird Greene, an entertaining second-grader who introduces challenging vocabulary words and tells "absolutely true" stories, finds a surprise room mother to bring cupcakes for the Thanksgiving pageant.

Pinkwater, Daniel Manus. *The Hoboken Chicken Emergency.* Aladdin Paperbacks, c1999. 108pp.
Arthur goes to pick up the turkey for Thanksgiving dinner but comes back with a 260-pound chicken.

Smith, Anne Warren. *Turkey Monster Thanksgiving.* Whitman, c2003. 103pp.
When her perfectionist classmate and neighbor plans an elaborate Thanksgiving dinner, Katie begins to wonder if the relaxed day she, her father, and her messy little brother usually enjoy means they are not a "real" family.

From Nancy J. Keane, *The Big Book of Children's Reading Lists: 100 Great, Ready-to-Use Book Lists for Educators, Librarians, Parents, and Children.* Westport, CT: Libraries Unlimited, 2006. Copyright © 2006 by Libraries Unlimited.

Christmas

Books for Children of All Ages

Brett, Jan. *Christmas Trolls.* Putnam, c1993. 32pp.
When Treva investigates the disappearance of her family's Christmas things, she finds two mischievous trolls who have never had a Christmas of their own.

Bunting, Eve. *December.* Harcourt Brace, c1997. 32pp.
A homeless family's luck changes after they help an old woman who has even less than they do at Christmas.

De Paola, Tomie. *The Legend of the Poinsettia.* Putnam, c1994. 32pp.
When Lucida is unable to finish her gift for the Baby Jesus in time for the Christmas procession, a miracle enables her to offer the beautiful flower we now call the poinsettia.

Kelley, Emily. *Christmas Around the World.* Carolrhoda Books, c2004. 48pp. (NF)
Describes Christmas traditions in Mexico, Ethiopia, China, Germany, Lebanon, Sweden, Australia, and Russia.

Krensky, Stephen. *How Santa Got His Job.* Simon & Schuster Books for Young Readers, c1998. 32pp.
Santa tries his hand at many jobs before finding the perfect career as the world's greatest gift giver.

Moore, Clement Clarke. *The Night Before Christmas.* Aladdin Paperbacks, 2000, c1997. 54pp.
The illustrator's Vermont farmhouse and her pets are featured in the illustrations of this well-known poem about an important Christmas Eve visitor.

Moore, Clement Clarke. *The Night Before Christmas.* Putnam, c1998. 32pp.
Presents the well-known poem about an important Christmas visitor.

Price, Moe. *The Reindeer Christmas.* Harcourt Brace, 1997, c1993. 32pp.
Elwin the elf helps Santa Claus find a faster way to deliver his gifts on Christmas Eve.

Primavera, Elise. *Auntie Claus.* Harcourt Brace, c1999. 36pp.
When her eccentric Auntie Claus leaves for her annual business trip, Sophie stows away in her luggage, travels with her to the North Pole, and discovers that her aunt is really Santa's sister and helper.

Rice, James. *Cowboy Night Before Christmas: Formerly Titled Prairie Night Before Christmas.* Pelican, c1990. 32pp.
When Santa's reindeer abandon their job in the midst of a Texas storm, he enlists the help of two lonely cowpokes so that he can finish his Christmas Eve rounds.

Rosen, Michael J. *Elijah's Angel: A Story for Chanukah and Christmas.* Harcourt Brace, 1997, c1992. 32pp.
At Christmas/Hanukkah time, a Christian wood-carver gives a carved angel to a young Jewish friend, who struggles with accepting the Christmas gift until he realizes that friendship means the same thing in any religion.

Sabuda, Robert. *The 12 Days of Christmas: A Pop-Up Celebration.* Little Simon, c1996. 12pp.
A sophisticated pop-up book that uses white paper cutouts by paper engineer Robert Sabuda to illustrate the traditional holiday song.

From Nancy J. Keane, *The Big Book of Children's Reading Lists: 100 Great, Ready-to-Use Book Lists for Educators, Librarians, Parents, and Children.* Westport, CT: Libraries Unlimited, 2006. Copyright © 2006 by Libraries Unlimited.

Christmas

Van Allsburg, Chris. ***The Polar Express.*** Houghton Mifflin, c1985. 32pp.
A magical train ride on Christmas Eve takes a boy to the North Pole to receive a special gift from Santa Claus.

Wilson, Karma. ***Bear Stays up for Christmas.*** Margaret K. McElderry Books, c2004. 34pp.
Bear's friends awaken him the day before Christmas and help him to stay awake as they bake fruitcakes, fill stockings, and sing carols; then, while they sleep, he prepares his own surprise.

Wojciechowski, Susan. ***The Christmas Miracle of Jonathan Toomey.*** Candlewick Press, 2002, c1995. 34pp.
The widow McDowell and her seven-year-old son Thomas ask the gruff Jonathan Toomey, the best wood-carver in the valley, to carve the figures for a Christmas crPche. Includes a reading on CD.

Books for Children Ages 8–12

Avi. ***The Christmas Rat.*** Atheneum Books for Young Readers, c2000. 135pp.
Alone in his apartment during Christmas vacation, eleven-year-old Eric finds himself caught in a battle between a strange exterminator and the rat he wants to kill.

Davis, C. L. ***The Christmas Barn.*** Pleasant, c2001. 177pp.
In 1930, when a snowstorm destroys their home in the mountains of Appalachia, twelve-year-old Roxie and her family move into the barn and prepare for a very unusual Christmas celebration.

Demi. ***The Legend of Saint Nicholas.*** Margaret K. McElderry Books, c2003. 34pp.
Recounts pivotal events in the history and life of Saint Nicholas, including how he came to be associated with Christmas and Santa Claus.

Greenwood, Barbara. ***A Pioneer Christmas: Celebrating in the Backwoods in 1841.*** Kids Can Press, c2003. 48pp.
In 1841, a pioneer family festively prepares for Christmas and eagerly awaits the arrival of their cousin and his pregnant wife, but their excitement turns to worry when a winter storm arrives with no sign of their very special guests. Includes several pioneer Christmas games and activities.

Grimes, Nikki. ***Under the Christmas Tree.*** HarperCollins, c2002. 32pp.
Presents twenty-three poems by Coretta Scott King Award winner Nikki Grimes in which she explores the many facets of Christmas, each with a color illustration.

Kuklin, Susan. ***The Harlem Nutcracker.*** Jump at the Sun/Hyperion Books for Children, c2001. 48pp.
A retelling of the classic story of Tchaikovsky's *Nutcracker* ballet, featuring an African American grandmother and her family and set in Harlem.

Marsden, Carolyn. ***Mama Had to Work on Christmas.*** Viking Press, c2003. 73pp.
Gloria's Christmas begins with frustration when she is forced to go to work with Mama, but by the end of the day, she appreciates her family and enjoys the holiday.

Osborne, Mary Pope. ***Christmas in Camelot.*** Random House, c2001. 115pp.
On Christmas Eve, Jack and Annie's tree house transports them to King Arthur's castle at Camelot, where they undertake a quest to the castle of the Otherworld.

Woodruff, Elvira. ***The Christmas Doll.*** Scholastic, 2001, c2000. 151pp.
As Christmas approaches, Lucy, a ten-year-old orphan living on the streets of London, is overjoyed to be given the job of sewing hearts for the dolls in ThimbleBee's Doll Shop.

From Nancy J. Keane, *The Big Book of Children's Reading Lists: 100 Great, Ready-to-Use Book Lists for Educators, Librarians, Parents, and Children.* Westport, CT: Libraries Unlimited, 2006. Copyright © 2006 by Libraries Unlimited.

Hanukkah

Books for Children of All Ages

Adler, David A. ***One Yellow Daffodil: A Hanukkah Story.*** Voyager Books/Harcourt Brace, 1999, c1995. 32pp.
During Hanukkah two children help a Holocaust survivor once again embrace his religious traditions.

Bunting, Eve. ***One Candle.*** Joanna Cotler Books, c2002. 32pp.
Every year a family celebrates Hanukkah by retelling the story of how Grandma and her sister managed to mark the day while in a German concentration camp.

Edwards, Michelle. ***Papa's Latkes.*** Candlewick Press, c2004. 32pp.
On the first Hanukkah after Mama died, Papa and his two daughters try to make latkes and celebrate without her.

Glaser, Linda. ***The Borrowed Hanukkah Latkes.*** Whitman, c1997. 32pp.
A young girl finds a way to include her elderly neighbor in her family's Hanukkah celebration.

Kimmel, Eric A. ***Asher and the Capmakers: A Hanukkah Story.*** Holiday House, c1993. 32pp.
On his way to get an egg for his mother the night before Hanukkah, a young boy encounters a group of mischievous fairies, who take him on an adventure to Jerusalem.

Kimmel, Eric A. ***Hershel and the Hanukkah Goblins.*** Holiday House, c1989. 32pp.
Relates how Hershel outwits the goblins that haunt the old synagogue and prevent the village people from celebrating Hanukkah.

Kimmel, Eric A. ***When Mindy Saved Hanukkah.*** Scholastic, 1998. 32pp.
A tiny Jewish family living behind the wall of a synagogue must battle a frightening cat if they want candles for their Hanukkah menorah.

Kimmel, Eric A. ***Zigazak!: A Magical Hanukkah Night.*** Doubleday Book for Young Readers, c2001. 32pp.
The rabbi of Brisk is able to teach the people of the town a lesson about good and evil when two devils arrive on Hanukkah night, intent on causing mischief.

Oberman, Sheldon. ***By the Hanukkah Light.*** Boyds Mills Press, c1997. 30pp.
A grandfather tells his grandchildren his own Hanukkah story from World War II.

Podwal, Mark H. ***The Menorah Story.*** Greenwillow Books, c1998. 24pp.
Discusses the story of the Hanukkah menorah, which commemorates the miraculous victory of the Maccabees over King Antiochus and his army.

Polacco, Patricia. ***The Trees of the Dancing Goats.*** Simon & Schuster Books for Young Readers, c1996. 32pp.
During a scarlet fever epidemic one winter in Michigan, a Jewish family helps make Christmas special for their sick neighbors by making their own Hanukkah miracle.

From Nancy J. Keane, *The Big Book of Children's Reading Lists: 100 Great, Ready-to-Use Book Lists for Educators, Librarians, Parents, and Children.* Westport, CT: Libraries Unlimited, 2006. Copyright © 2006 by Libraries Unlimited.

Hanukkah

Schotter, Roni. ***Hanukkah!*** Little, Brown, c1990. 32pp. (NF)
Describes the meaning and traditions of Hanukkah as five children and their family celebrate the holiday.

Spinner, Stephanie. ***It's a Miracle!: A Hanukkah Storybook.*** Atheneum Books for Young Readers, c2003. 43pp.
Every night of Hanukkah, Grandma tells a story at bedtime. Includes the Hanukkah legend, blessings, and a glossary.

Yorinks, Arthur. ***Arthur Yorinks's the Flying Latke.*** Simon & Schuster Books for Young Readers, c1999. 32pp.
A family argument on the first night of Chanukah results in a food fight and a flying latke, which is mistaken for a flying saucer.

Books for Children Ages 8–12

A Hanukkah Treasury. H. Holt, c1998. 99pp. (NF)
Presents stories, songs, recipes, and activities related to the celebration of Hanukkah.

Hesse, Karen. ***The Stone Lamp: Eight Stories of Hanukkah Through History.*** Hyperion Books for Children, c2003. 32pp. (NF)
Relates eight incidents from throughout the history of Judaism, each followed by a free-verse poem, told in the voice of a child from that time, who is celebrating one night of Hanukkah and the resilience of the Jewish people.

Hoyt-Goldsmith, Diane. ***Celebrating Hanukkah.*** Holiday House, c1996. 31pp. (NF)
Presents the history, traditions, and significance of Hanukkah as it is celebrated by a Jewish family in San Francisco.

Rocklin, Joanne. ***The Very Best Hanukkah Gift.*** Dell Yearling, 2001, c1999. 114pp.
Young Daniel Bloom waits for Hanukkah with excited anticipation—despite his mother's zucchini latke experiments—and wishes that he could get over his fear of dogs so that his sister, who loves dogs, could get one. Includes recipes for potato and zucchini latkes.

Rosen, Michael J. ***Elijah's Angel: A Story for Chanukah and Christmas.*** Harcourt Brace, 1997, c1992. 32pp.
At Christmas/Hanukkah time, a Christian wood-carver gives a carved angel to a young Jewish friend, who struggles with accepting the Christmas gift until he realizes that friendship means the same thing in any religion.

Zalben, Jane Breskin. ***The Magic Menorah: A Modern Chanukah Tale.*** Simon & Schuster Books for Young Readers, c2001. 56pp.
Stanley does not look forward to spending another Chanukah with all his relatives, but when an old man comes out of a tarnished menorah in the attic and grants Stanley three wishes, he changes his mind.

From Nancy J. Keane, *The Big Book of Children's Reading Lists: 100 Great, Ready-to-Use Book Lists for Educators, Librarians, Parents, and Children.* Westport, CT: Libraries Unlimited, 2006. Copyright © 2006 by Libraries Unlimited.

Kwanzaa

Books for Children of All Ages

Chocolate, Deborah M. Newton. ***Kwanzaa.*** Children's Press, c1990. 31pp. (NF)
Discusses the holiday in which African Americans celebrate their roots and cultural heritage.

Gnojewski, Carol. ***Kwanzaa: Seven Days of African-American Pride.*** Enslow, c2004. 48pp. (NF)
Presents the history and meaning behind the observance of Kwanzaa.

Katz, Karen. ***My First Kwanzaa.*** H. Holt, c2003. 28pp.
A girl describes how she and her family celebrate the seven days of Kwanzaa.

Morninghouse, Sundaira. ***Habari Gani? = What's the News? A Kwanzaa Story.*** Open Hand Publishing (distributed by Talman), c1992. 32pp.
A family celebrates each day of Kwanzaa.

Porter, A. P. ***Kwanzaa.*** Carolrhoda Books, c1991. 56pp. (NF)
Describes the origins and practices of Kwanzaa, a holiday created to remind African Americans of their history and their origins.

Saint James, Synthia. ***The Gifts of Kwanzaa.*** Whitman, c1994. 32pp. (NF)
Explains the meaning of the African American holiday, discussing the seven symbols and principles contemplated on each night of the celebration, which runs from December 26 through January 1.

Washington, Donna L. ***The Story of Kwanzaa.*** HarperCollins, c1996. 32pp. (NF)
Describes the tradition and customs of Kwanzaa and includes activities.

Books for Children Ages 8–12

Goss, Linda. ***It's Kwanzaa Time!*** Putnam, 2002, c1995. 72pp. (NF)
Stories, recipes, and activities introduce the holiday of Kwanzaa and the ways in which it is celebrated.

Hoyt-Goldsmith, Diane. ***Celebrating Kwanzaa.*** Holiday House, c1993. 32pp. (NF)
Text and photographs depict how a Chicago family celebrates the African American holiday.

Johnson, Dolores. ***The Children's Book of Kwanzaa: A Guide to Celebrating the Holiday.*** Atheneum Books for Young Readers, c1996. 159pp. (NF)
A guide to the origins, principles, symbols, and celebration of the African American holiday.

Medearis, Angela Shelf. ***Seven Spools of Thread: A Kwanzaa Story.*** Whitman, c2000. 40pp.
When they are given the seemingly impossible task of turning thread into gold, the seven Ashanti brothers put aside their differences, learn to get along, and embody the principles of Kwanzaa. Includes information on Kwanzaa, West African cloth weaving, and instructions for making a belt.

From Nancy J. Keane, *The Big Book of Children's Reading Lists: 100 Great, Ready-to-Use Book Lists for Educators, Librarians, Parents, and Children.* Westport, CT: Libraries Unlimited, 2006. Copyright © 2006 by Libraries Unlimited.

Military Parents

Books for Children of All Ages

Appelt, Kathi. *Oh My Baby, Little One.* Harcourt, c2000. 30pp.
A mother explains to her child all the ways her love remains even while she's away.

Crary, Elizabeth. *Mommy, Don't Go.* Parenting Press, c1996. 30pp.
Illustrates the use of problem-solving skills, critical thinking, and conflict resolution through an example of mother-child separation.

Greenfield, Eloise. *Talk about a Family.* HarperTrophy, 1993, c1978. 60pp.
Genny is eager for her eldest brother's return from military service, convinced that he can fix everything, even the growing rift between their parents.

Hoff, Syd. *Captain Cat.* HarperTrophy, c1993. 46pp.
A cat makes friends with a soldier and learns about military life when he joins the army.

Mead, Alice. *Soldier Mom.* Farrar, Straus & Giroux, c1999. 151pp.
Eleven-year-old Jasmyn gets a different perspective on life when her mother is sent to Saudi Arabia at the beginning of the Persian Gulf War, leaving her and her baby half-brother behind in Maine in the care of her mother's boyfriend.

Pelton, Mindy L. *When Dad's at Sea.* Whitman, c2004. 32pp.
Emily, whose father is a Navy pilot, has to deal with the separation of her family while her dad is deployed aboard a ship.

Penn, Audrey. *The Kissing Hand.* Child Welfare League of America, c1993. 32pp.
When Chester the raccoon is reluctant to go to kindergarten for the first time, his mother teaches him a secret way to carry her love with him.

Spinelli, Eileen. *While You Are Away.* Hyperion Books for Children, c2004. 32pp.
Three children whose parents are serving in the military think about the special things they do together to keep from being sad and dream about the day they will be with their parents again.

Ward, S. *I Live at a Military Post.* PowerKids Press, c2000. 24pp. (NF)
A third-grader describes what it is like living with his family at Fort Belvoir in Fairfax, Virginia.

Zolotow, Charlotte. *If You Listen.* Running Press, c2002. 32pp.
A mother reassures her little girl there is a way to know that someone far away loves you.

From Nancy J. Keane, *The Big Book of Children's Reading Lists: 100 Great, Ready-to-Use Book Lists for Educators, Librarians, Parents, and Children.* Westport, CT: Libraries Unlimited, 2006. Copyright © 2006 by Libraries Unlimited.

Months

Books for Children of All Ages

Barner, Bob. ***Parade Day: Marching Through the Calendar Year.*** Holiday House, c2003. 32pp.
Easy rhyming text describes a parade celebrating each month of the year, followed by information about different calendars, the months, and how to make one's own calendar.

Blackstone, Stella. ***Jump Into January: A Journey Around the Year.*** Barefoot Books, c2004. 26pp.
A short verse for each month of the year encourages the reader to find objects hidden in the pictures that depict that month's activities, such as ear muffs and pine trees in January, or scooters and a picnic bench in June.

Bunting, Eve. ***Sing a Song of Piglets: A Calendar in Verse.*** Clarion Books, c2002. 32pp.
From skiing in January to surfing in July, two energetic piglets romp through the months of the years in this calendar in verse.

Hague, Kathleen. ***Calendarbears: A Book of Months.*** H. Holt, c1997. 27pp.
During each month of the year, a different bear takes part in an activity that is seasonally appropriate.

Hayles, Marsha. ***Pajamas Anytime.*** Putnam, c2005. 32pp.
Each month of the year presents a special occasion on which pajamas are the perfect thing to wear.

Lobel, Anita. ***One Lighthouse, One Moon.*** Greenwillow Books, c2000. 40pp.
Presents the days of the week, the months of the year, and numbers from one to ten through the activities of a cat and people in and around a lighthouse.

Murphy, Patricia J. ***Months.*** Capstone, c2005. 24pp. (NF)
An introduction to the concept of the months of the calendar, in simple text with illustrations; includes information on the seasons and how the calendar is divided. Includes a glossary.

Nelson, Robin. ***Months.*** Lerner, c2002. 23pp. (NF)
Color photos and simple text introduce the months of the year, naming a characteristic of each, such as which month is the shortest and which one begins the summertime.

Roth, Susan L. ***My Love for You All Year Round.*** Dial Books for Young Readers, c2003. 32pp.
Two mice describe their love in terms of the special characteristics of each month of the year.

Sendak, Maurice. ***Chicken Soup with Rice: A Book of Months.*** Harper & Row, c1962. 30pp.
Describes how nice it is to eat chicken soup with rice during every month of the year.

Spinelli, Eileen. ***Here Comes the Year.*** H. Holt, c2002. 26pp.
Describes in rhyme the special qualities that characterize each month of the year.

Tompert, Ann. ***Harry's Hats.*** Children's Press, c2004. 31pp.
A young boy has fun doing various activities that depend on the hat he is wearing each day of the week.

Updike, John. ***A Child's Calendar: Poems.*** Holiday House, c1999. 29pp.
A collection of twelve poems describing the activities in a child's life and the changes in the weather as the year moves from January to December.

From Nancy J. Keane, *The Big Book of Children's Reading Lists: 100 Great, Ready-to-Use Book Lists for Educators, Librarians, Parents, and Children.* Westport, CT: Libraries Unlimited, 2006. Copyright © 2006 by Libraries Unlimited.

Pirates

Books for Children of All Ages

Cannon, A. E. ***Let the Good Times Roll with Pirate Pete and Pirate Joe.*** Viking Press, c2004. 32pp.
Pirate Pete and Pirate Joe visit the Pirate Queen and have fun playing games and going to Disco Dan's House of Pins until it is bedtime and the Pirate Queen becomes just their mother once again.

Cannon, A. E. ***On the Go with Pirate Pete and Pirate Joe.*** Viking Press, c2002. 32pp.
Pirate Pete and Pirate Joe go out for seafood with their cat, Studley, and their dog, Dudley.

Dubowski, Cathy East. ***Pirate School.*** Grosset & Dunlap, c1996. 48pp.
At Pirate School, Pete learns to act like a pirate and fight it out, but when he and a classmate find the treasure at the same time, pirate rules don't seem to work.

Fox, Mem. ***Tough Boris.*** Harcourt Brace, c1994. 32pp.
Although he is a very tough pirate, Boris von der Borch cries when his parrot dies.

Helquist, Brett. ***Roger the Jolly Pirate.*** HarperCollins, c2004. 36pp.
While his shipmates face their toughest enemy, Roger has a chance to prove himself in a most unlikely way after being banished, as usual, below decks during the fighting.

Jaspersohn, William. ***The Scrimshaw Ring.*** Vermont Folklife Center (distributed by Independent Publishers Group), c2002. 32pp.
A young boy living in Newport, Rhode Island in 1710 enjoys imaginary adventures with make-believe pirates, until the day real pirates come ashore for evil purposes and leave him a remarkable memento. Includes ideas for activities related to family heirlooms.

Kimmel, Eric A. ***The Erie Canal Pirates.*** Holiday House, c2002. 32pp.
A boat captain and his men battle Bill McGrew and his pirate crew on the Erie Canal, in this rhyming tale inspired by a folksong.

Laurence, Daniel. ***Captain and Matey Set Sail.*** HarperCollins, c2001. 62pp.
Despite their frequent disagreements, two pirates share many adventures.

Lichtenheld, Tom. ***Everything I Know About Pirates: A Collection of Made-Up Facts, Educated Guesses, and Silly Pictures About Bad Guys of the High Seas.*** Simon & Schuster Books for Young Readers, c2000. 34pp.
Presents made-up facts, educated guesses, and silly pictures about pirates.

Long, Melinda. ***How I Became a Pirate.*** Harcourt, c2003. 36pp.
Jeremy Jacob joins Braid Beard and his pirate crew and finds out about pirate language, pirate manners, and other aspects of their life.

McPhail, David M. ***Edward and the Pirates.*** Little, Brown, c1997. 32pp.
Once Edward has learned to read, books and his vivid imagination provide him with great adventures.

Priest, Robert. ***The Old Pirate of Central Park.*** Houghton Mifflin, c1999. 32pp.
A retired pirate and a retired queen engage in a thunderous battle to gain control of the Central Park sailboat pond.

From Nancy J. Keane, *The Big Book of Children's Reading Lists: 100 Great, Ready-to-Use Book Lists for Educators, Librarians, Parents, and Children.* Westport, CT: Libraries Unlimited, 2006. Copyright © 2006 by Libraries Unlimited.

Pirates

Smallcomb, Pam. ***Camp Buccaneer.*** Aladdin Paperbacks, c2002. 58pp.
After spending summer vacation learning to be a real pirate at Camp Buccaneer, Marlon feels much better prepared to return to school and face Carla, the bully who has pestered her since kindergarten.

Tucker, Kathy. ***Do Pirates Take Baths?*** Whitman, c1994. 32pp.
Humorous rhyming answers to eleven questions about the life of pirates.

Walker, Richard. ***The Barefoot Book of Pirates.*** Barefoot Books, c1998. 63pp.
A collection of seven tales of swashbuckling pirates from different cultures around the world.

Books for Children Ages 8–12

Adkins, Jan. ***What If You Met a Pirate?: An Historical Voyage of Seafaring Speculation.*** Roaring Brook Press, c2004. 32pp.
Pictures and text describe what pirates were really like, especially the pirates of the sixteenth, seventeenth, and eighteenth centuries.

Barry, Dave. ***Peter and the Starcatchers.*** Hyperion Books for Children, c2004. 451pp.
Peter, an orphan boy, and his friend Molly fight off thieves and pirates to keep the secret safe away from the diabolical Black Stache and his evil associate, Mister Grin.

Cowell, Cressida. ***How to Be a Pirate.*** Little, Brown, c2005. 211pp.
Follows the further adventures and misadventures of Hiccup Horrendous Haddock the Third as his Viking training continues and his father leads a stranger and the Hairy Hooligans to the Isle of Skullions in search of a pirate's treasure.

Farman, John. ***The Short and Bloody History of Pirates.*** Lerner, 2002, c2000. 96pp. (NF)
A humorous presentation of the history and life of pirates from the mid-seventeenth to mid-eighteenth centuries.

Fienberg, Anna. ***Horrendo's Curse.*** Annick Press (distributed in the United States by Firefly Books), c2002. 158pp.
For as long as he can remember, pirates have come to Horrendo's village to steal every twelve-year-old boy, and as Horrendo approaches his twelfth year, he eagerly awaits his chance for adventure on the high seas.

Masefield, John. ***Jim Davis.*** Scholastic, c2002. 224pp.
Jim Davis is a twelve-year-old boy whose life takes a terrifying turn when he stumbles upon a ring of bloodthirsty pirates.

Scieszka, Jon. ***The Not-So-Jolly Roger.*** Viking Press, c1991. 57pp.
Blackbeard, the meanest pirate ever, has our accidental time travelers cornered. Should Fred, Sam, and Joe the Time Warp Trio join his pirate crew, or become shark munchies?

Yolen, Jane. ***The Ballad of the Pirate Queens.*** Harcourt Brace, 1998, c1995. 32pp.
Two women who sailed with Calico Jack Rackham and his pirates in the early 1700s do their best to defend their ship while the men on board are busy drinking.

From Nancy J. Keane, *The Big Book of Children's Reading Lists: 100 Great, Ready-to-Use Book Lists for Educators, Librarians, Parents, and Children.* Westport, CT: Libraries Unlimited, 2006. Copyright © 2006 by Libraries Unlimited.

Baseball

Books for Children of All Ages

Adler, David A. ***The Babe & I.*** Harcourt Brace, c1999. 32pp.
While helping his family make ends meet during the Great Depression by selling newspapers, a boy meets Babe Ruth.

Bildner, Phil. ***Shoeless Joe & Black Betsy.*** Simon & Schuster Books for Young Readers, c2002. 40pp.
Shoeless Joe Jackson, said by some to be the greatest baseball player ever, goes into a hitting slump just before he is to start his minor league career, so he asks his friend to make him a special bat to help him hit.

Burleigh, Robert. ***Home Run: The Story of Babe Ruth.*** Harcourt, 2003, c1998. 31pp.
A poetic account of the legendary Babe Ruth as he prepares to make a home run.

Curtis, Gavin. ***The Bat Boy & His Violin.*** Simon & Schuster Books for Young Readers, c1998. 32pp.
Reginald is more interested in practicing his violin than in his father's job managing the worst team in the Negro Leagues, but when Papa makes him the bat boy and his music begins to lead the team to victory, Papa realizes the value of his son's passion.

Gibbons, Gail. ***My Baseball Book.*** HarperCollins, c2000. 24pp. (NF)
An introduction to baseball, describing the equipment, playing field, rules, players, and process of the game.

Hopkinson, Deborah. ***Girl Wonder: A Baseball Story in Nine Innings.*** Atheneum Books for Young Readers, c2003. 34pp.
In the early 1900s, Alta Weiss, a young woman who knows from an early age that she loves baseball, finds a way to show that she can play, even though she is a girl.

Isadora, Rachel. ***Luke Goes to Bat.*** Putnam, c2005. 32pp.
Luke is not very good at baseball, but his grandmother and sports star Jackie Robinson encourage him to keep trying.

Isadora, Rachel. ***Max.*** Aladdin Books, c1987. 32pp.
Max finds a new way to warm up for his Saturday baseball game—his sister's dancing class.

Isadora, Rachel. ***Nick Plays Baseball.*** Putnam, c2001. 32pp.
Uses the story of Nick and his teammates' championship baseball game to provide an introduction to aspects of the game of baseball, including equipment, player positions, and rules.

Johnson, Angela. ***Just Like Josh Gibson.*** Simon & Schuster Books for Young Readers, c2004. 32pp.
A young girl's grandmother tells her of her love for baseball and the day they let her play in the game even though she was a girl.

From Nancy J. Keane, *The Big Book of Children's Reading Lists: 100 Great, Ready-to-Use Book Lists for Educators, Librarians, Parents, and Children.* Westport, CT: Libraries Unlimited, 2006. Copyright © 2006 by Libraries Unlimited.

Baseball

Kusugak, Michael. ***Baseball Bats for Christmas.*** Annick Press, c1990. 23pp.
Describes Christmas in 1955 in Repulse Bay, when two little boys find a bat to play baseball with on the Arctic circle.

Mammano, Julie. ***Rhinos Who Play Baseball.*** Chronicle Books, c2003. 25pp.
Baseball-playing rhinos crack dingers out of the park, rip grass-cutting grounders across the field, and rally in the bottom of the ninth. Includes a glossary of "catch phrases."

Moss, Marissa. ***Mighty Jackie: The Strike-out Queen.*** Simon & Schuster Books for Young Readers, c2004. 32pp. (NF)
In 1931, seventeen-year-old Jackie Mitchell pitches against Babe Ruth and Lou Gehrig in an exhibition game, becoming the first professional female pitcher in baseball history.

Patrick, Jean L. S. ***The Girl Who Struck Out Babe Ruth.*** Carolrhoda Books, c2000. 48pp. (NF)
A retelling of the day Jackie Mitchell, a seventeen-year-old female professional baseball player, struck out the New York Yankees best hitters, Babe Ruth and Lou Gehrig, in an exhibition game in 1931.

Tavares, Matt. ***Mudball.*** Candlewick Press, c2005. 32pp.
During a rainy Minneapolis Millers baseball game in 1903, Little Andy Oyler has the chance to become a hero by hitting the shortest and muddiest home run in history.

Tavares, Matt. ***Zachary's Ball.*** Candlewick Press, 2000. 32pp.
Dad takes Zachary to his first Boston Red Sox game, where they catch a ball and something magical happens.

Thayer, Ernest Lawrence. ***Casey at the Bat: A Ballad of the Republic Sung in the Year 1888.*** Simon & Schuster Books for Young Readers, c2003. 33pp.
An illustrated version of the famous poem.

Uhlberg, Myron. ***Dad, Jackie, and Me.*** Peachtree, c2005. 32pp.
In Brooklyn, New York, in 1947, a boy learns about discrimination and tolerance as he and his deaf father share their enthusiasm for baseball and the Dodgers' first baseman, Jackie Robinson.

Winter, Jonah. ***Roberto Clemente: Pride of the Pittsburgh Pirates.*** Atheneum Books for Young Readers, c2005. 36pp. (NF)
A children's illustrated biography of baseball great Roberto Clemente, who played for the Pittsburg Pirates from 1955 until his untimely death in an airplane crash in 1972.

Books for Children Ages 8–12

Bowen, Fred. ***Winners Take All.*** Peachtree, c2000. 104pp.
When Kyle fakes a catch, his baseball team goes on to win the league championship, but Kyle doesn't feel good about winning by cheating. Includes a section on the sportsmanship of Christy Mathewson, a pitcher who played professional baseball in the early 1900s.

From Nancy J. Keane, *The Big Book of Children's Reading Lists: 100 Great, Ready-to-Use Book Lists for Educators, Librarians, Parents, and Children.* Westport, CT: Libraries Unlimited, 2006. Copyright © 2006 by Libraries Unlimited.

Baseball

Buckley, James. ***Play Ball!*** DK Publishing, c2002. 48pp. (NF)
Photographs and text, including tips from professional players, show how to warm up, select the right equipment, and play baseball.

Butcher, Kristin. ***Cairo Kelly and the Mann.*** Orca Book Publishers, c2002. 172pp.
Kelly Romani and his friend Midge risk disqualification from the baseball playoffs when they attempt to convince the league to allow their favorite umpire to officiate.

Coleman, Janet Wyman. ***Baseball for Everyone: Stories from the Great Game.*** Harry N. Abrams in association with the American Folk Art Museum, c2003. 48pp. (NF)
An illustrated history of baseball, covering the origins of the game, some of its best-known players, and significant changes in rules and practices throughout the nineteenth and twentieth centuries.

Cooney, Doug. ***I Know Who Likes You.*** Simon & Schuster Books for Young Readers, c2004. 217pp.
When Swimming Pool's mother insists she graduate from charm school or give up baseball, Ernie, the reluctant team manager, and Dusty, the catcher, pull together to help the team and their friend.

Jennings, Patrick. ***Out Standing in My Field.*** Scholastic, c2005. 165pp.
Fifth-grader Ty Cutter, named after baseball great Ty Cobb, has lots of enthusiasm for the game but very little talent, which makes life difficult for him and his father, who is the coach of Ty's team.

Naylor, Phyllis Reynolds. ***Boys in Control.*** Delacorte Press, c2003. 143pp.
Once again the Hatford brothers and the Malloy sisters find themselves pitted against each other, when embarrassing pictures of the boys turn up in the girls' basement, and the boys try to figure out how to get them back.

Smith, Charles R., Jr. ***Diamond Life: Baseball Sights, Sounds, and Swings.*** Orchard Books, c2004. 31pp. (NF)
Presents photographs and brief writings that celebrate the joys of baseball.

Tavares, Matt. ***Oliver's Game.*** Candlewick Press, c2004. 26pp.
Oliver's grandfather tells him the story of how he almost joined the Chicago Cubs baseball team.

Weatherford, Carole Boston. ***A Negro League Scrapbook.*** Boyds Mills Press, c2005. 48pp. (NF)
Uses historical photographs and text to explore what it was like to play in baseball's Negro League, and provides information about some of the League's most distinguished players.

Will, Sandra. ***Baseball for Fun!*** Compass Point Books, c2003. 48pp. (NF)
Describes the basic rules, skills, and important people and events in the sport of baseball.

Winter, Jonah. ***Beisbol!: Latino Baseball Pioneers and Legends.*** Lee & Low Books, c2001. 32pp. (NF)
Profiles fourteen Latino baseball stars who played in Latin America or the United States.

From Nancy J. Keane, *The Big Book of Children's Reading Lists: 100 Great, Ready-to-Use Book Lists for Educators, Librarians, Parents, and Children.* Westport, CT: Libraries Unlimited, 2006. Copyright © 2006 by Libraries Unlimited.

Basketball

Books for Children of All Ages

Barber, Barbara E. ***Allie's Basketball Dream.*** Lee & Low Books, c1996. 32pp.
Determined in her effort to play basketball, a young African American girl gives it one more shot, with the support of a special friend.

Cooper, Floyd. ***Jump!: From the Life of Michael Jordan.*** Philomel Books, c2004. 40pp. (NF)
A picture book based on the story of how basketball great Michael Jordan worked for years to become good enough to beat his toughest competitor—his older brother Larry—at hoops.

Helmer, Diana Star. ***The History of Basketball.*** PowerKids Press, c2000. 24pp. (NF)
Relates the history of basketball from the 1890s to today, including discussion of prominent teams, women's teams, and the National Basketball Association.

Klingel, Cynthia Fitterer. ***Basketball.*** Child's World, c2001. 24pp. (NF)
Illustrations and simple text describe the fun a child has playing basketball.

Kuklin, Susan. ***Hoops with Swoopes.*** Jump at the Sun/Hyperion Books for Children, c2001. 32pp. (NF)
A story of Sheryl Swoopes and basketball—the moves and motion, heart and soul.

Martin, Bill. ***Swish!*** H. Holt, 2000 c1997. 32pp.
The Cardinals and the Blue Jays, two girls' basketball teams, play a close and intense game, told in simple, rhyming text with illustrations.

Mattern, Joanne. ***Lebron James: Young Basketball Star.*** Mitchell Lane Publishers, c2005. 32pp. (NF)
A brief biography of LeBron James, the first pick in the 2003 National Basketball Association draft, discussing his childhood in Ohio, his high school success, and his rookie year with the Cleveland Cavaliers.

Mills, Claudia. ***Gus and Grandpa at Basketball.*** Farrar, Straus & Giroux, c2001. 47pp.
Gus enjoys basketball practice, but the noise and pace of real games bother him, until his grandpa gives him some good advice.

Noble, Trinka Hakes. ***Jimmy's Boa and the Bungee Jump Slam Dunk.*** Dial Books for Young Readers, c2003. 32pp.
Jimmy's boa constrictor creates havoc in his gym class, and his antics leads to the formation of an unusual basketball team.

Smith, Charles R. ***Let's Play Basketball!*** Candlewick Press, c2004. 20pp.
A basketball asks to be taken outside to play.

From Nancy J. Keane, *The Big Book of Children's Reading Lists: 100 Great, Ready-to-Use Book Lists for Educators, Librarians, Parents, and Children.* Westport, CT: Libraries Unlimited, 2006. Copyright © 2006 by Libraries Unlimited.

Basketball

Books for Children Ages 8–12

Burgan, Michael. ***Great Moments in Basketball.*** World Almanac Library, c2002. 48pp. (NF)
Recounts ten high points in the history of basketball, including Wilt Chamberlain's 100-point game, eight consecutive NBA championships won by the Boston Celtics, and the Houston Comets winning the first four WNBA championships.

Eule, Brian. ***Basketball for Fun!*** Compass Point Books, c2003. 48pp. (NF)
Describes the basic rules, skills, and important people and events in the sport of basketball.

Jordan, Deloris. ***Salt in His Shoes: Michael Jordan in Pursuit of a Dream.*** Simon & Schuster Books for Young Readers, c2000. 32pp. (NF)
A young Michael Jordan puts salt in his shoes, hoping it will help him grow tall enough to become a famous basketball player.

Mantell, Paul. ***Nothin' But Net.*** Little, Brown, c2003. 136pp.
When thirteen-year-old Tim Daniels gets a chance to go to basketball camp, he is faced with trying to be accepted by the popular players but remaining true to his friend, who has become the butt of practical jokes.

O'Malley, Kevin. ***Mount Olympus Basketball.*** Walker, c2003. 32pp.
Zeus, Hera, Athena, Poseidon, and Hades pull some dirty tricks as they face off against Hercules, Jason, Odysseus, Achilles, and Theseus, in this gods versus mortals basketball game in ancient Greece.

Richardson, Charisse K. ***The Real Slam Dunk.*** Dial Books for Young Readers, c2005. 68pp.
Marcus, hoping to become a professional basketball player when he grows up, is surprised to learn his idol, superstar Jason Carter, is a big believer in getting a college education.

Smith, Charles R. ***Hoop Kings: Poems.*** Candlewick Press, c2004. 37pp.
A collection of twelve poems that celebrate contemporary basketball stars, including Shaquille O'Neal, Allen Iverson, and Kobe Bryant.

Smith, Charles R. ***Hoop Queens: Poems.*** Candlewick Press, c2003. 35pp.
A collection of twelve poems that celebrate contemporary women basketball stars, including Yolanda Griffith, Chamique Holdsclaw, and Natalie Williams.

Walters, Eric. ***Triple Threat.*** Orca, c2004. 162pp.
After Nick and Kia are kicked off a basketball court by bullies, they get revenge by finding a perfect teammate for a tough game of three on three.

Walters, Eric. ***Underdog.*** Orca, c2004. 167pp.
Nick and Kia have their work cut out for them when Ashton, new kid on the squad, shows little interest and is not much of a team player.

From Nancy J. Keane, *The Big Book of Children's Reading Lists: 100 Great, Ready-to-Use Book Lists for Educators, Librarians, Parents, and Children.* Westport, CT: Libraries Unlimited, 2006. Copyright © 2006 by Libraries Unlimited.

Football

Books for Children of All Ages

Allard, Harry. ***Miss Nelson Has a Field Day.*** Houghton Mifflin, c1985. 32pp.
The notorious Miss Swamp reappears at the Horace B. Smedley School, this time to shape up the football team and make them win at least one game.

Barber, Tiki. ***By My Brother's Side.*** Simon & Schuster Books for Young Readers, c2004. 32pp. (NF)
Introduces twin brothers Tiki and Ronde Barber, who worked hard to overcome obstacles and become National Football League stars, one as running back for the New York Giants, the other as cornerback for the Tampa Bay Buccaneers.

Carlson, Nancy L. ***Louanne Pig in Making the Team.*** Carolrhoda Books, c1985. 32pp.
Though she plans to try out for cheerleading, Louanne Pig helps her friend Arnie try out for football, with surprising results.

Fauchald, Nick. ***Touchdown!: You Can Play Football.*** Picture Window Books, c2004. 24pp. (NF)
A brief introduction to the game of football as intended to be played by children.

Kessler, Leonard P. ***Kick, Pass, and Run.*** HarperCollins, c1996. 64pp.
After observing a boys' football game, a group of animals organizes its own teams and game.

Martin, Bill. ***Little Granny Quarterback.*** Boyds Mills Press, c2001. 32pp.
Granny envisions what it would be like to be a star football player, as she was when she was young.

Books for Children Ages 8–12

Bee, Clair. ***Fiery Fullback.*** Broadman & Holman, c2002. 197pp.
Chip Hilton, all American, struggles to restore harmony in State University's football team after Greg Hansen, a divisive new player, joins their roster.

Christopher, Matt. ***The Dog That Stole Football Plays.*** Little, Brown, 1997, c1980. 44pp.
A boy and his psychic dog are able to steal plays from the opposing football team.

Goin, Kenn. ***Football for Fun!*** Compass Point Books, c2003. 48pp. (NF)
Describes the basic rules, skills, and important people and events in the sport of football.

From Nancy J. Keane, *The Big Book of Children's Reading Lists: 100 Great, Ready-to-Use Book Lists for Educators, Librarians, Parents, and Children.* Westport, CT: Libraries Unlimited, 2006. Copyright © 2006 by Libraries Unlimited.

Football

Hale, Bruce. ***This Gum for Hire: from the Tattered Casebook of Chet Gecko, Private Eye.*** Harcourt, c2002. 115pp.

To save his own skin, private eye Chet Gecko sets out to solve the mystery of Emerson Hicky Elementary School's disappearing football players.

Haywood, Carolyn. ***Betsy and the Boys.*** Harcourt, 2004, c1945. 140pp.

Betsy enjoys the adventures of starting the fourth grade with a new teacher, but she runs into trouble when she tries to join the boys on the football team.

Korman, Gordon. ***No More Dead Dogs.*** Hyperion Books for Children, c2000. 180pp.

Eighth-grade football hero Wallace Wallace is sentenced to detention attending rehearsals of the school play where, in spite of himself, he becomes wrapped up in the production and begins to suggest changes that improve not only the play but his life as well.

Levy, Elizabeth. ***Tackling Dad.*** HarperCollins, c2005. 134pp.

When Cassie tries out for the middle school football team, she faces unexpected opposition from her father, a former professional football player.

Suen, Anastasia. ***The Story of Football.*** PowerKids Press, c2002. 24pp. (NF)

Examines the origins of American football, looks at how the game has changed over the years, and discusses its development into a professional sport.

From Nancy J. Keane, *The Big Book of Children's Reading Lists: 100 Great, Ready-to-Use Book Lists for Educators, Librarians, Parents, and Children.* Westport, CT: Libraries Unlimited, 2006. Copyright © 2006 by Libraries Unlimited.

Gymnastics

Books for Children of All Ages

Hoban, Lillian. *Arthur's Birthday Party.* HarperTrophy, 2000, c1999. 64pp.
Arthur the chimpanzee is determined to be the best all-around gymnast at his gymnastics birthday party.

Holabird, Katharine. *Angelina and Alice.* Pleasant, c2001. 25pp.
Angelina and her best friend Alice discover the importance of teamwork when their acrobatics are the hit of the gymnastics show at the village fair.

Kalman, Bobbie. *Gymnastics.* Crabtree, c1997. 32pp. (NF)
Introduces the basics of gymnastics, covering techniques, equipment, and routines.

Taylor, Sean. *Boing!* Candlewick Press, c2004. 54pp.
A man known as the Great Elastic Marvel has an unexpected adventure when his jump on a trampoline takes him out his apartment window.

Books for Children Ages 8–12

Blackall, Bernie. *Gymnastics.* Heinemann Library, c1998. 32pp. (NF)
Introduces gymnastics, discussing its history, American highlights, skills, stretching exercises, equipment, events, and safety aspects.

Ditchfield, Christin. *Gymnastics.* Children's Press, c2000. 47pp. (NF)
Describes the history, equipment, events, and scoring of gymnastics.

Jensen, Julie. *Beginning Gymnastics.* Lerner, c1995. 80pp. (NF)
An introduction to gymnastics, covering apparatus, routines, and important skills. Includes information on competitions, as well as on the sport's history.

Kalman, Bobbie. *Gymnastics in Action.* Crabtree, c2003. 32pp. (NF)
Describes the basic movements and techniques of gymnastics.

From Nancy J. Keane, *The Big Book of Children's Reading Lists: 100 Great, Ready-to-Use Book Lists for Educators, Librarians, Parents, and Children.* Westport, CT: Libraries Unlimited, 2006. Copyright © 2006 by Libraries Unlimited.

Hockey

Books for Children of All Ages

Bach, Mary. ***Termites.*** R.C. Owen Publishers, c1998. 16pp.
A children's book for early readers about a little girl who learns to skate and becomes a member of the hockey team.

Bouchard, Dave. ***That's Hockey.*** Orca, c2002. 32pp.
Etienne teaches his cousin an unusual way of playing street hockey during the winter.

Carter, Anne. ***The F Team.*** Orca, c2003. 32pp.
Fanny and her friends organize their own hockey team, which they call the F Team, and they intend to give the A Team a big surprise.

Dubowski, Cathy East. ***The Big Sweep.*** Simon Spotlight/Nickelodeon, c2003. 32pp.
Otto competes in a street hockey game with Lars, who has a new and expensive hockey stick.

Klein, Abby. ***Don't Sit on My Lunch!*** Blue Sky Press, c2005. 91pp.
When first-grader Freddy decides to try out for peewee hockey, his archenemy, the school bully Max, decides to also try out for the one slot left on the team.

Leonetti, Mike. ***Number Four, Bobby Orr!*** Raincoast Books, Publishers Group West, c2003. 32pp.
Joey and his dad love hockey, but when Joey hurts his leg he wonders if he will ever play hockey again, until a visit from his hero, Bobby Orr of the Boston Bruins, lifts his spirits.

Maloney, Peter. ***The Magic Hockey Stick.*** Dial Books for Young Readers, c1999. 34pp.
When her parents win Wayne Gretzky's hockey stick at a charity auction, a young girl begins playing with it and becomes her team's star.

McGugan, Jim. ***Bridge 6.*** Stoddart Kids (distributed in the United States by General Distribution Services), c1999. 32pp.
A weekly hockey game is the scene of an escalating power struggle between a young girl's two older brothers. Afraid her family is coming apart, she cleverly thinks of a way for everyone to win.

Tibo, Gilles. ***Alex and the Game of the Century.*** Picture Window Books, c2005. 32pp.
Alex, challenged to a face-off by Big Pelo to determine which of them is the hockey champion of the world, gets some unexpected help.

From Nancy J. Keane, *The Big Book of Children's Reading Lists: 100 Great, Ready-to-Use Book Lists for Educators, Librarians, Parents, and Children.* Westport, CT: Libraries Unlimited, 2006. Copyright © 2006 by Libraries Unlimited.

Hockey

Books for Children Ages 8–12

Carter, Anne. ***In the Clear.*** Orca, c2001. 133pp.
After surviving the horrors of polio, Caroline is ashamed of her leg brace and limp and dreams of playing hockey, but first she must overcome her fears.

Christopher, Matt. ***Penalty Shot.*** Little, Brown, c1997. 163pp.
Jeff, already worried about losing his place on the hockey team because of low grades, suddenly finds himself the victim of sabotage in the form of forged papers.

Jensen, Julie. ***Beginning Hockey.*** Lerner, c1996. 80pp. (NF)
An introduction to the sport of ice hockey, including its history, equipment, techniques, and terminology.

Lewis, Maggie. ***Morgy Coast to Coast.*** Houghton Mifflin, c2005. 132pp.
After moving to Massachusetts and starting fourth grade, Morgy continues to experience a lot of changes in his life, including learning to play hockey and the trumpet, and adopting a greyhound named Dante.

McDonnell, Christine. ***Ballet Bug.*** Puffin Books, 2003, c2001. 86pp.
When Bea becomes interested in ballet, she starts taking classes, auditions for *The Nutcracker,* and makes a new best friend, but she also must cope with some nasty classmates and a possible conflict between playing hockey and dancing.

From Nancy J. Keane, *The Big Book of Children's Reading Lists: 100 Great, Ready-to-Use Book Lists for Educators, Librarians, Parents, and Children.* Westport, CT: Libraries Unlimited, 2006. Copyright © 2006 by Libraries Unlimited.

Skiing

Books for Children of All Ages

Calhoun, Mary. ***Cross-Country Cat.*** Mulberry Books, 1986, c1979. 40pp.
When he becomes lost in the mountains, a cat with the unusual ability of walking on two legs finds his way home on cross-country skis.

Eckart, Edana. ***I Can Ski.*** Children's Press, c2003. 24pp.
When a young girl and her mother go skiing, the mother demonstrates how to ski properly and safely.

Jones, Melanie Davis. ***I Can Ski!*** Children's Press, c2003. 31pp.
A boy goes to ski school and learns to ski.

Klingel, Cynthia Fitterer. ***Downhill Skiing.*** Child's World, c2003. 24pp. (NF)
A simple introduction to downhill skiing.

Mayer, Gina. ***Just a Snowy Vacation.*** Golden Books, c2001. 24pp.
Little Critter and his family go on a vacation to Critter Mountain Ski Resort.

Books for Children Ages 8–12

Brimner, Larry Dane. ***Skiing.*** Children's Press, c1997. 47pp. (NF)
Illustrates the various styles of skiing, from cross country to downhill, as well as kinds of equipment and clothing.

Crossingham, John. ***Skiing in Action.*** Crabtree, c2005. 32pp. (NF)
Introduces the techniques, equipment, rules, and safety requirements of skiing.

Italia, Bob. ***Skiing on the Edge.*** Abdo (distributed by Rockbottom Books), c1993. 32pp. (NF)
Discusses the equipment, training, and maneuvers used in freestyle skiing, a sport recently added to the winter Olympic competitions.

Jefferis, David. ***Snow Sports.*** Raintree Steck-Vaughn, c2002. 32pp. (NF)
Photographs and simple text introduce young readers to a variety of extreme snow sports, including snow boarding, skiing, snowmobiling, and bobsledding.

From Nancy J. Keane, *The Big Book of Children's Reading Lists: 100 Great, Ready-to-Use Book Lists for Educators, Librarians, Parents, and Children.* Westport, CT: Libraries Unlimited, 2006. Copyright © 2006 by Libraries Unlimited.

Soccer

Books for Children of All Ages

Bellingham, Brenda. ***Lilly Makes a Friend.*** Formac Publishing (distributed in the United States by Orca), c2004. 62pp.
Davy, a blind boy in the kindergarten class, wants to play soccer, so Lilly and her friends try to find some way for them all to play together without Davy getting hurt.

Berenstain, Stan. ***Too Small for the Team.*** Random House, c2003. 88pp.
Although she is a very good soccer player, Sister Bear isn't allowed to try out for the team until she is bigger, so she signs up to be the team manager in hopes of proving herself to the coach.

Browne, Anthony. ***Willy the Wizard.*** Candlewick Press, 2003, c1995. 32pp.
Willy the chimpanzee loves to play soccer, but he is never picked for a team, until a stranger gives him some shoes that he is certain are magic.

Brug, Sandra Gilbert. ***Soccer Beat.*** Margaret K. McElderry Books, c2003. 32pp.
Illustrations and rhyming text describe the action of an animal soccer game.

Burleigh, Robert. ***Goal.*** Silver Whistle, c2001. 32pp.
Illustrations and poetic text describe the movement and feel of a fast-paced game of soccer.

Catalanotto, Peter. ***Dylan's Day Out.*** Orchard Books, 1993, c1989. 32pp.
In a story where almost everything is black and white, Dylan, a Dalmatian, escapes from his home and becomes involved in a soccer game between penguins and skunks.

Couric, Katie. ***The Blue Ribbon Day.*** Doubleday, c2004. 32pp.
When Carrie is disappointed by not making the school soccer team, she turns her attention to creating a science fair project.

Fauchald, Nick. ***Score!: You Can Play Soccer.*** Picture Window Books, c2004. 24pp. (NF)
A brief introduction to the basic moves and plays of a soccer game.

Finchler, Judy. ***You're a Good Sport, Miss Malarkey.*** Walker, c2002. 32pp.
The children on a newly formed soccer team love their coach, Miss Malarkey, who doesn't know much about the game except how to make it fun, but the school principal and parents have other ideas.

Foreman, Michael. ***Wonder Goal!*** Farrar, Straus & Giroux, c2003. 24pp.
A boy describes what it feels like to score a goal that makes his soccer teammates stop teasing him.

From Nancy J. Keane, *The Big Book of Children's Reading Lists: 100 Great, Ready-to-Use Book Lists for Educators, Librarians, Parents, and Children.* Westport, CT: Libraries Unlimited, 2006. Copyright © 2006 by Libraries Unlimited.

Soccer

Gibbons, Gail. ***My Soccer Book.*** HarperCollins, c2000. 24pp. (NF)
Briefly describes the equipment, terminology, rules, positions, and plays of one of the world's most popular games.

Gikow, Louise. ***The Big Game.*** Children's Press, c2004. 31pp.
A child who has trouble with some of the soccer skills finds an important role as goalie.

Hamm, Mia. ***Winners Never Quit!*** HarperCollins, c2004. 26pp.
When she quits the soccer team because she couldn't score a goal, Mia must learn the hard way that being a team player is more important than winning or losing.

Helmer, Diana Star. ***The History of Soccer.*** PowerKids Press, c2000. 24pp. (NF)
Traces the sport of soccer from its reputed origin to its current level of popularity, introducing its rules, governing bodies, roles for women, and international competitions.

Klingel, Cynthia Fitterer. ***Soccer.*** Child's World, c2001. 24pp. (NF)
Illustrations and simple text describe the fun a child has playing soccer.

London, Jonathan. ***Froggy Plays Soccer.*** Viking Press, c1999. 32pp.
Although Froggy is very excited when his Dream Team plays in the city soccer championship, he makes a mistake on the field that almost costs the team the game.

Mammano, Julie. ***Rhinos Who Play Soccer.*** Chronicle Books, c2001. 26pp.
Rhinoceroses play a game of soccer as Team Rhino meets the All Stars. Includes a list of soccer vocabulary.

Murcia, Rebecca Thatcher. ***David Beckham: Soccer Megastar.*** Mitchell Lane Publishers, c2005. 32pp. (NF)
A biography of international soccer champion David Beckham; chronicles his life and career from his childhood in England to his success in the world of soccer.

Murphy, Stuart J. ***Game Time.*** HarperCollins, c2000. 33pp.
Calendars and clocks keep track of passing time as the Huskies prepare for and compete in the championship soccer game against the Falcons.

Posner, Pat. ***Princess Fidgety Feet.*** Gingham Dog Press, c2003. 26pp.
When Miss Posy trains Princess Bridget to keep her feet still, Bridget fears that she will not be able to play soccer.

From Nancy J. Keane, *The Big Book of Children's Reading Lists: 100 Great, Ready-to-Use Book Lists for Educators, Librarians, Parents, and Children.* Westport, CT: Libraries Unlimited, 2006. Copyright © 2006 by Libraries Unlimited.

Soccer

Books for Children Ages 8–12

Christopher, Matt. ***The Comeback Challenge.*** Little, Brown, c1996. 144pp.
Mark, center for his middle school's soccer team, the Scorpions, must cope with his parents' divorce and a teammate who holds a grudge against him.

Christopher, Matt. ***Soccer Scoop.*** Little, Brown, c1998. 133pp.
When a cartoon appears in the school newspaper making fun of his tendency to talk a lot, Mac, the goalie for the Cougars soccer team, is determined to find out who is responsible.

Goin, Kenn. ***Soccer for Fun!*** Compass Point Books, c2003. 48pp. (NF)
Describes the basic rules, skills, and important people and events in the sport of soccer.

Greene, Stephanie. ***Owen Foote, Soccer Star.*** Clarion Books, c1998. 88pp.
Eight-year-old Owen and his best friend Joseph face a test of their game skills and their friendship when they join a neighborhood soccer league.

Joosse, Barbara M. ***The Losers Fight Back: A Wild Willie Mystery.*** Clarion Books, c1994. 97pp.
With some help from his detective partner King Kyle in Cleveland, Wild Willie and his friend Lucy figure out how to turn their soccer team into winners.

Suen, Anastasia. ***The Story of Soccer.*** PowerKids Press, c2002. 24pp. (NF)
Provides information about early kicking games, focusing on the development of soccer, and looks at how the sport has been popularized by the Olympics and in countries around the world.

Ungs, Tim. ***Superstars of Men's Soccer.*** Chelsea House, c1998. 64pp. (NF)
Provides historical background on men's soccer and profiles champions such as Pele Diego Maradona and the 1994 U.S. team.

Wukovits, John F. ***The Composite Guide to Soccer.*** Chelsea House, c1999. 64pp. (NF)
Traces the history of soccer, from its beginnings, to its first stars and championship games, to the notable players of today.

From Nancy J. Keane, *The Big Book of Children's Reading Lists: 100 Great, Ready-to-Use Book Lists for Educators, Librarians, Parents, and Children.* Westport, CT: Libraries Unlimited, 2006. Copyright © 2006 by Libraries Unlimited.

If you liked Lemony Snicket, try . . .

- Spiderwick Chronicles (series) by Tony DiTerlizzi and Holly Black.
  Simon & Shuster Books for Young Readers.
- The Eddie Dickens Trilogy (series) by Philip Ardagh
  Henry Holt
- The Edge Chronicles (series) by Paul Stewart
  David Fickling Books
- Unlikely Exploit (series) by Philip Ardagh
  Henry Holt.
- *The Witches* by Roald Dahl
  Puffin
- *Matilda* by Roald Dahl
  Puffin
- *Dial-a-Ghost* by Eva Ibbotson
  Puffin

From Nancy J. Keane, *The Big Book of Children's Reading Lists: 100 Great, Ready-to-Use Book Lists for Educators, Librarians, Parents, and Children.* Westport, CT: Libraries Unlimited, 2006. Copyright © 2006 by Libraries Unlimited.

If you liked Lemony Snicket, try . . .

- Spiderwick Chronicles (series) by Tony DiTerlizzi and Holly Black.
  Simon & Shuster Books for Young Readers.
- The Eddie Dickens Trilogy (series) by Philip Ardagh
  Henry Holt
- The Edge Chronicles (series) by Paul Stewart
  David Fickling Books
- Unlikely Exploit (series) by Philip Ardagh
  Henry Holt.
- *The Witches* by Roald Dahl
  Puffin
- *Matilda* by Roald Dahl
  Puffin
- *Dial-a-Ghost* by Eva Ibbotson
  Puffin

From Nancy J. Keane, *The Big Book of Children's Reading Lists: 100 Great, Ready-to-Use Book Lists for Educators, Librarians, Parents, and Children.* Westport, CT: Libraries Unlimited, 2006. Copyright © 2006 by Libraries Unlimited.

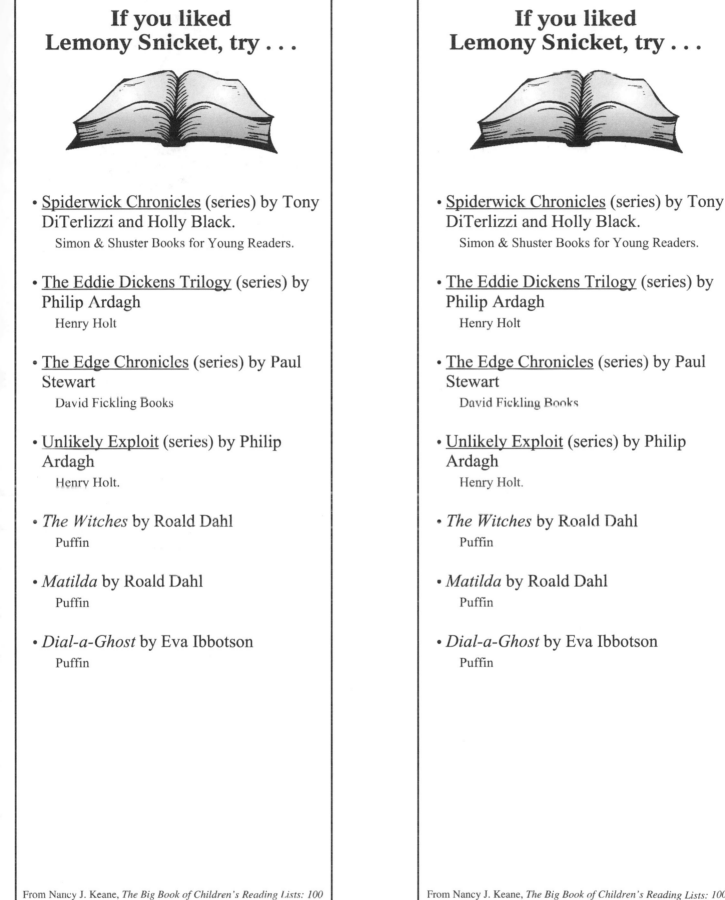

If you liked Magic Tree House, try . . .

- Blast to the Past (series) by Stacia Deutsch
  Aladdin Paperbacks
- Horrible Harry (series) by Suzy Kline
  Puffin
- Pee Wee Scouts (series) by Judy Delton
  Bantam Doubleday
- Secrets of Droon (series) by Tony Abbott
  Scholastic
- Time-traveling Twins (series) by Diane Stanley
  Joanna Cotler Books
- Time Warp Trio (series) by Jon Scieszka
  Viking

From Nancy J. Keane, *The Big Book of Children's Reading Lists: 100 Great, Ready-to-Use Book Lists for Educators, Librarians, Parents, and Children.* Westport, CT: Libraries Unlimited, 2006. Copyright © 2006 by Libraries Unlimited.

If you liked Magic Tree House, try . . .

- Blast to the Past (series) by Stacia Deutsch
  Aladdin Paperbacks
- Horrible Harry (series) by Suzy Kline
  Puffin
- Pee Wee Scouts (series) by Judy Delton
  Bantam Doubleday
- Secrets of Droon (series) by Tony Abbott
  Scholastic
- Time-traveling Twins (series) by Diane Stanley
  Joanna Cotler Books
- Time Warp Trio (series) by Jon Scieszka
  Viking

From Nancy J. Keane, *The Big Book of Children's Reading Lists: 100 Great, Ready-to-Use Book Lists for Educators, Librarians, Parents, and Children.* Westport, CT: Libraries Unlimited, 2006. Copyright © 2006 by Libraries Unlimited.

If you liked Tale of Despereaux, try . . .

- *Chasing Redbird* by Sharon Creech
  HarperCollins
- *Chasing Vermeer* by Blue Balliett
  Scholastic
- *How Angel Peterson Got His Name* by Gary Paulson
  Wendy Lamb Books
- *Ida B: And Her Plans to Maximize Fun, Avoid Disaster, and (Possibly) Save the World* by Katherine Hannigan.
  Greenwillow Books
- *Inkheart* by Cornelia Funke
  Scholastic
- *Mysterious Matter of I.M. Fine* by Diane Stanley
  HarperCollins
- *Once Upon a Marigold* by Jean Ferris
  Harcourt
- *Time Stops for No Mouse* by Michael Hoeye
  G.P. Putnam's Sons
- *When Zachary Beaver Came to Town* by Kimberly Willis
  Henry Holt

From Nancy J. Keane, *The Big Book of Children's Reading Lists: 100 Great, Ready-to-Use Book Lists for Educators, Librarians, Parents, and Children.* Westport, CT: Libraries Unlimited, 2006. Copyright © 2006 by Libraries Unlimited.

If you liked Tale of Despereaux, try . . .

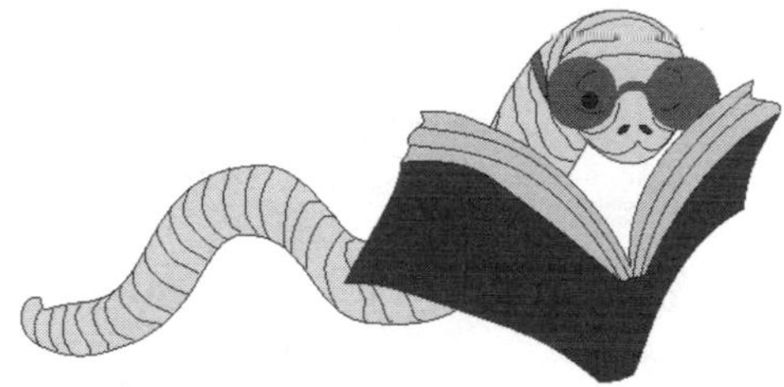

- *Chasing Redbird* by Sharon Creech
  HarperCollins
- *Chasing Vermeer* by Blue Balliett
  Scholastic
- *How Angel Peterson Got His Name* by Gary Paulson
  Wendy Lamb Books
- *Ida B: And Her Plans to Maximize Fun, Avoid Disaster, and (Possibly) Save the World* by Katherine Hannigan.
  Greenwillow Books
- *Inkheart* by Cornelia Funke
  Scholastic
- *Mysterious Matter of I.M. Fine* by Diane Stanley
  HarperCollins
- *Once Upon a Marigold* by Jean Ferris
  Harcourt
- *Time Stops for No Mouse* by Michael Hoeye
  G.P. Putnam's Sons
- *When Zachary Beaver Came to Town* by Kimberly Willis
  Henry Holt

From Nancy J. Keane, *The Big Book of Children's Reading Lists: 100 Great, Ready-to-Use Book Lists for Educators, Librarians, Parents, and Children.* Westport, CT: Libraries Unlimited, 2006. Copyright © 2006 by Libraries Unlimited.

If you liked Lilly's Purple Plastic Purse, try . . .

- *The Bag I'm Taking to Grandma's* by Shirley Neitzel
  Greenwillow
- *The Shopping Basket* by John Burningham
  Candlewick
- *The Mitten* by Jan Brett
  Putnam
- *I Unpacked My Grandmother's Trunk* by Susan Ramsay Hoguet
  Dutton

From Nancy J. Keane, *The Big Book of Children's Reading Lists: 100 Great, Ready-to-Use Book Lists for Educators, Librarians, Parents, and Children.* Westport, CT: Libraries Unlimited, 2006. Copyright © 2006 by Libraries Unlimited.

If you liked Lilly's Purple Plastic Purse, try . . .

- *The Bag I'm Taking to Grandma's* by Shirley Neitzel
  Greenwillow
- *The Shopping Basket* by John Burningham
  Candlewick
- *The Mitten* by Jan Brett
  Putnam
- *I Unpacked My Grandmother's Trunk* by Susan Ramsay Hoguet
  Dutton

From Nancy J. Keane, *The Big Book of Children's Reading Lists: 100 Great, Ready-to-Use Book Lists for Educators, Librarians, Parents, and Children.* Westport, CT: Libraries Unlimited, 2006. Copyright © 2006 by Libraries Unlimited.

Scary books for little ones

- *Big Spooky House* by Donna Washington
  Jump at the Sun/Hyperion
- Black Lagoon Series by Mike Thayer
  Scholastic
- *Ghost Eye-Tree* by Bill Martin
  Henry Holt
- *In the Haunted House* by Eve Bunting
  Clarion
- *Little Old Lady Who Was Not Afraid of Anything* by Linda Williams
  HarperCollins
- *Psssst!, It's Me the Bogeyman* by Barbara Park
  Aladdin
- *Scary Stories to Tell in the Dark* by Alvin Schwartz
  HarperCollins

From Nancy J. Keane, *The Big Book of Children's Reading Lists: 100 Great, Ready-to-Use Book Lists for Educators, Librarians, Parents, and Children.* Westport, CT: Libraries Unlimited, 2006. Copyright © 2006 by Libraries Unlimited.

Scary books for little ones

- *Big Spooky House* by Donna Washington
  Jump at the Sun/Hyperion
- Black Lagoon Series by Mike Thayer
  Scholastic
- *Ghost Eye-Tree* by Bill Martin
  Henry Holt
- *In the Haunted House* by Eve Bunting
  Clarion
- *Little Old Lady Who Was Not Afraid of Anything* by Linda Williams
  HarperCollins
- *Psssst!, It's Me the Bogeyman* by Barbara Park
  Aladdin
- *Scary Stories to Tell in the Dark* by Alvin Schwartz
  HarperCollins

From Nancy J. Keane, *The Big Book of Children's Reading Lists: 100 Great, Ready-to-Use Book Lists for Educators, Librarians, Parents, and Children.* Westport, CT: Libraries Unlimited, 2006. Copyright © 2006 by Libraries Unlimited.

Let's go on a treasure hunt!

- *Garbage Juice for Breakfast* by Patricia Reilly Giff (Bantam, 1989)

  Dawn and her friend Lizzie are eager to get started on the camp treasure hunt.

- *How I Became a Pirate* by Melinda Long (Harcourt, 2003)

  Jeremy Jacob joins Braid Beard and his pirate crew and finds out about pirate language, pirate manners, and other aspects of their life . . . complete with a treasure map with an X on it!

- *Surprise!* By Mercer Mayer (McGraw-Hill, 2002)

  When Little Critter wakes up on his birthday, he finds a series of notes leading him on a treasure hunt around the house, with a wonderful surprise at the end.

- *Toot and Puddle: A Present for Toot* by Hollie Hobbie (Little, Brown, 1998)

  When he just about gives up trying to find the right birthday gift for Toot in Pip's Pet Shop, Puddle needs to look no further because the special present finds him.

- *Tooth Fairy's First Night* by Anne Bowen (Carolrhoda, 2005)

  Sally the Tooth Fairy's first day on the job is a challenge when a toothless little girl hides her tooth and makes Sally follow a series of clues to find it.

- *X Marks the Spot* by Lucille Recht Penner (Kane, 2002)

  Upon moving to their grandfather's house, two boys discover a treasure map in the attic and must learn how to use it to find their surprise.

From Nancy J. Keane, *The Big Book of Children's Reading Lists: 100 Great, Ready-to-Use Book Lists for Educators, Librarians, Parents, and Children.* Westport, CT: Libraries Unlimited, 2006. Copyright © 2006 by Libraries Unlimited.

Let's go on a treasure hunt!

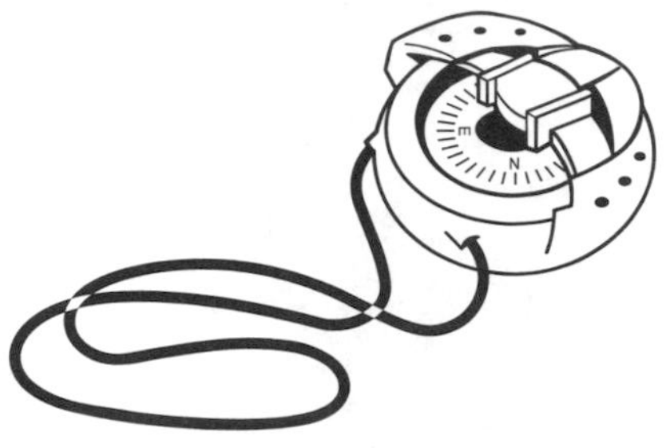

- *Garbage Juice for Breakfast* by Patricia Reilly Giff (Bantam, 1989)

  Dawn and her friend Lizzie are eager to get started on the camp treasure hunt.

- *How I Became a Pirate* by Melinda Long (Harcourt, 2003)

  Jeremy Jacob joins Braid Beard and his pirate crew and finds out about pirate language, pirate manners, and other aspects of their life . . . complete with a treasure map with an X on it!

- *Surprise!* By Mercer Mayer (McGraw-Hill, 2002)

  When Little Critter wakes up on his birthday, he finds a series of notes leading him on a treasure hunt around the house, with a wonderful surprise at the end.

- *Toot and Puddle: A Present for Toot* by Hollie Hobbie (Little, Brown, 1998)

  When he just about gives up trying to find the right birthday gift for Toot in Pip's Pet Shop, Puddle needs to look no further because the special present finds him.

- *Tooth Fairy's First Night* by Anne Bowen (Carolrhoda, 2005)

  Sally the Tooth Fairy's first day on the job is a challenge when a toothless little girl hides her tooth and makes Sally follow a series of clues to find it.

- *X Marks the Spot* by Lucille Recht Penner (Kane, 2002)

  Upon moving to their grandfather's house, two boys discover a treasure map in the attic and must learn how to use it to find their surprise.

From Nancy J. Keane, *The Big Book of Children's Reading Lists: 100 Great, Ready-to-Use Book Lists for Educators, Librarians, Parents, and Children.* Westport, CT: Libraries Unlimited, 2006. Copyright © 2006 by Libraries Unlimited.

If you liked I Spy books, try . . .

- *Animalia* by Graham Base
  H.N. Abrams
- *Can You See What I See?* by Walter Wick
  Scholastic
- *Great Animal Search* by Caroline Young
  Usborne
- *Look Alikes* by Joan Steiner
  Little, Brown
- *Magic Eye* by N E. Thing Enterprises
  Andrews and McMeel
- *Pigs 1 to 10* by Arthur Geisert
  Houghton Mifflin
- *Pigs A to Z* by Arthur Geisert
  Houghton Mifflin
- *Where's the Bear?* by Jan Bruegel
  J. Paul Getty Museum
- *Where's Waldo?* by Martin Handford
  Candlewick Press

From Nancy J. Keane, *The Big Book of Children's Reading Lists: 100 Great, Ready-to-Use Book Lists for Educators, Librarians, Parents, and Children.* Westport, CT: Libraries Unlimited, 2006. Copyright © 2006 by Libraries Unlimited.

If you liked I Spy books, try . . .

- *Animalia* by Graham Base
  H.N. Abrams
- *Can You See What I See?* by Walter Wick
  Scholastic
- *Great Animal Search* by Caroline Young
  Usborne
- *Look Alikes* by Joan Steiner
  Little, Brown
- *Magic Eye* by N E. Thing Enterprises
  Andrews and McMeel
- *Pigs 1 to 10* by Arthur Geisert
  Houghton Mifflin
- *Pigs A to Z* by Arthur Geisert
  Houghton Mifflin
- *Where's the Bear?* by Jan Bruegel
  J. Paul Getty Museum
- *Where's Waldo?* by Martin Handford
  Candlewick Press

From Nancy J. Keane, *The Big Book of Children's Reading Lists: 100 Great, Ready-to-Use Book Lists for Educators, Librarians, Parents, and Children.* Westport, CT: Libraries Unlimited, 2006. Copyright © 2006 by Libraries Unlimited.

Books about horses

- *Chico* by Sandra Day O'Connor
  Dutton Children's Books
- *Great Horses* by Gloria Skurzynski
  National Geographic Society
- *Gib and the Gray Ghost* by Zikpha Keatley Snyder
  Dell Yearling
- *The Girl on the High-diving Horse* by Linda Oatman High
  Philomel Books
- *Harry's Pony* by Barbara Ann Porte
  HarperCollins
- *Jigsaw Pony* by Jessie Haas
  Greenwillow Books
- *Lara and the Gray Mare* by Kathleen Duey
  Dutton Children's Books
- *Little Horse* by Betsy Cromer Byars
  Holt
- *Sky* by Pamela Porter
  Groundwood Books
- *Winter Pony* by Krista Ruepp
  North-South Books

From Nancy J. Keane, *The Big Book of Children's Reading Lists: 100 Great, Ready-to-Use Book Lists for Educators, Librarians, Parents, and Children.* Westport, CT: Libraries Unlimited, 2006. Copyright © 2006 by Libraries Unlimited.

Books about horses

- *Chico* by Sandra Day O'Connor
  Dutton Children's Books
- *Great Horses* by Gloria Skurzynski
  National Geographic Society
- *Gib and the Gray Ghost* by Zikpha Keatley Snyder
  Dell Yearling
- *The Girl on the High-diving Horse* by Linda Oatman High
  Philomel Books
- *Harry's Pony* by Barbara Ann Porte
  HarperCollins
- *Jigsaw Pony* by Jessie Haas
  Greenwillow Books
- *Lara and the Gray Mare* by Kathleen Duey
  Dutton Children's Books
- *Little Horse* by Betsy Cromer Byars
  Holt
- *Sky* by Pamela Porter
  Groundwood Books
- *Winter Pony* by Krista Ruepp
  North-South Books

From Nancy J. Keane, *The Big Book of Children's Reading Lists: 100 Great, Ready-to-Use Book Lists for Educators, Librarians, Parents, and Children.* Westport, CT: Libraries Unlimited, 2006. Copyright © 2006 by Libraries Unlimited.

Books about summer camp

- *Agnes Parker—Happy Camper?* By Kathleen O'Dell
  Dial
- *Annabel the Actress Starring in Camping It Up* by Ellen Conford
  Simon & Schuster Books for Young Readers
- *Beany Goes to Camp* by Susan Wojciechowski
  Candlewick Press
- *Fat Camp Commandos* by Daniel Pinkwater
  Scholastic
- *Molly Saves the Day: A Summer Story* by Valerie Tripp
  Pleasant Company
- *Rainy* by Sis Boulos Dean
  Henry Holt
- *Truly Winnie* by Jennifer Jacobson
  Houghton Mifflin

From Nancy J. Keane, *The Big Book of Children's Reading Lists: 100 Great, Ready-to-Use Book Lists for Educators, Librarians, Parents, and Children.* Westport, CT: Libraries Unlimited, 2006. Copyright © 2006 by Libraries Unlimited.

Books about summer camp

- *Agnes Parker—Happy Camper?* By Kathleen O'Dell
  Dial
- *Annabel the Actress Starring in Camping It Up* by Ellen Conford
  Simon & Schuster Books for Young Readers
- *Beany Goes to Camp* by Susan Wojciechowski
  Candlewick Press
- *Fat Camp Commandos* by Daniel Pinkwater
  Scholastic
- *Molly Saves the Day: A Summer Story* by Valerie Tripp
  Pleasant Company
- *Rainy* by Sis Boulos Dean
  Henry Holt
- *Truly Winnie* by Jennifer Jacobson
  Houghton Mifflin

From Nancy J. Keane, *The Big Book of Children's Reading Lists: 100 Great, Ready-to-Use Book Lists for Educators, Librarians, Parents, and Children.* Westport, CT: Libraries Unlimited, 2006. Copyright © 2006 by Libraries Unlimited.

If you liked Because of Winn Dixie, try . . .

- *The Field of the Dogs* by Katherine Paterson
  HarperTrophy
- *Gooseberry Park* by Cynthia Rylant
  Scholastic
- *Henry and Ribsy* by Beverly Cleary
  Morrow Junior Books
- *It Only Looks Easy* by Pamela Swallow
  Roaring Brook Press
- *Kavik the Wolf Dog* by Walt Morey
  Puffin
- *No More Dead Dogs* by Gordon Korman
  Hyperion Books for Children
- *Red Dog* by Bill Wallace
  Holiday House
- *Shiloh* by Phyllis Reynolds Naylor
  Atheneum Books for Young Readers
- *When Mack Came Back* by Brad Strickland
  Dial Books for Young Readers

From Nancy J. Keane, *The Big Book of Children's Reading Lists: 100 Great, Ready-to-Use Book Lists for Educators, Librarians, Parents, and Children.* Westport, CT: Libraries Unlimited, 2006. Copyright © 2006 by Libraries Unlimited.

If you liked Because of Winn Dixie, try . . .

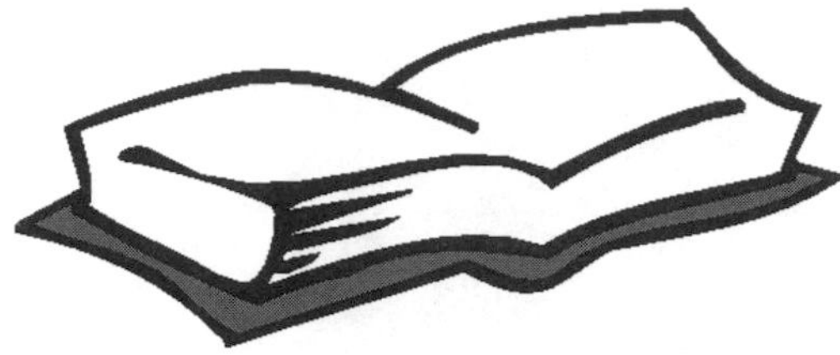

- *The Field of the Dogs* by Katherine Paterson
  HarperTrophy
- *Gooseberry Park* by Cynthia Rylant
  Scholastic
- *Henry and Ribsy* by Beverly Cleary
  Morrow Junior Books
- *It Only Looks Easy* by Pamela Swallow
  Roaring Brook Press
- *Kavik the Wolf Dog* by Walt Morey
  Puffin
- *No More Dead Dogs* by Gordon Korman
  Hyperion Books for Children
- *Red Dog* by Bill Wallace
  Holiday House
- *Shiloh* by Phyllis Reynolds Naylor
  Atheneum Books for Young Readers
- *When Mack Came Back* by Brad Strickland
  Dial Books for Young Readers

From Nancy J. Keane, *The Big Book of Children's Reading Lists: 100 Great, Ready-to-Use Book Lists for Educators, Librarians, Parents, and Children.* Westport, CT: Libraries Unlimited, 2006. Copyright © 2006 by Libraries Unlimited.

If you like books about angels, try . . .

- *Angels, Angels Everywhere* by Larry Libby
  Zonderkidz
- *Calling the Shots* by Annie Dalton
  Avon
- *Cassandra's Angel* by Gina Otto
  Illumination Arts Pub
- *Cat Heaven* by Cynthia Rylant
  Blue Sky Press
- *The Christmas Rat* by Avi
  Atheneum Books for Young Readers
- *City Angel* by Eileen Spinelli
  Dial Books for Young Readers
- *Grandpa's Angel* by Jutta Bauer
  Candlewick Press
- *Harvey Angell Beats Time* by Diana Hendry
  Aladdin Paperbacks
- *Isabelle and the Angel* by Thierry Magnier
  Chronicle Books
- *Little Angels' Alphabet of Love* by Joan Walsh Anglund
  Simon & Schuster Books for Young Readers
- *What Night Do the Angels Wander?* by Phoebe Stone
  Little, Brown

From Nancy J. Keane, *The Big Book of Children's Reading Lists: 100 Great, Ready-to-Use Book Lists for Educators, Librarians, Parents, and Children.* Westport, CT: Libraries Unlimited, 2006. Copyright © 2006 by Libraries Unlimited.

If you like books about angels, try . . .

- *Angels, Angels Everywhere* by Larry Libby
  Zonderkidz
- *Calling the Shots* by Annie Dalton
  Avon
- *Cassandra's Angel* by Gina Otto
  Illumination Arts Pub
- *Cat Heaven* by Cynthia Rylant
  Blue Sky Press
- *The Christmas Rat* by Avi
  Atheneum Books for Young Readers
- *City Angel* by Eileen Spinelli
  Dial Books for Young Readers
- *Grandpa's Angel* by Jutta Bauer
  Candlewick Press
- *Harvey Angell Beats Time* by Diana Hendry
  Aladdin Paperbacks
- *Isabelle and the Angel* by Thierry Magnier
  Chronicle Books
- *Little Angels' Alphabet of Love* by Joan Walsh Anglund
  Simon & Schuster Books for Young Readers
- *What Night Do the Angels Wander?* by Phoebe Stone
  Little, Brown

From Nancy J. Keane, *The Big Book of Children's Reading Lists: 100 Great, Ready-to-Use Book Lists for Educators, Librarians, Parents, and Children.* Westport, CT: Libraries Unlimited, 2006. Copyright © 2006 by Libraries Unlimited.

If you like unicorns, try . . .

- *I Wished for a Unicorn* by Robert Heidbreder
  Kids Can Press
- *The Mountains of the Moon* by Kathleen Duey
  Aladdin
- *Nicolo's Unicorn* by Sylvaine Nahas
  Watson-Guptill
- *The Unicorn* by Emily Rodda
  HarperCollins
- *Where Have the Unicorns Gone?* By Jane Yolen
  Aladdin
- *Wizard at Work* by Vivian Vande Velde
  Harcourt

From Nancy J. Keane, *The Big Book of Children's Reading Lists: 100 Great, Ready-to-Use Book Lists for Educators, Librarians, Parents, and Children.* Westport, CT: Libraries Unlimited, 2006. Copyright © 2006 by Libraries Unlimited.

If you like unicorns, try . . .

- *I Wished for a Unicorn* by Robert Heidbreder
  Kids Can Press
- *The Mountains of the Moon* by Kathleen Duey
  Aladdin
- *Nicolo's Unicorn* by Sylvaine Nahas
  Watson-Guptill
- *The Unicorn* by Emily Rodda
  HarperCollins
- *Where Have the Unicorns Gone?* By Jane Yolen
  Aladdin
- *Wizard at Work* by Vivian Vande Velde
  Harcourt

From Nancy J. Keane, *The Big Book of Children's Reading Lists: 100 Great, Ready-to-Use Book Lists for Educators, Librarians, Parents, and Children.* Westport, CT: Libraries Unlimited, 2006. Copyright © 2006 by Libraries Unlimited.

Index

About the Author

NANCY J. KEANE is Library Media Specialist at Rundlett Middle School in Concord, New Hampshire. She is author of *Booktalking Across the Curriculum: The Middle Years* (Libraries Unlimited, 2002) and several other titles, and she is recipient of the 2004 Association for Library Service to Children (ALSC)/Sagebrush Education Resources Literature Program Award. For more than a decade, she has hosted a popular booktalk Web site (www.nancykeane.com).